WILCO

GREG KOT

BROADWAY BOOKS
NEW YORK

LEARNING HOW TO DIE

PRINTED IN THE UNITED STATES OF AMERICA

Library of Congress Cataloging-in-Publication Data
Kot, Greg.   Wilco : learning how to die / Greg Kot.— 1st ed.   p. cm.
1. Wilco (Musical group)   2. Rock groups—Illinois.   I. Title.
ML421.W52K68 2004   782.42166'092'2—dc22   2004040686

ISBN 0-7679-1558-5

10 9 8 7 6

FOR DEB, KATIE, AND MARISSA

CONTENTS

CHAPTER 1

"YOU HAVE TO LEARN HOW TO DIE"

Jeff Tweedy was sobbing as he sang. He and his bandmates in Wilco were coming off a grueling tour that had seen them play too many shows too far from home for far too long, and now they had just finished up four days of recording sessions in an Austin, Texas, studio. Listening to the playback, Tweedy could measure the toll. He could hear the depression and exhaustion in his voice, the misgivings about the life he had made for himself. Music was both the best thing that had ever happened to him and the worst. It kept him away from his wife and family for long stretches, and now he was beginning to doubt everything: his music, his marriage, the sound of his own voice. The songs held no answers; they simply channeled what was in his heart and mind. Both, frankly, had seen better, brighter days. "I dreamed about killing you again last night, and it felt alright to me." He heard himself sing the words as they marched past him; rather than cushioning or muffling the lyrics, the music seemed to highlight them, making them even more difficult to bear. All Jeff Tweedy could think was, "I've failed. I've let the band down. I sound like the most depressed person in the world."

But he hadn't failed. He had taken the first blind leap into an album that would prove to be one of the defining moments of his and Wilco's career. *Summerteeth* would expose his inner world to an almost unbearable degree but, with the help of his bandmates, somehow turn it into life-affirming music.

A couple of years later, Tweedy would write a song called "War on War," in which he would sing, "You have to learn how to die, if you wanna wanna be alive."

In that Austin recording studio, Tweedy died a little. It was a feeling he already knew intimately. There was the moment Jay Farrar took the band they had built together, Uncle Tupelo, and tore it apart by telling Jeff Tweedy he couldn't stand working with him anymore. The moment Tweedy turned an alternative-country concert for a club full of Johnny Cash fans into a punk-rock kamikaze mission. The night Tweedy baited a British audience until they wanted to tear his fool Yankee head off. And still to come would be the moment when he found his record label didn't want the best record he'd ever made.

Beneath the facade of the small-town newspaper-delivery boy that he once was, the kid who wouldn't speak unless he was spoken to, Jeff Tweedy brings a self-confidence that cannot be ignored or denied. It can be willful and sometimes almost cruel, but it is not indiscriminate or random. The personality can best be glimpsed and assessed through the music, because Tweedy is a songwriter of knee-buckling honesty. The emotions in his songs examine the heart of darkness that, to some degree, lurks in all of us. His great subject is intimacy—with a lover, with a friend, with music itself—and its price. His songs teeter between bliss and oblivion: "There is something wrong with me"; "I've got reservations about so many things, but not about you"; "I am trying to break your heart"; "Playing Kiss covers, beautiful and stoned."

He can ice the listener's blood with a scream; there are nights when "Misunderstood" sounds like a back-alley mugging, when his howl "I want to thank you all for nothin', nothin' at all" repeats until the veins rise like blue fault lines down his neck. Or he can cut our hearts out with a whisper. "She's a Jar" climaxes with a line that lands with a sickening thud, a corpse being dropped from a third-floor window, but it's sung with the understatement of an undertaker: "She begs me not to hit her." Left unanswered is precisely what kind of holocaust the character in this song had to live through to deliver that line with such matter-of-factness. Not knowing is almost a relief.

In the way they marry the everyday with the surreal, the opaque with the anthemic, the acerbic with the melodic, Tweedy's songs evoke the work of the great songwriters, not so much the usual suspects (Neil Young, Woody Guthrie, Bob Dylan) as the lost punks, iconoclasts, and misfits who put the color in Tweedy's life between the headphones. Tweedy learned to be a great listener before he became a great songwriter and musician, and he developed a connoisseur's taste: Pere Ubu's Peter Laughner, the Minutemen's D. Boon, the English folkies Nick Drake and Bill Fay. With these rock outsiders Tweedy shares a certain daring, a way of looking at the world that demands more of it and more of himself, sometimes at a steep cost. Tweedy's cry "Maybe all I need is a shot in the arm" on *Summerteeth* echoes the desperation of Nick Drake as he sang in the darkness of a British recording studio just weeks before entering a psychiatric rest home, murmuring about the world's fading beauty, even though unable to lift his face off the studio floor.

With each Wilco album—including two *Mermaid Avenue* collaborations with Billy Bragg on the lyrics of Woody Guthrie—Tweedy and his band have pushed their music to measure up against those lost giants. They've done what few bands in the post-Nirvana rock 'n' roll world have managed: to better themselves with each album. It's not a stretch to imagine Dylan and the Band bashing out a Tweedy song such as "Dreamer in My Dreams" in the basement of Big Pink. And it's possible to get so lost in the closing moments of Wilco's ensemble performances in "Reservations" or "One by One" that time melts away.

"Jeff is one of the few people I am envious of as a writer," says Gary Louris, whose band the Jayhawks helped restore the art of songwriting to 1990s rock. "I don't mean to be a curmudgeon, but there's very little that impresses me when I listen to new stuff. Whether it's the White Stripes or whoever the band of the moment is supposed to be, I think, 'That's kinda cool, but compare it to the greatest stuff in rock and it pales.' I try to look at things like that in perspective, stacked against the best of all time, and I think Jeff ranks up there. You can put his stuff against anyone's, and as a songwriter he doesn't have to back down to anyone. He lives the music, more than anyone I know. He's immersed in music, and it shows."

R.E.M.'s Peter Buck simply calls Tweedy "one of the best songwriters of his generation."

It took time. For a shy small-town kid from the Midwest, to risk failure in the name of artistic expression is to contradict a lifetime's worth of social schooling. But the thirty-four-year-old man who wrote "War on War" isn't that far removed from the fourth grader who brandished a cassette copy of Bruce Springsteen's *Born to Run* one day at school and informed his classmates that it was his creation. It was as if the kid weren't challenging his classmates to believe so much as himself.

With his high-school friend Jay Farrar in Uncle Tupelo, Tweedy forged a style of music that both embodied and repudiated the small-town life he had known in Belleville, Illinois, a blue-collar town surrounded by farms and strip mines thirty miles southeast of St. Louis. Together they steered the band with a tight-lipped refusal to pander, a deft songwriting touch, and voices that sounded like they could've fit comfortably alongside the plainspoken misfits on Harry Smith's *Anthology of American Folk Music*. But whereas Farrar was already a fully formed musical talent at the time of Uncle Tupelo's first album, Tweedy grew into a formidable songwriter incrementally. On Uncle Tupelo's fourth album, *Anodyne*, in 1993, he was finally sharing the songwriting load equally with Farrar, matching him song for quality song. Uncle Tupelo's twang punk sowed seeds for an alternative-country movement that would become a fad by 1995, spawning a spate of major-label signings of Tupelo-like bands, a still-thriving Internet community of fans, and the fanzine *No Depression*, named after the Carter Family song that had provided the title for Uncle Tupelo's 1990 debut album. But Uncle Tupelo wasn't around to enjoy the spoils. The band's bitter breakup would prove a watershed in Tweedy's development as an artist: within months he took the remaining members of Uncle Tupelo into the studio and began shaping a musical personality that would take him far beyond the alt-country world that he and Farrar had been credited with creating.

It was no accident that Tweedy's abilities as a songwriter and arranger caught up to his ambitions in Wilco; by the time Uncle Tupelo broke up, John Stirratt and Ken Coomer had begun to evolve into a swinging rhythm section, and the versatility of the musicians added and subtracted along the way—Max Johnston, Jay Bennett, Bob Egan, Leroy Bach, Glenn Kotche, Mikael Jorgensen—paved new avenues for Tweedy's songs. In its raunchiest moments, Wilco celebrated rock for rocking's sake: the Keith Richards–worthy riff high-stepping out of "Casino Queen," the fractured guitar solo in "I'm the Man Who Loves You," the Velvet Underground–worthy throb of "I'm Always in Love." The band mastered the simple joy and immediacy of a pop song, in the spacious arms-wide-open wonder of "California Stars," or the sing-along that drunkenly smiles at crushing small-town routine in "Passenger Side." What's most intriguing, however, is a more recent development: Wilco's increasing aptitude for exploring the shadows. On their 2002 album, *Yankee Hotel Foxtrot*, they make music that evokes the feeling of being between worlds, of searching for consolation on a planet that feels lonelier than ever even as it becomes more packed with distractions, information, and convenience stores. It's all there in "Ashes of American Flags," the sound of 3 a.m. solitude, of Miles Davis's "Blue in Green" or the Flamingos' "I Only Have Eyes for You," music so intimate it's like a whisper in the listener's ear.

At its best, the music industry was complicit in such exchanges, a conduit between the most profound musicians of an era and the most ravenous music fans. When Wilco signed to Reprise Records in 1994 and became part of the Warner Brothers empire, it was joining a group of labels with a long, rich history of supporting not just musical giants such as Frank Sinatra, Neil Young, and R.E.M. but mavericks such as Van Dyke Parks, Ry Cooder, and Randy Newman. It was an artist-driven label run by music aficionados, and Wilco fit right in with the philosophy: to sign artists with a genuine vision that would be developed over a dozen albums, rather than quick-hit wonders designed to cash in on a trend. Then it all went wrong.

It was Wilco's lot to develop into a creative force at a time when the monetary value of music soared to an all-time high even as its artistic worth plummeted lower than Christina Aguilera's leather hip-huggers.

Against the backdrop of a $156 billion merger between America Online and Time Warner in 2000, bands such as Wilco—whose entire catalog for the conglomerate had sold about 1.5 million copies—became expendable. At least that's what two Reprise executives believed in the spring of 2001, when they decided to take a pass on Wilco's fourth album, *Yankee Hotel Foxtrot*.

It was a signpost of a trend that impinged on all the arts, especially music: For the last decade, the intelligence of America's listening audience had been tacitly ridiculed by the multinational corporations that make, market, and filter most of the music we hear. A band's worth was determined no longer by its artistic reach, its potential to create music of lasting significance, but by how rapidly it could find a huge audience. It didn't matter whether that audience was seduced by a designer fashion line, an acting role in a Hollywood movie, a tie-in with a video game, or, perchance, a compact disc as long as the corporate shareholders got their quarterly dose of good news. Of the Big Five corporations that ran the music industry at the time of the AOL–Time Warner merger, none was in it exclusively for the music; they had spread their financial claims across a diverse range of products, from cell phones to wine coolers, and music was just another widget on the assembly line.

The trend toward simpler music, quicker success, and more instantly marketable artists presumed that America had become a nation of indifferent, inattentive listeners and it should get the music it deserved. In turn, the multinationals poured big bucks into manufacturing pop stars, even those who couldn't sing or play a lick. Of course, prefab pop was at least as old as the Monkees and Menudo, but now the stakes were higher than ever: $14 million alone to make sure that everyone knew that Jennifer Lopez had a new album of pitch-corrected pop songs on the market. That left little or no cash to promote "difficult" artists, who were seen as self-indulgent prima donnas who could not be easily molded into multimillion sellers.

"Jeff Tweedy is a twat," one former major-label president told me at the height of the singer's travails with Reprise. Though acknowledging the enduring merit of Wilco's music, the executive—who didn't even work for Warner Brothers—marveled at Wilco's desire to make "indulgent albums" for what had become the music industry's largest corporation. "It's unacceptable at this time for any artist to behave the way he does. Who does he think he is? Neil Young?"

Perhaps. Neil Young once got sued by his label in the 1980s for making what the gravely disappointed executive David Geffen called "unrepresentative" albums—in other words, they didn't sell well enough. Two decades later, the stakes for Wilco and Reprise were even higher. The business of making music generates more than $12 billion a year, more annual revenue than even the movie industry. Yet as teen consumers are being tempted by diversions other than CDs—DVDs, cable TV, home video games, and, most insidious of all, personal computers—the Big Five, and the newly bloated AOL Time Warner in particular, are on a mission to cut not just the nonprofitable acts but even some of the ones who aren't profitable enough.

Into the latter camp fell Wilco. Wilco's sin wasn't that it was a drain on Time Warner's budget; here was a band, after all, that was pulling down more than $1 million a year on tour and therefore required no handouts from the label to stay on the road. But it simply wasn't big enough soon enough to suit the new demands of a business looking for instant megastars and cross-promotional celebrities. In the year after the merger was announced, AOL Time Warner's value had sagged by more than $50 billion. At a time when the blockbuster hit mattered more than ever, anything less—even a band emerging as one of the most important American rock bands of the last ten years—was deadweight.

So for music lovers who were paying attention to these dispiriting machinations, it was not particularly startling when Reprise rejected *Yankee Hotel Foxtrot* in July 2001. The real surprise came next. Rather than water down the music to meet its record company's demands for a more commercial album containing more radio-friendly songs, the band left Reprise, began streaming *Foxtrot* on its Web site—essentially giving its music away—and performed its new songs on a national tour.

The Chicago quintet's industry end around was a risky move

that turned into an artistic and commercial coup. When *Yankee Hotel Foxtrot* was finally released nine months later on Nonesuch Records (ironically, another, albeit smaller, subsidiary of the same AOL Time Warner conglomerate to which Reprise belongs), it was already one of the year's most widely discussed albums, a cause célèbre in the media, and a major embarrassment for the once-venerated Reprise, which underwent a leadership overhaul in the wake of Wilco's departure. *Foxtrot* sold more than 55,000 copies in its first week and debuted at number 13 on the *Billboard* pop-album chart; it has since sold more than 400,000 copies. Those figures are career bests for Wilco, but they're merely commercial validation for the one thing the record industry has misplaced in its rush to cut costs and bolster revenue: the music.

At times in Jeff Tweedy's life, it seemed as though music was the *only* thing that mattered. Along the way he has butted heads with equally strong-willed artists, tripped beneath the wheel of drugs and alcohol, let friends slip away, fired bandmates without notice, and struggled through the ups and downs of marriage. He has been human, in other words. His music resonates because it embraces that truth, especially the flaws.

Flaws, accidents, and failure are as essential to great music as instruments and voices. Rock 'n' roll is amplified self-expression. It is music so personal and unashamed that it couldn't be made by anyone else. It's not so much what notes are played as how they are played. It's the high wire Jeff Tweedy walks when he jumps into a guitar solo. Or the moment when Wilco drops the volume to an uncomfortable whisper in a noisy bar, as if the band were slowly undressing in front of a roomful of hooting strangers. It's the ongoing response to the question once posed in song by the Who's Pete Townshend: "Can you see the real me?" The artist's most difficult challenge is finding "the real me" rather than an idealized "me" or a copy of someone else's "me."

Jeff Tweedy has spent three-quarters of his life barging through unmarked doors in search of an answer, and his songs, from "Screen Door" to "Reservations," mark his journey. In many ways, that search makes him all wrong for what the music industry has become at the outset of the twenty-first century. He is not a celebrity or a larger-than-life character. He is not even an artist his most ardent fans can always embrace, because his music is less about meeting expectations than about upsetting them, including his own. In a business increasingly geared toward quarterly profits, Jeff Tweedy is a tough sell. But sometimes tough sells shake our souls in a way that no one else can. More than anything else, this is the story of an artist and a band that defied everything and everyone to put the music first.

CHAPTER 2

"SPEED BECAME AN END IN ITSELF"

At age fourteen in the fall of 1981, Jeff Tweedy was maimed by rock 'n' roll. He watched his new friend Jay Farrar, the kid he'd just met in freshman English class at Belleville Township High School West, pick up an electric guitar and bang out what sounded like just about the best version of Gang of Four's "I Found That Essence Rare" he'd ever heard. Farrar was tearing it up in a garage band called the Plebes with his older brothers Wade and Dade. Jeff, a kid who rarely spoke when adults were around, stood next to the speakers, trying to look like he belonged, trying to look older and cooler than he actually was. But all that unraveled when the Farrar brothers' music kicked him in the face, an unseen force that flung his body into a frenzy of involuntary motion.

It was a small-town junior-high-school dance, but for Tweedy it might as well have been the Rolling Stones at Madison Square Garden. The set list consisted mostly of punk, new-wave, and garage-rock songs, played with sloppy fervor and at withering volume: the Romantics' "What I Like About You," learned off the original Bomp single, and double-time Sonics, Generation X, and Stones covers, among others. Tweedy had no real idea whether the

Plebes were any good, but they were loud, and, most of all, he had a personal stake in their success: not only did he personally know the lead-guitar player; he'd carried his amplifier into the show. Up till then, he could only imagine himself playing guitar in a rock 'n' roll band. Now he could see firsthand how it was done, and he wanted in.

"I just went nuts," Jeff Tweedy says of that day. "Danced like a freakin' idiot. Before that moment, I don't think I had ever seen a rock band live. I had never been to a concert. I had been to weddings and seen bands that played all '40s stuff, but I had never been attacked by a garage band playing punk-rock songs. I was just completely blown away in awe—in awe of Jay, in awe of his brothers, in awe of the idea that this could be happening, that I was part of their inner circle in some way. They were just cool. Cooler than me. They were empowered in the way that I imagined myself to be empowered."

Jeffrey Scott Tweedy was born in Belleville, Illinois, on August 25, 1967, eight months after Jay Farrar, though sometimes the spread between the two would seem much wider once adulthood began to define them.

"He was an afterthought, a surprise baby," his mother, Jo Ann Tweedy, says of Jeff. He was indulged like an only child, with three significantly older siblings—Debra Ann, born in 1952; Steven Kent, 1955; and Robert Gregory, 1957—who were more like doting aunts and uncles. Deb outfitted him in dresses when Jeff was a baby, because she'd pined for a sister. Steve would later buy Jeff guitars. Greg would help maintain the beat-up vans that kept Jeff's bands on the road.

Jeff's father, Bob, had been working on the Alton & Southern Railroad in East St. Louis since before he was old enough to vote; by the time he retired in 1995, he'd put in forty-six years at the switching yard, advancing to a series of management positions that required him to be on call through most weekends and made him a relatively remote presence in his children's lives. Jo Ann, the high-school sweetheart he married in 1952, when both were attending Belleville West, designed kitchens while raising their children in cramped quarters until a three-bedroom bungalow on Fortieth Street became available in 1967. The family bought it at auction for sixteen thousand dollars. This was the house Jeff Tweedy would grow up in, with a swing on the front porch, a two-car garage out back, and an attic big enough to accommodate not only Jeff's bedroom but the practice space where he and Jay would hack out an identity as a band while a handful of neighborhood kids watched.

Eric Rujanitz is a police officer's son who lived across the street from the Tweedys. "We lived in a neighborhood of one-income families, people that pulled down thirty to thirty-five thousand dollars a year and had four kids, a dog, a cat, and two cars," he says. "Nobody was coal-miner's-daughter poor, but we were also pretty sheltered from people who were rich. It wasn't until I got to high school and met a few kids whose dads were lawyers, and only then did I start to realize we didn't really have that big of a house, or have that much money."

A blue-collar town of about forty thousand people, Belleville is surrounded by farms and low rolling hills, stitched with railroad tracks, and has been insulated from economic hardship since the nineteenth century by a network of strip mines, breweries, mills, and foundries. Countless corner taverns served up four-dollar take-home buckets of beer for factory workers heading home. On summer nights, the Tweedys' block would teem with kids tossing Frisbees or baseballs while parents grilled burgers and bratwurst on their barbecues and downed beers. The local economy was slowing down, with the Stag brewery downtown on its last legs (it would close before the end of the 1980s), but it wasn't much different from many other small midwestern towns: white, working-class, and relatively sheltered from what were readily seen by most of the locals as the scourges of big-city life—underachieving schools, crime, traffic, poverty, and integration.

But by the time Jeff Tweedy and Jay Farrar were in their early teens, most of those industries and traditions had collapsed, leaving the town largely dependent on service jobs in the local hospitals and schools and nearby Scott Air Force Base.

"It wasn't a happy place to be in the '80s," Jay Farrar says. "It really wasn't. This was the era of the poor indoor skating parks, so there wasn't that much to do outside of playing sports or playing music."

"Downtown dried up, the nice department stores closed, and people started migrating east," Bob Tweedy says. "Now you got pawnshops and used-car lots and a lot of vacant storefronts. There's not a heck of a lot left in this town. Everybody is trying to get used to being integrated, and a lot of the old German folks in town don't take to that kindly. There are no jobs here. The city is dying."

Yet the Tweedys didn't budge from their home in central Belleville. "The attitude growing up was definitely to get out of there," Jeff Tweedy says. "One of the only things to do was bitch about Belleville. But it's not much different now from the way it was then. My family is still there, and that's all anybody ends up having. I used to call it boring, mundane in newspaper stories, and I'd get stopped by the cops and they'd say, 'Did you really mean those things you said about Belleville, Jeff?' And I'd say I wouldn't be here if it wasn't boring and mundane. My parents would've moved if it was too exciting."

Tweedy escaped Belleville whenever he visited his attic bedroom. Its centerpiece was a poster of the midwestern rock heroes Cheap Trick, with Rick Nielsen brandishing a five-necked guitar like some mischievous medieval wizard. On his dresser was a crude little Fisher stereo. He picked through the leftovers in his siblings' record collections after they went off to college, and discovered everything from his sister's Herman's Hermits 45s to his brother's dorm albums: Edgar Froese and Amon Düül next to Leo Sayer and Harry Chapin. "I was physically attracted to Paul McCartney's picture on the Beatles' White Album," Tweedy recalls. "The Beatles were so charismatic. The pictures of all four of them in that album were so beautiful, especially the one of Paul. I remember thinking that's what I wanted to look like."

He soaked up knowledge furtively at magazine racks, losing himself in record reviews in *Rolling Stone* and *Trouser Press* while his mother shopped; then he'd scrounge and scrape to get the albums that sounded most appealing. A friend's grandmother used to keep quarters in mason jars on her back porch, so the boys helped themselves to several pocketfuls of the change and went shopping: Jeff picked up X's *Wild Gift*. A rave in *Rolling Stone* of the Clash's *London Calling* prompted Jeff to tag along with his mom to a local Target store in hopes of finding the prize. And there it was: a violent black-and-white cover photograph of the Clash's Paul Simonon laying waste to his bass guitar onstage. Jeff was concerned his mom would never let him buy it, but she did, of course; there was little that Jo Ann Tweedy denied her son when it came to pursuing his music.

Jo Ann was the neighborhood den mother, and Jeff and his friends found her comfortable to be around. Her devotion to her son's music would span the decades: she bought him his first guitars, collected door money at his first gigs, fronted the rent on his first recording space, clipped and saved mountains of articles about his exploits, and attended every show within driving distance, no matter how ill or busy she was. Only three days after being released from the hospital in November 2002, when blocked arteries caused her EKG reading to flat-line and doctors had to scramble to save her, she defied physicians and family members and attended a tour-closing Wilco show in St. Louis.

Jo Ann Tweedy was the reserved, soft-spoken complement to her husband, the no-nonsense taskmaster and partymeister. Though not a particularly large man, Bob could take over a room by walking into it; with piercing blue eyes, the strong hands and forearms of a railroad man, and a booming voice, he had stage presence, even though he never learned to play an instrument.

At gatherings of the extended Tweedy clan, hootenannies broke out once the beer started to flow, and Bob would be right in the middle of them. Jeff was a silent witness, sitting in the corner watching the adults guzzle, grin, and stumble their way through an assortment of old country tunes, folk ballads, and spirituals like "The Battle Hymn of the Republic." Bob Tweedy's cousin Herb Henson had been a country radio and television star in the 1950s, and Bob's barrel-chested brother Bill was the guitar-playing catalyst for many of the picking sessions at family gatherings. None of Jeff's siblings played an instrument, but Bob Tweedy loved to be around music and would throw open his home to just about anyone with a guitar who wanted to drink beer, laugh, and sing songs. One day Jeff's guitar-playing friend Brian Henneman showed up while Jeff was on tour with Uncle Tupelo, and Bob

invited him not only to stay for a few cold ones but to plug in his
gear so Bob could bellow Neil Young songs, "Turkey in the
Straw," and "I've Been Working on the Railroad." Henneman
ended up staying fifteen hours, camped out in the Tweedys' living
room, playing just about every song he knew twice, sustained by
egg sandwiches, pizza, and several cases of beer.

Jeff's curiosity took a few years to translate into actually playing music. When Jeff was six years old, his mother bought him an
acoustic guitar and later paid for a half-dozen guitar lessons, which
left him discouraged but not any less obsessed. "I took *Born to Run*
to school on a cassette that I copied off a record and told everybody that it was my band," Jeff says. "Most everybody was just
shaking their heads at me. So I'd hang out with the kids that would
tolerate that kind of delusion. And I still do." He laughs. "I still
only hang out with the kids that will tolerate that degree of psy-
chosis.

"For me, I was reveling as much in the music as in the idea of
that coming out of me. I don't think I made those philosophical
connections as a kid, but that's what I was doing. And I still do that
to this day. That's one of the primary experiences I have listening
to music, whether it's Steve Reich or Gram Parsons. Does it trans-
port me to some other place, create a flow in my mind, and, most
important, do I automatically start to picture myself playing those
two notes on the piano, and what kind of feeling would that be to
have that coming out of me?"

But it wasn't until Jeff took a bad tumble off his bike and
ripped open a fist-sized wound in his leg at the end of eighth grade
that he began to apply himself to learning guitar. "I was lying in
bed for a few weeks," he says, "so I took the guitar from the closet.
I thought I better learn how to play this thing before people figure
out I can't." The goal wasn't to master fancy solos but to get just
good enough to strum a song.

"I saw the life my dad had, and I knew I didn't want it,"
Tweedy says. "He had to take care of a family basically since he was
seventeen, and the only real outlet he had was a twelve-pack after
working all day. I saw the guitar as *my* outlet."

Armed only with knowledge of a few basic barre chords, Jeff
Tweedy knew what he wanted to do. He just didn't know how to

take the next step. Then, in freshman English class in the fall of 1981, he met Jay Farrar, a tight-lipped kid who had difficulty looking anyone in the eye. "We were assigned to turn to the person next to us, interview them, and then write an essay about them," Tweedy recalls. "Jay and I didn't interview each other, but I remember hearing the essay about him: 'This is Jay. Jay's favorite rock group is the Sex Pistols.' And the kid next to me reads mine. 'This is Jeff. His favorite record is by the Ramones.' In Belleville, it was shocking to meet another kid that was into punk rock."

Jay Farrar was struck by a similar feeling of instant kinship. "It's like the two visitors from Mars, as far as everyone else was concerned," he recalls. "We felt like the only two people listening to that type of music."

But the friendship didn't exactly catch fire. "Bonding experiences with Jay Farrar are so subtle they're more accumulative," Tweedy says. "At some point I'm like, 'I guess he likes me.' I flattered myself. He actually called me one time, and it was a big deal, because it meant that it always wasn't going to be me calling him. It was really tough to tell what he thought of anyone. I was insecure about that, and I still am to an extent."

Jay Farrar grew up in farm country south of Belleville in a house filled with musical instruments, stacks of folk, country, and classic-rock albums, and three guitar-playing older brothers: Wade, Dade, and John. His dad, Jim "Pops" Farrar, traced his lineage to the Ozark Mountains in Arkansas and was a merchant marine who rarely left a port without collecting a new song: Irish folk ballads, German drinking songs, polkas, and sea chanteys. Once in a while Pops's brother and an old Army buddy would get together in the house to play music—on dueling squeeze-boxes. "It was three accordion players wheezing away at once, playing waltzes, polkas, reworking these old folk songs, an odd and unpredictable mix that, looking back on it, was quite a trip for a nine- or ten-year-old kid to experience firsthand," Farrar says. His mother, Darlene, was a much better musician than Pops technically, a skilled guitarist and singer who passed her talents—and her self-effacing manner—to her sons. But Pops also had an impact. He wasn't much for hitting all the right chords, but his philosophy would prove integral to Jay's lifelong attitude toward music: "Just find an individual way and do the best you can."

Jay was one of a kind right from the start; he made his public performing debut at age five dressed in a pint-sized suit and tie when he played "Dixie" on harmonica at a Millstadt Grade School PTA meeting. After listening to Rolling Stones, Beatles, and punk records with his older brothers, Jay had begun gravitating toward his mother's acoustic folk albums by his late teens. His curiosity led him to music "that had the same intensity as punk rock but was more versatile, because it could be done with the same intensity at quieter volume levels," Farrar says. "I liked the impromptu-jam aspect of it, the idea of people playing acoustic instruments together in a room without anything between the listener and them."

By seventh grade, Jay Farrar had become competent enough on the guitar to hang with his older brothers at their garage band's rehearsals. Dade played bass, and Wade morphed into a wiry, blond Belleville incarnation of Iggy Pop, a manic singer who cannon-balled off the stage onto the dance floor, wailed on harmonica, and left the girls breathless.

"I don't remember all of us sitting down at once, but in twos and threes," Wade says of the Farrar-family jam sessions. "Our oldest brother, John, gravitated toward jazz and classical, while our dad was of the opinion that three chords were enough for every-body. John didn't follow his advice, but his guitars and amps got passed down, and that's what we learned on. When Jay discovered old Beatles records, he went in a different direction than John. Growing up with musicians, I know what it takes to be a great one. You have to sit in your room for hours and hours a day, just you and your instrument. I didn't have that discipline, but Jay did."

Jeff ingratiated himself with the Farrars enough that he was asked to join the band, even though he wasn't much of a rhythm-guitar player and was too shy to sing. But the Plebes needed another high-school-age member to qualify for a local Battle of the Bands, and Jeff was in. By that time the band had started to veer toward rockabilly, but the newest member would have none of it. He may not have been able to play his instrument, he may not

have been much of a singer, and he may have had the least senior-
ity, but he knew what he wanted his band to sound like.

"Jeff started getting the bookings—the newest guy in the band,
the youngest guy in the band did the bookings!" Wade Farrar says.
"He had much different goals than the rest of us: the things he
wanted to do, the places he wanted to play, the sacrifices he wanted
to make. He wanted to get us over to St. Louis and play clubs,
where we were really gonna have to pay our dues because no one
knew who we were. He took over for Dade, who wanted to play
more rockabilly. Jeff didn't. Jeff was in the band for two months,
and Dade was my brother, but Dade was the guy who left the
band."

Before his departure, Dade brought the last in a string of
drummers to the band: Mike Heidorn, the younger brother of the
girl Dade Farrar was dating at the time. Heidorn was a classmate of
Jeff Tweedy's and Jay Farrar's at Belleville West, though neither
knew him very well and both considered him kind of an oddball.
Mike was garrulous, energetic, and outwardly enthusiastic—a personality that couldn't have been more opposite that of his new
bandmates. But he had a three-piece drum kit that he had salvaged
from a garage sale for sixty-five dollars, and though he was self-
taught, he was a loose, limber natural talent on the kit. After one
rehearsal in the basement of Pops Farrar's house, he was in.

With the ouster of Dade Farrar and the addition of Mike Heidorn, the Plebes morphed into the Primitives, taking their name
from a 1965 garage-rock song by the long-forgotten Groupies; the
new band was also occasionally known as the Primatives, with an
a, due to a misspelling on a business card. However it was spelled,
the name fit the sound. "I remember looking the word up in the
dictionary, and there wasn't a word [of the definition] that didn't
describe what we were trying to do," Wade Farrar says.

The third definition of "primitive" in the *New Shorter Oxford
English Dictionary* certainly fitted the quartet: "having a quality or
style associated with an early or ancient period or stage; old-
fashioned; simple, unsophisticated; undeveloped, crude."

It wasn't particularly fashionable to be a punk rocker in
Belleville. St. Louis's rock scene was stultifying in its conservatism,
bereft of bands playing original music, and dominated by a rock

station heavy on Styx, REO Speedwagon, and classic rock. It seemed possible to count the punk devotees at Belleville West on the fingers of two hands in the early 1980s. Refusal to bow down at the altar of Ted Nugent or Van Halen could win you a mugging at the hands of the denim-jacketed taste police.

"I wore a new-wave tie to a gig once in 1981—I didn't wear makeup, but I still got beat up," Wade Farrar says. "They thought I was glammed up, which by Belleville standards I guess I was. Right before you'd get punched, you'd hear, 'Deep Purple, ass-hole!' "

The Primitives responded to their teenage version of hell by focusing exclusively on high-octane, blues-based garage rock pumped through vintage Vox amplifiers. They soon became part of a small scene that included like-minded bands such as the Blue Moons and Joe Camel and the Caucasians. The idea was to play everything faster and louder, so that the crowd wouldn't just move, it would lose its collective mind in a blur of sweat, alcohol, and three-chord adrenaline: the Kinks' "You Really Got Me"; the Isley Brothers' "Shout"; Vince Taylor's rockabilly obscurity "Brand New Cadillac," via the spit-and-vinegar reinvention on the Clash's London Calling; even the occasional revved-up Buck Owens or Johnny Cash song.

"Speed became an end in itself," Wade Farrar says, "because it allowed us to make anything our own. At the time, I don't think we liked country all that much, because it was something our parents listened to. But when we'd finish playing 'Act Naturally,' my dad would yell, 'Play that "I'm gonna be a big star" song again.' We got it off one of his Buck Owens records, but he liked our version. As long as the crowd could dance, they liked whatever we played."

Soon the band was drawing hundreds of people and making two thousand dollars a gig for its shows at the Liederkranz, a century-old wedding hall in Millstadt, five miles south of Belleville. Jo Ann Tweedy collected the three-dollar cover fee in one of her Tupperware bowls. Under-age drinking was rampant under the not-so-watchful eye of a single off-duty police officer, and the floor would be sticky with suds, sweat, and grime as the Primitives drove themselves and the audience to the brink of exhaustion.

The band occasionally shared the bill with a like-minded band of shaggy-haired, flannel-shirted outcasts from another out-of-the-way blue-collar enclave: the Blue Moons from Festus, Missouri. The band was led by Brian Henneman, a gifted guitarist and song-writer who would later serve as something of a roadie, sideman, and instigator for Uncle Tupelo before going on to make a series of acclaimed albums with the Bottle Rockets.

"We were coming from a similar place: garage covers, really raw versions of 'Get off My Cloud' and 'Louie Louie,'" Henneman recalls. "But the Primitives were more intense, better in every way. Seeing them the first time, my reaction was, 'Damn, we gotta work harder than we are.' They were just kids, but they were slamming it."

Jay Farrar's guitar was the biggest brick in the wall of sound, buzzing with string-snapping fuzz-toned aggression. "It sounded like the solos on those early Kinks records," Henneman says. "It was somehow clean and dirty at the same time. He had these country licks, a dash of Buck Owens, but at the same time he'd be chopping away. Stand in front of his amplifier, and you were in for a good whipping." Jay would also occasionally give his brother a breather and sing a few lead vocals, usually on blitzkrieg-bop versions of "Hang on Sloopy" and the Stones' "Hang Fire." It was a prelude of things to come. "I was singing from the get-go because no one else had the nerve to do it," Wade Farrar says. "So I never noticed how good Jay's voice was until he sang 'Hang on Sloopy.' It's a silly song, but when he sang it, it wasn't silly anymore."

Off Wade's left shoulder, Jeff Tweedy was now a crude but able abuser of the bass guitar, and he provided an onstage visual counterpoint for the delirium on the dance floor. He pinballed and pogo-hopped in front of Heidorn's drums and occasionally stepped up to the microphone to inject a background scream. He was a cherub living in his own little "Wayne's World" of noise.

When Tweedy wasn't rehearsing with the band, the after-school hours he had once devoted to playing baseball and soccer were now spent hanging around at Record Works, the sole Belleville outlet for punk-rock singles. There he was offered his first joint, had lost his virginity to a twenty-five-year-old clerk by the time he was fifteen, and immersed himself in albums by the

Minutemen, Hüsker Dü, and Public Image Ltd. At night in his attic bedroom, he'd go to sleep with the drums of Martin Atkins and the voice of John Lydon on P.I.L.'s *Flowers of Romance* ushering in his dreams.

"I would vividly imagine how awesome it would be to be playing 'Pretty Vacant' at my high school and singing like Johnny Rotten and scaring the fuck out of the people who didn't like me," Tweedy recalls. "There were other kids worse off than me, but I wallowed in my own self-pity plenty. There were always feelings of not being loved by the right girls, or being ignored by the right people."

Music was a way of setting himself apart, of joining an elite group, even if that group consisted of only a handful of punk-rock aficionados. He helped himself to records from the Belleville Public Library, such as Elvis Costello's *My Aim Is True* and old Alan Lomax field recordings and Folkways records. "The attitude was that there's nobody else in this town that's gonna want this, let alone be cool enough to appreciate it the way I can," Tweedy explains. "Jay Farrar was guilty of that as well. We had an elitist attitude toward those records, like we deserved them more than anybody else."

Mike Heidorn tagged along. "There would be parties at the rich kids' houses, football team parties or whatever, and we'd go because there's nothing else going on," he says. "We played into these personas as the flannel guys who would crash your party, spill beer on your carpet, and take over your stereo. They'd be playing Fleetwood Mac or Journey, and we'd scratch the record as we took it off the turntable and put on one of our Black Flag or Minutemen tapes, something that we thought was more rockin'. We'd get kicked out of there within an hour every time."

Even in the Primitives' hierarchy, Mike, Jeff, and Jay went relatively unrecognized. They were the boys in the band. Wade Farrar, the older, more outwardly confident, and charismatic front man, was the star.

"I always thought Wade would have been the guy out of all of them to do something in music, because he was a super front guy," says Darin Gray, another disenfranchised punk-rock kid from nearby Edwardsville, Illinois, who befriended Jeff and started showing up regularly at Primitives gigs. "The rest of the guys were great musicians—better than anyone else we knew of that age— but they just kind of stood there and played, maybe sang a little bit, but I never thought it would be those guys that would go on and do something in music."

Without Wade Farrar it's doubtful Jay, Jeff, and Mike would initially have felt confident enough to step onstage. But Wade didn't have their single-minded drive and ambition. He was work- ing toward an engineering degree at Southern Illinois University Edwardsville, about thirty miles northeast of town, and there was never enough study time. He would immerse himself in stacks of computer paper backstage before Primitives gigs in a feverish attempt to keep up with his mounting homework. He was also pil- ing up student loans, and out of desperation he tried to join the Army. He told everyone he was leaving the band, only to find that through a paperwork screwup the Army wasn't going to accept his application. Then Heidorn broke his collarbone goofing around with his friends after a concert in 1986, which effectively sidelined the Primitives. Jay Farrar and Tweedy weren't about to stop play- ing, however. Within weeks they were meeting over at Heidorn's house to write songs and practice.

When Wade began to catch up on his studies a few months later, he was itching to play music again. On weekends, maybe, just for kicks, like old times. Jay, Jeff, and Mike had bigger plans. "I went back to the guys and said, 'Let's get together and jam some- time,'" Wade recalls. "They just looked at me funny and didn't say a word. I found out later they already had a new band."

CHAPTER 3

"I GOT DRUNK AND I FELL DOWN"

Before there was the band, there was the cartoon: a beer-brandishing Fat Elvis. The rock 'n' roll icon from Tupelo, Mississippi, reclines on a sofa chair, wearing his rhinestone Vegas jumpsuit and a pair of bunny slippers. Jeff Tweedy, Jay Farrar, and Mike Heidorn cracked up when their high-school friend Chuck Wagner showed them the cartoon he'd drawn. It helped confirm their decision: the two words the trio had randomly juxtaposed from two columns of nouns on a yellow legal pad would stick. "Uncle," meet "Tupelo."

The songs the young trio were writing were far more earnest than Wagner's Fat Elvis cartoon, which adorned flyers for the first handful of Uncle Tupelo concerts but, sadly, never ascended to the level of an official band logo. Whereas the Primitives focused mainly on covers that would work their crowds into a mindless sweat, Uncle Tupelo coalesced around the idea of writing songs that would hold up under more intense scrutiny. "The Primitives were all about let's go crazy and dance," their friend Nick Sakes says. "With Uncle Tupelo, it's like they discovered sadness, and the songs all of a sudden became way more serious."

In mainstream rock, 1987 was the year of Bon Jovi's "Livin' on a Prayer" and U2's *Joshua Tree* album. But Farrar and Tweedy were more tuned in to the lacerating, heart-on-sleeve indie rock of the Replacements, the Minutemen, X, Jason and the Scorchers, and Hüsker Dü. Another favorite, Soul Asylum, was the subject of an interview Tweedy conducted in high school while moonlighting as a music journalist for the St. Louis fanzine *Jet Lag*.

"They were cooler than me, even if they were acting like jerks," Tweedy says of his encounter with the Minneapolis indie rockers, which took place outside Mississippi Nights, the big rock club on the riverfront in St. Louis. "I might as well have begged for it. I brought them a case of Stag beer from Belleville, and they were making time with my girlfriend. I never did transcribe that interview."

Tweedy took a halfhearted stab at college, mostly because his parents insisted on it. His two oldest siblings had gotten multiple college degrees, while his brother Greg had gone on to work at the railroad, where he was injured on the job and was eventually forced to retire with a disability settlement.

"I couldn't see Jeff out there walking down a train track between a couple of boxcars at three in the morning," Bob Tweedy says. "What could Jeff do for a living? It was a complete blank. His mother didn't know either, until much later." Bob Tweedy shakes his head when he thinks about the life that he anticipated for his youngest son if he didn't get a college degree. "Jeff didn't believe in putting gas or oil in a car," he says. "I don't think he ever looked under the hood of an automobile."

Bob Tweedy still remembers the late-night phone call he got from Jeff after his son's high-school prom. Jeff's seven-hundred-dollar green Volkswagen Rabbit had blown an engine in a bad section of town, the outskirts of East St. Louis.

"Jeff, didn't you see any red dashboard lights come on?"

"Yeah, Dad. The oil light came on."

"And you kept driving?"

"Yup."

"He ran it into the ground," Bob Tweedy says. "He did that more than once. He wouldn't tell you anything is wrong as long as it would move."

It came as a major blow when Jeff said he was quitting college after a couple of desultory years at Southern Illinois University Edwardsville and Belleville Area College. Bob Tweedy stomped his feet and raised his voice until his face burned. Jeff said little, his mind set, his resolve unwavering. At nineteen he had decided to put music ahead of everything—even his relationship with his father.

"To me, Jeff and the band were just making a lot of noise," Bob Tweedy says. "I didn't think it would go anywhere. I raised a ton of hell, but Jeff's mind was made up. I was jumping up and down, but, polite as can be, Jeff told me how it had to be."

Jo Ann Tweedy, as usual, smoothed the way for her youngest son. "Jeff was transfixed by music," she says. "The band was taking him away from everything. I thought, if he falls flat on his face, he falls flat on his face. What can you tell a nineteen-year-old kid who's in love? Stop being in love?"

Love, however, did not pay the rent. While raising their sights as songwriters and performers in a succession of decrepit apartments and practice spaces, the boys worked part-time jobs to keep the money flowing for life's essentials: records, pizza, beer. During high school, Jay Farrar had worked at his mother's used bookstore in downtown Belleville. Mostly, this required him to prop his feet up on the couch and plow through her collection of English lit classics and Beat novels. Heidorn made his rent money as a printer for the local newspaper, the Belleville *News-Democrat*. But Tweedy ended up with the most fortuitous job of all. He landed a clerking position at one of the few cutting-edge record stores in St. Louis, Euclid Records, which was managed by a music fanatic named Tony Margherita, who is seven years older than Tweedy. Years later, Margherita could have been cast in the movie *High Fidelity* as one of the record-store music snobs; he was tall, diffident, even intimidating, with black horn-rimmed glasses and a discriminating ear. He could be downright condescending when it came to arguing about music. Uncle Tupelo was okay, for a local band.

"At that point, they were like a family, in all the good ways and the dysfunctional ways," Margherita says. "They had a serious side, but they were basically having a lot of fun. Frankly, they were drinking—a lot. I didn't really take them seriously for a long time."

Tweedy begged Margherita to see the band, and when he

finally agreed, what he saw didn't knock him out: a fuzz-toned roar that buried the melodies. But an acoustic performance at a charity event in the winter of 1988 was a different matter. "Up till then it had just been a bunch of kids playing with a lot of energy and volume," Margherita says. "But I walked out of there that night thinking that I should do everything I could to help these guys. I could finally hear the songs."

Margherita took over as the band's de facto manager, picking up many of Tweedy's duties as the guy who pestered club owners for gigs. And he pushed the trio to get into a studio and make a demo tape so that they could pry open a few doors at record labels.

"Jeff's social capabilities were essential to the success of the band at every level, and most importantly because it got Tony Margherita into the fold," says Chris King. King would go on to play in the St. Louis indie band Enormous Richard and run his own record label, Skuntry, which would record the music of Pops Farrar a few years before the patriarch's death in 2002. With Enormous Richard, he found himself picking Margherita's brain plenty of times for advice and knowledge, which the manager gladly shared. "I got to know a lot of bands that were as good as Uncle Tupelo, but none of them had Tony Margherita on the phone for them," King says. "His greatest gift was his ability to say no. He knew that you had to withhold a little bit to be desirable, and, working at the record store, he dealt with lots of labels, so he knew who to talk to and what they wanted to hear. He's just a good poker player."

Margherita had to become expert at bluffing. Like the band, he didn't really know what the hell he was doing. He had a degree from Washington University in urban studies, but his only job in the "music business," aside from that at Euclid Records, had been driving a delivery truck for another St. Louis record store. Even while employed at Euclid, he was painting houses to make ends meet. But Margherita was sure of one thing: Tupelo had the goods. By this time, Tweedy, Farrar, and Heidorn had written their first batch of originals, including "I Got Drunk" and "Screen Door," two songs that couldn't have been more different in outlook or approach yet somehow fit together to create an achingly sincere portrait of the band's little world.

"I Got Drunk" came out brawling, a full-on electric two-step that downshifted into a banjo-led acoustic finale. It began with Heidorn spitting out his first and only lyric contribution to an Uncle Tupelo song—"I got drunk and I fell down"—while his bandmates were jamming on a riff, and in a matter of minutes the verse was fleshed out by Farrar. He sang in a voice cracking with weariness and desperation, a last go-round from the back of one of their town's ubiquitous gin mills. Jay Farrar sounded like Belleville's world-weariest twenty-year-old:

> I grabbed me a fifth
> I poured me a shot
> I thought about all the things
> That I haven't got.

Tweedy's "Screen Door," on the other hand, was a vision of rustic innocence, a sunny little would-be folk song delivered in a shaky voice by a kid making the best of his surroundings:

> Down here, where we're at
> All we do is sit out on the porch
> Play our songs, like nothing's wrong
> Sometimes friends come around, they all sing along.

"I only knew how to play to my abilities as a musician, and I was very limited as a musician and a singer," Tweedy says. "I couldn't play a lot of other people's music on the guitar, so I would make up my own, simple things, and slowly figure out how to play them and turn them into a song. In a lot of ways the songwriting now isn't that different, but the raw material back then that I had to work with was so little, so spartan. 'Screen Door' was among the first songs I wrote. I remember sitting on the floor skipping class at SIU-Edwardsville, writing those stupid lyrics, trying to wrap those lyrics onto what I was trying to play on the guitar, and get good enough at it that I could play it for Jay."

Tweedy made a virtue of his limitations because they forced him to sing about the only world he knew: his own. It was a small planet; the number of people who cared about the band or the type of music it was attempting to master could easily have fit inside the three-bedroom second-floor apartment he shared with his bandmates on Eleventh Street in downtown Belleville. Visitors were inevitably greeted by a stack of empty pizza boxes at the door, dirty dishes were frequently piled in a plastic garbage bag until someone got around to washing them, and the refrigerator was well stocked with beer and perhaps a stray ketchup or mustard bottle. The furniture, such as it was, was a frightening collection of garage-sale and Dumpster reclamations. In winter, Tweedy's uninsulated six-by-eight-foot room off the kitchen would get so cold that he'd go to bed wearing a hooded parka and thermal gloves.

Plaster flaked off the walls, and the all-weather carpet was stained with stale beer and tobacco chew. But the place brimmed with instruments, recording equipment, cool records—everything from mountain-soul collections to SST-label post-punk—and highly opinionated music aficionados. It became a sanctuary, an unofficial clubhouse for the area's disenfranchised punk rockers, most of them scattered in southwestern Illinois towns such as Edwardsville, Wood River, and Chester. Nick Sakes and Darin Gray, future members of avant-punkers the Dazzling Killmen, were frequent visitors, as was David Dethrow, who would later play drums for country punks Caution Horse. They joined the band's small circle of confidants and cheerleaders, privy to every gig before it was announced and every song before it was performed in public.

"It was just such a small community of people, especially on the east side [of the Mississippi], where we all felt so isolated," Darin Gray says. "When we went to high school, nobody was into the bands we were into, so if you could find one person like that, you'd cling to them, just to have someone to relate to and make your world a little less small, to feel a little more comfortable in our own skins. We would drive hours to hang out together."

Nick Sakes booked Tupelo's first show, a sloppy forty-minute set in 1987 at the Corner Tavern in Edwardsville; it was witnessed by thirty people, most of whom were there to see the headliners, Das Damen. "I begged them to play, even though they kept saying they weren't ready," Sakes says. "They were right. They were rusty, they played a lot of covers [Dylan's "Knockin' on Heaven's

Door," Cream's "White Room"], but we were all hungry to see some bands that we could call our own, so it didn't matter."

Even in the late 1980s, when thriving independent rock scenes had sprung up in cities from Seattle to Athens, Georgia, St. Louis offered little to young bands playing original music. Nightlife was dominated by the strip of bars and clubs along the cobblestoned nine-block stretch of Laclede's Landing on the Mississippi River. "Living in St. Louis was like being stuck in that movie *Groundhog Day*, where the guy keeps reliving the same day over and over," says Wade Farrar. "Every day for thirty years you'd turn on the radio in St. Louis, and it'd still be the '70s."

"It was like a giant frat scene with lots of Budweiser and bad cover bands with bad '80s hair—like every bad teen movie party that you can imagine," says Richard Byrne, who was just starting out as the music editor of the local counterculture weekly, *The Riverfront Times*. New music with any sort of punk edge or artistic aspiration was barely tolerated, let alone encouraged; the Landing club owners were more interested in hiring bands that would provide a sleek backdrop for drinking and that were appealing to women. One of the few original bands that actually caught on was the Eyes, later renamed the Pale Divine, a pretty-boy Goth-rock outfit that eventually scored a major-label deal.

"Girls would line up for blocks to get into their shows," recalls Steve Scariano, a longtime record-store fixture in St. Louis who also played guitar in several underground bands. "We'd go down to the Landing and laugh at the enemy, so to speak, but Jeff also wanted to prove to them that he was better, that he and his band were better. The Eyes were making gobs of money, selling out shows at places like Kennedy's. The first time we went to see them, Jeff went off on them. I'm like, 'What do you care? Your band is so much better! Why do you give a fuck about those guys?' But the spark in his eyes was like, 'I'm better than them. The world needs to see that; the world needs to hear that.' It was there then, and it's still there now."

Cicero's would be Tweedy's proving ground, and Uncle Tupelo's. It was a dingy basement bar below a pizza joint on Delmar Boulevard, a few hundred feet from the Washington University campus on St. Louis's west side. Cicero's began booking the band, and by the tail end of 1988 the first signs of a viable music community distinct from the Landing's frat-party fare had begun to emerge. The dirty little secret of any "scene" is that it doesn't take a nation of millions to make one. A few dozen people will do, especially if they're the right people. In the case of St. Louis, circa 1989, the ingredients included a club (Cicero's), a handful of bands (Uncle Tupelo, Brian Henneman's Chicken Truck, Three Merry Widows, Three Foot Thick, Enormous Richard), a couple of tuned-in record stores (Euclid Records, Vintage Vinyl), and a complicit media (the community radio station KCOU and *The Riverfront Times*'s Richard Byrne).

"Cicero's gave the freakiest folks a chance to play, and in a one alt-newspaper town where the daily is completely ignoring this music, I had a lot of jack and I used it," Byrne says. "To the point where I was being almost irresponsible about it, by ignoring bands who, at least in terms of ticket sales, were much more successful, like the Eyes. So I had a column, and the record-store guys were talking, and there was a university within walking distance of Cicero's, and suddenly things were happening that had nothing to do with the Landing. People were coming to University City to see new music by new bands."

Within a year, the scene had mushroomed to the point where it could sustain the first of two *Out of the Gate* compilations of local underground bands. Cicero's was fast becoming St. Louis's answer to a circuit of clubs around the Midwest that catered to indie rock: Gabe's Oasis in Iowa City; the Blue Note in Columbia, Missouri; Lounge Ax in Chicago; Jake's in Bloomington, Indiana. Much like the Cavern Club, where the Beatles first got their start, Cicero's— which has since relocated to a spiffier location across the street— was as musty as an old man's unventilated basement and as homely as a three-legged dog. On nights when Uncle Tupelo played, claustrophobia reigned, and the city fire code was left in tatters: pipes dripped from amid the exposed floor joists across the six-and-a-half-foot ceiling, and when the audience crept past the 150 mark, it stood shoulder to shoulder from the bar at the bottom of the stairs to the three-inch stage at the base of the L-shaped room. A potentially lethal steel beam above the stage menaced any singer over six feet tall, and when it rained, water pooled near the electrical outlets.

"I'm five eight, and I'd hit my head sometimes in there," says René Saller, who years before becoming *The Riverfront Times*'s music editor fronted a twee country band named 60 Hertz Hum that occasionally opened for Uncle Tupelo. "It would drip, and there would be ominous crackling sounds from the electrical wires. I was always afraid I'd be electrocuted like in *Carrie* while I was singing. I did get shocked on several occasions. It was incredibly dangerous, but I'd drink enough to relax down there and forget what a dungeon it was. Unless you showed up two hours early, you couldn't get into some shows."

Brian Henneman and his bands were Cicero's regulars. "It was the worst place in St. Louis to see a band," Henneman says, "but it was the place every band wanted to play because it was always the best experience any of us ever had on a stage. Nobody ever complained that they couldn't see the band. It was more like you could hear 'em and feel 'em, and you were drunk or high or both, and the music was loud, and that was enough."

In the early days, the same core of about fifty people attended show after show. Cicero's had played host to some accomplished punk and post-punk bands, but until Uncle Tupelo came along, this stretch of Delmar had yet to see a homegrown act with the fire to match out of towners such as the Lyres or Jason and the Scorchers. Uncle Tupelo's performances became calendar-circling events, a matter of civic pride for the devotees.

"We were in their face," Steve Scariano says. "You could grab Jay's arm. The people who were there were going crazy, just drunk, and every time it was a ball. Right off the bat they had this group of a few dozen people who would show up at every show, encouraging them, these nurturing older brothers and sisters who were right in front of them every time, going crazy. They had charisma, even though they didn't move a lot onstage. A lot of it had to do with being the 'anti' of every other thing that was happening in town. This is the only band we have that was ours, that wasn't slick. Back then, you know how [the Replacements' Paul] Westerberg was the coolest guy in the world? It was that kind of cool, a Replacements-type thing."

Before one show, Scariano subjected Byrne to a face-to-face, spittle-flying tirade because he believed the critic wasn't paying the local boys enough attention. Byrne soon made up for it; he wrote about the band so frequently that he became the object of derision in some of the media-watchdog columns around town, many of which couldn't understand why he was lavishing so much attention on a band that no one outside the University City neighborhood seemed even to have heard of. It was just another reason to care about the band even more, as far as the faithful were concerned. Byrne, undaunted, turned every show into a must-see event in his column.

His enthusiasm was understandable. When Uncle Tupelo was onstage, there was no mistaking the band's priorities: songs, passion and sincerity, and the unspoken belief that everything else was an afterthought. The trio worked through several pitchers of draft beer onstage, and several more before and after. Heidorn soaked through his T-shirt, a lit cigarette bounced off his lips, and he paused to chug beers between songs. His kick drum didn't have much oomph, but he danced across the top of his kit with a dexterity that could be awe inspiring, lurching songs backward and forward like a driver wrestling a balky race car. He machine-gunned snare-drum fills and punctuated choruses with cymbal-sizzling authority. Farrar didn't just play his guitar; he attacked it through sweat-soaked bangs and broke enough strings every gig to defy any roadie to keep up with him. For Farrar, there was no such thing as a half-assed note.

"I went to the last gig with the Primitives, and Jay broke every string on every guitar in the house, and he borrowed my Tele-caster," Brian Henneman says. "Maybe that was a sign of the future, because he picked that thing up and you could really hear him. It was like a bull rampaging through a china shop. It was like, wow! He bought that guitar from me. He came to my house and showed me his bank-account statement; he had taken all of his money out to pay for it: $125. He used every penny he had left to buy a guitar."

Tweedy visibly gained confidence with almost every show, filling in the background harmonies, taking more chances with his bass playing, and, through a combination of alcohol and persistence, mustering the courage to push his thin, nicotine-scarred baritone through the din on a few lead vocals.

The trio dabbled in adding a fourth musician a couple of times, but it never worked out to anyone's satisfaction. "They were three guys who had been playing all through high school together, who were listening to the same records, who were living together— they were the three musketeers," Scariano says. "Their chemistry was so incredibly natural nobody else could have been in that band back then."

In the summer of 1989, lubricated by beer and growing self-confidence as songwriters and performers, the band was the freest it would ever be. At one gig, the normally reserved Farrar called attention to his bandmate who was wrestling with a broken bass string: "Ladies and gentlemen, this is John Paul Jones on bass guitar!"

While Tweedy grinned sheepishly, Farrar uncorked the guitar riff from Led Zeppelin's "Communication Breakdown," and the crowd giggled in acknowledgment of the reference. Later there were more uncharacteristic in-jokes from Farrar. U2's *Rattle and Hum* had come out the previous year, and it included several pompous speeches from Bono. Farrar began introducing every song that night with a Bono quote: "This is not a rebel song . . ."

"Jesus, Jay!" Tweedy exclaimed as Farrar persisted, both amazed and exasperated at his bandmate's sudden burst of giddiness.

The audacity extended to the music: a version of Bob Dylan's "Knockin' on Heaven's Door" that bridged hardcore punk and dub reggae, Bad Brains–style, and a hillbilly reinterpretation of the Stooges' "I Wanna Be Your Dog."

"They were acting like themselves, no airs, and the impact was as much physical and visual as it was musical," Chris King says. "They were all good-looking guys, shy yet charismatic. Heidorn was back there drinking, smoking, and smackin' the shit out of that snare on every fourth beat. I don't want a rock drummer who looks like he should be in a jazz band or at home taking care of his baby. I always thought the number-one ingredient of a rock drummer is they have to look like there's no place on earth they'd rather be than behind that kit, and that was Mike Heidorn. Jeff was the sort of guy who bounced off the wall, jumped up and down, shouted into the microphone. He later cultivated the image of a diffident, hard-to-reach artist, but that wasn't how he came up. He came up as the greeter of the band, the drinker, the enthusiast, the guy who loved to be in a band, the guy who was making the flyers and was working the crowd."

"They were great from the start, even when they were really drunk and self-indulgent and doing goofy stuff, especially Jeff, who would do totally melodramatic things onstage," says Cicero's regular René Saller. "I remember leaving one time in disgust. He was dating this woman Natasha, and they had this very tempestuous relationship. She apparently showed up at the gig, and he saw her in the audience and freaked out and said, 'This is a song about killing women, and I'm sending it out to Natasha,' and they'd do [the Soft Boys'] 'I Wanna Destroy You.' He was probably joking, but I still thought he went too far. He was in his early twenties, and everybody had those moments back then. Although Jay never did anything like that. Jay was always just perfect. He'd say something here and there. He's pretty much that way now. Jeff was the rock star. He had more charisma. He'd do things like take off his shirt. He was super skinny at the time, and he knew that girls liked him. I can't believe it was just because it was hot in there. Jay would never do that. It just wasn't his style."

Yet offstage Tweedy was still having trouble reconciling his own doubts about his abilities and his innate modesty with his rapidly rising stature in the St. Louis indie-rock hierarchy.

Heather Crist was a twenty-year-old Washington University student when Cicero's talent buyer, Risa Fite, entrusted her with checking I.D.'s at the club's upstairs entrance. "I remember this guy came in and I carded him because he looked like he was twelve," Crist says. "Then I told him what the cover charge was, and he says, 'Oh, Risa doesn't usually charge me a cover, because I work at Euclid Records.' I let him in, but I told Risa about it. She says, 'I don't care if he works at Euclid Records. I don't make him pay a cover because that's Jeff and he's in Uncle Tupelo.' I remember when they first started, when he first started getting popular, it was really uncomfortable for him to be recognized off the stage."

Tweedy hung out at Cicero's several nights a week, running up a tab of hundreds of dollars that had Cicero's owner, Shawn Jacobs, occasionally calling for a reckoning that never came. The staff loved Uncle Tupelo, and they especially loved Tweedy, who made the bar his second home. He and Crist developed such a close bond that several of their friends assumed they were dating, though they never did. When he wasn't at the bar or playing with the band, Tweedy would call her at two or three in the morning, waking her up just to talk. "Jeff craved human contact," Crist says. "He would always apologize when he called so late—he was the most apologetic person I ever knew—but you could tell he was lonely. He didn't try to hide how he was feeling."

It was easy to read Jeff Tweedy. When he was among his friends, his emotions—like his songs at the time—were up-front, almost embarrassingly transparent. But within the complex emotional architecture of Uncle Tupelo, communication was not nearly so direct. Even though the trio were roommates who played in the same band, they shared little else. "Me and Jeff would joke to each other without Jay hearing: 'Hey, Mike, want to go and rap about our feelings tonight?' " Heidorn says.

The chill would sometimes spill over into the living-room rehearsals. "There was a lot of unspoken communication in the band," Heidorn says. "If Jay wanted us to learn a particular cover song, he wouldn't tell us, he'd just point the speakers out toward the kitchen and play the song on his stereo for a week. Or Jeff would sit around and play something on an acoustic guitar for a few days. It was more like we were absorbing the music rather than learning it. At practice, the buck always stopped with Jay. Me and Jeff would learn a song and we'd say, 'Let's try this.' Jeff would start the song on bass, I'd play the drums, and sometimes Jay would say, 'Give me the guitar, Jeff.' Or he wouldn't say anything, and we'd move on to the next song. So Jay in that respect dictated what we did."

But when Jay Farrar did commit to a piece of music, he did so with the zeal of a true believer. Music for Jay Farrar was sacred ground. "Years later, when Jay and I were Son Volt, we weren't getting along for a day, and I remember playing the songs differently that night—not worse, just differently," Heidorn says. "I didn't miss any beats, but I just didn't play them with any of those extra accents I usually gave them. That was the only time in my whole life that he ever got really pissed off at me. Jay came offstage and said to me, 'You can call me an ass, but don't take it out on the music. Never mess with the music.' "

Plenty of musical tributaries converged in Uncle Tupelo's early recordings, but one of the most prominent was Neil Young—the off-the-cuff, midnight-of-the-soul Young of *Tonight's the Night* and *On the Beach*, as well as the hippie balladeer of *Harvest* and the primitive guitar genius of "Down by the River."

"You can't overestimate Young's influence on that whole scene," says the journalist Richard Byrne. "I would say the main reason I got what was happening was because I was a huge *Tonight's the Night* fan, and *Tonight's the Night* was the album for all of these guys, for Brian Henneman, for Jay Farrar, for Jeff Tweedy. They were hearing the country and folk stuff that they grew up around, and they were listening to all their SST punk records, and Neil crystallized it for them."

If so, Farrar and Tweedy came at Young from opposite directions—or from different sides of Tweedy's "Screen Door." Tweedy wrote about the world inside that door, Farrar about the one outside it. Jay Farrar didn't write love songs. He spoke through the voices of regular folks who didn't share in America's wealth, who were just scraping by or barely hanging on: barflies, factory workers, jobless outcasts. Farrar felt more comfortable speaking through those characters than he did pouring out his innermost feelings about the girl who got away. Tweedy felt completely out of his realm writing about broader, populist issues, so he focused on the complex feelings stirred by a never-ending series of relationships with women. "He went through them like tissue paper," Saller says. It allowed Tweedy to play Grant Hart to Farrar's Bob Mould, to build a partnership in the tradition of Hüsker Dü, a band that fed off the tension and contrasts between its two primary songwriters.

"I convinced myself that one of the reasons the band was connecting was because there was a difference between us," Tweedy says. "I was in awe of Jay Farrar, but I couldn't be him, and for me to try to write songs like him would've been a joke. I think Jay Farrar is a very old soul, a very old man, and he always has been, ever since I first saw him in English class. He has the weight of the world on his shoulders. There never seemed like there could be a frivolous moment playing music with a person like that, unless there was a disclaimer. In Uncle Tupelo's live shows, alcohol became the disclaimer if things got a little too celebratory. There was a concern about the world, that we had to do something. But the music we were emulating was nowhere near as serious as we made it out to be, except some of the folk stuff. There was a Dylan fixation too. Dylan definitely never played to his age-group. He played down to his age-group. He modeled himself after an old man, and so did Jay Farrar."

And it was Farrar's songwriting, singing, and guitar playing that drew the most attention in the band's early days. But even Farrar acknowledges that the songwriting and recording process was much more collaborative than initially perceived by some listeners. "Over time Jeff and I found it easier to write separately and bring our songs to the band," he says. "There were a few exceptions. For 'So Called Friend,' Jeff wrote most of the lyrics and I wrote most of the music. In 'Graveyard Shift,' there was some input from Jeff on the music. Mostly it was an editing process, where Jeff or I would bring in a song and the others would suggest things, mostly in the musical structure."

These "edits" would prove crucial. If Farrar focused primarily on lyrics and chord changes, Tweedy and Heidorn brought the dynamics that gave the songs their manic pop thrill. Tweedy was already predisposed to the explosive stop-start arrangements that would soon become the band's signature from listening to the Minutemen, and Heidorn's energetic self-taught style was perfectly suited for it. Much in the way the Who had turned Keith Moon's idiosyncrasies as a drummer into a strength, Tweedy and Farrar exploited Heidorn's nervous energy to create songs that had the same push-pull tension as their songwriting.

"I wrote songs and lyrics the way I did because I wanted our songs to fit together," Tweedy says. "We were driving in the same direction as a band, listening to the same records. But things came a lot quicker to Jay. So I became skilled at arranging. Jay would crank out the songs, and my contribution was to boil them down, to figure out what was the most impactful way to get the song to work. The arrangements on the first couple records are insane, and I still don't know how we pulled some of them off. A lot of it had to do with Mike Heidorn. Nobody could duplicate his parts."

After a series of dim-sounding demos, in 1989 the trio traveled to Champaign, Illinois, where they laid down ten tracks in the attic studio of the pop rocker Adam Schmitt. Heidorn wasn't wild about the experience; he didn't like hearing his bandmates' instruments through headphones and lamented that he couldn't make visual contact with them. "It's something I got used to after about seven records," he says, "but initially I think the music suffered a bit because I needed Jay and Jeff to be close to me. I wanted to see their right legs twitching as they built up to a chorus so I could give it the energy it deserved."

The resulting cassette, which the band dubbed *Not Forever, Just for Now*, is far from definitive. On the cover is a white Rickenbacker guitar, the type some of the chiming folk-rock bands of the 1960s had used, most notably the Beatles and the Byrds, and the cassette had a dry, sparse sound that only hinted at the band's power as a live act. But the songs were unusually well developed, with contrasting acoustic and electric shades; they included the longtime live staples "I Got Drunk" and "Screen Door" and early takes on a fistful of songs that would appear on their first album: "Whiskey Bottle," "Flatness," "Train," "Before I Break."

The growing batch of original songs got them gigs in an ever-widening radius of towns. When Margherita signed on as manager, one of his few stipulations was that the trio take any gig it could within driving distance to establish a presence outside St. Louis. The manager's strategy was simple but sound: he never saw Uncle Tupelo as a local band, and he parceled out their hometown dates sparingly once his boys began selling out Cicero's. It wasn't unusual for them to drive great distances to play for twenty-five dollars and not many more people. Among their first out-of-town gigs was at the University of Mississippi in Oxford, where the future Uncle Tupelo and Wilco bassist, John Stirratt, was attending college. It was through his connections that the university booked the band, and he nearly regretted it when the award-winning author Barry Hannah, a writer in residence at the university, tried to bully his way onstage, trumpet in hand.

"Tony Margherita had to physically remove Barry, who was notorious for demanding to sit in with every band that came through town," Stirratt says. "He was in his gonzo phase, and he couldn't play a note. Tony almost had to fight him to get him off there."

The trip also had an ulterior motive: the band got to visit Elvis Presley's birthplace in nearby Tupelo. But this, too, was something of a letdown. "Only the door frames are original, and it's been moved," Tweedy lamented in a postcard to his parents. "Tupelo is a really disappointing town to have as a namesake."

The road was an opportunity to build confidence and win fans, one at a time, a sometimes arduous, frequently dispiriting exercise for a young band from a nowhere town without a record deal. Typical was a ten-hour round-trip to Nashville to play for twenty-curiosity seekers in a bar that had lost its beer, wine, and dancing licenses. "What's left?" Tweedy asked. Margherita couldn't even persuade the owner to comp the band three rum and Cokes (the bar could still serve hard alcohol). But the trio stormed through "Cocaine Blues" and "Graveyard Shift" so righteously that the thin but liquored-up crowd collectively defied the dancing ban. No arrests were made, everybody got drunk, and Uncle Tupelo had packed up and rolled back into Belleville by dawn.

The relentless touring and the steady procession of demos did not go completely unnoticed by the music-business powers, great and small. But most record-label talent scouts didn't hear anything in the trio's sound that suggested this would be an easy sell. Uncle Tupelo straddled the divide between the countrified punk of early 1980s bands such as Green on Red, Jason and the Scorchers, and X—none of whom had bum-rushed the charts—and the Pacific Northwest grunge of Mudhoney and Nirvana, which was still years away from breaking through.

But listeners and fans who weren't thinking strictly in terms of numbers and sales heard something fresh. The *CMJ New Music Report*, an influential tip sheet for college radio deejays and indie-label talent scouts, singled out the *Not Forever, Just for Now* demo for a lead review: "mature, developed, seriously thought-out songwriting . . . a world of lonely train tracks and empty bottles, populated by people who live in box cars and bars, and who'd whup the tar out of any buckskin-vested poseur . . . more hard-bitten, hard-won wisdom than any urban cowboy." The ripe imagery was typical of the initial wave of East Coast hyperbole that greeted the band, a series of backhanded compliments that suggested Uncle

Tupelo had just rolled off a hay wagon and Belleville was the Midwest's answer to Appalachia, complete with moonshine stills and barefoot children living in log cabins without running water.

The review brought Margherita a few calls, the most ardent coming from Giant Records—a New York–based indie label on the verge of changing its name to Rockville. The *Not Forever, Just for Now* cassette was greeted with enthusiasm by the two-person staff: Debbie Southwood-Smith and Jeff Pachman, who handled all the day-to-day details of running the label for the owners, Barry Tenenbaum and Jay Fialkov. "It was the best tape submitted to the label all year," Pachman says. When the pair saw the band on the road, they were even more impressed, eventually bringing them to New York for a show at CBGB in July 1989 and at the Continental Divide during the College Music Journal conference in October.

"They were living in the van, touring their asses off," Pachman says. "There wasn't even time to do the laundry. So you'd see, day 1, T-shirt with logo in the front; day 2, same T-shirt with logo in the back; day 3, same T-shirt with logo inside out. They were drunk when they played the Continental—Jeff fell off the stage and onto a table—and they were great. There were maybe ten people in the audience as drunk as they were. I hadn't had my socks blown off by a band like that since the first time I saw the Replacements."

With a deal in the works, at least one thing had to change.

"They had this unbelievably shitty van, a 1970 Econoline," Tony Margherita says. "I drove, and I remember the steering wheel had so much play. I said, 'If we get home from this trip, we're getting another van, because I'm too young to die.' Jeff and I went scouring used lots, and we found this Chevy van. We wanted to trade the Econoline, so we brought it to the dealer for a test drive. He got out of the van and said, 'Are you boys religious?' He gave us fifty bucks for it. We got the Chevy van, which ended up being unbelievable. We drove it for years. Blue Chevy van. Old Blue. We drove that one to Boston."

There they would record the album that, for better or worse, would jump-start not just their career but an entire musical movement.

CHAPTER 4

Uncle Tupelo's first album, *No Depression*, was recorded in ten days on a crime-infested street in the dead of a Boston winter. It's still notable for several reasons, not the least of which is how casually it blended country fiddle, banjo, and mandolin with punk's biting Doberman guitars and shrapnel-spraying drums, sometimes all within the confines of the same song. Hardcore-punk polka beats shared the same grimy dance floor with waltzes and two-steps. The Carter Family shook hands with Dinosaur Jr. It was a striking first step for three young men from a place that, as far as the rest of the music world was concerned, might as well have been nowhere.

"Hometown, same town blues / Same old walls closing in," Jay Farrar sings as the album opens with "Graveyard Shift." Variations of that theme have been the foundation of countless rock 'n' roll careers and records, from Del Shannon's "Runaway" to Steve Earle's "Guitar Town." The lyrics are nearly as grim as anything written by Dock Boggs, but the music goes down kicking and clawing, a wall of distortion and stuttering rhythm over which Farrar's voice sails. It's not a screeching punk-rock voice but a wail that wells up from underneath a note and rises to snatch it. With this voice, despair is dignified, the possibility of defeat ennobled, the inevitability of death embraced.

"Factory Belt" equates blue-collar life with a lingering death; it crashes down in a feedback hailstorm, the sound of the factory belt fraying until it snaps. And then there's "Whiskey Bottle," set in a gin mill where the patrons try to drown out "the sound of people chasing money, and money getting away." There are also Leadbelly's outlaw murder ballad "John Hardy" and the Carter Family's 1936 country classic "No Depression," a vision of the afterlife that promises relief from the turmoil and hardship described in virtually every other song on the album.

Brian Henneman once referred to Jay Farrar as "the griever," a young man who wore an old man's scars, and it's the griever's voice and songs that dominate *No Depression*, that give it weight and purpose beyond the vast majority of rock albums released in 1990. But without Jeff Tweedy the album would lose something vital: the perspective of a man who, spiritually at least, is much younger than Jay Farrar, who hasn't yet learned how to grieve but approaches life with a mixture of fear, confusion, and naive optimism (" 'Cause things don't get better," he sings on "Flatness," "but some people do").

Given the youth of the songwriters—Farrar and Tweedy were barely of legal drinking age when most of the songs were written—it's no surprise that some of the lyrics come off as painfully earnest. Farrar telegraphs his *Grapes of Wrath* punches ("This is for the broken-spirited man"), and Tweedy indulges in callow self-mythologizing ("Down here where we're at, everybody is equally poor"). "I laugh about how we romanticized it," Tweedy says. "To my credit, I think Jay probably wrote a few more songs geared toward that than I did. I wrote the song about being drafted when there was no draft ['That Year']."

But these are beginner's mistakes, the residue of aiming too high too soon, of taking a stab at writing songs as profound as those of Son House, Woody Guthrie, or the *Nebraska*-era Bruce Springsteen without the life experience to pull it off. *No Depression* is energized by that ambition, its sincerity and innocence, the way songs about alcoholism, joblessness, and feeling trapped are redeemed by empathy, and the music itself. The very act of making music that rocks this hard transcends—or at least momentarily eclipses—the hardships described in many of the songs. Even the acoustic tunes are played with a bruised, brash intensity that wipes out the hints of folkie sanctimony.

"I hate purists or fundamentalists of any kind, and to me one of the things that was great about Uncle Tupelo in the beginning was they weren't purists," says Sean Slade, the Boston music veteran who co-produced *No Depression* with his partner, Paul Q. Kolderie. "They throw all this stuff into a song, but they pulled it off. It was totally sincere and authentic. They were singing about their lives and things they cared about with rock energy."

Slade and Kolderie split about one thousand dollars out of a paltry thirty-five-hundred-dollar budget for co-producing *No Depression*. The rest went to cover studio expenses. Though they have since produced many more lucrative and high-profile albums, including breakthroughs by Hole (*Live Through This*), Radiohead (*Pablo Honey*), and the Mighty Mighty Bosstones (*Let's Face It*), there are few recordings they've enjoyed more than *No Depression*. The pair had built a reputation for recording cheap, loud, no-frills indie records for the likes of Dinosaur Jr., the Pixies, Buffalo Tom, and the Volcano Suns in the 1980s. Both art-history graduates of Yale University, Kolderie and Slade were part of the post-punk do-it-yourself intelligentsia: smart, funny, easy-to-be-around guys who played in new-wave bands and then set up a relatively inexpensive recording facility for underground bands at Fort Apache in Boston.

At the time Uncle Tupelo rolled into town, Fort Apache was running two studios. Rockville couldn't afford to pay for the relatively posh twenty-four-track facility in Cambridge, so Tupelo had to settle for the smaller studio in the drug-infested, crime-riddled Roxbury neighborhood in south Boston. Tweedy, Farrar, and Heidorn admired the fuzz-toned guitar mayhem Kolderie and Slade had captured on Dinosaur Jr.'s *Bug*, so they were willing to give their co-producers the benefit of the doubt when it came to making suggestions. Though they liked what they heard on the *Not Forever, Just for Now* cassette, Kolderie and Slade introduced a couple of wrinkles that helped sharpen the trio's attack on *No*

Depression. Rather than emphasize the roots-rock signifiers in Uncle Tupelo's sound, the producers wanted to erase or at least tweak them. In so doing, they took the album to a place it might not otherwise have reached.

First, Slade handed Tweedy a long-necked Epiphone Embassy bass with a richer tone and gave Farrar the 1961 Gibson Les Paul SG Junior that J. Mascis had played on *Bug.* "Mascis loved that guitar—he called it 'instant rock,' " Slade says. "It was perfect for those big power chords that are all over the album."

Then there was the matter of Farrar's harmonica playing, which distinguished some of the *Not Forever, Just for Now* tracks. Too much like Springsteen, Slade and Kolderie argued. Instead, they wanted to substitute a pedal steel guitar to provide the country shadings on "Factory Belt" and "Whiskey Bottle." They recruited a rock guitarist named Rich Gilbert, who had played in the post-punk bands Human Sexual Response and the Zulus. "I liked the idea that he wasn't this Nashville cat, but a slash-and-burn guitarist who was playing pedal steel as kind of a hobby," Slade says. "The idea was not to play any traditional country licks but to take a different angle on it."

The band members were arrayed so they could face one another, which came as a relief to Heidorn. Now he'd finally have eye contact with his bandmates in the recording studio, and it would prove crucial to the album's ebb-and-flow dynamics. Technically the recording is less than perfect, with a few bum notes and a monolithic eight-track sound that is the antithesis of most pristine, Los Angeles–produced rock recordings of the era. But nobody was disappointed.

"Jeff was and is a very good bass player, but a lot of the interplay was between Jay and Mike—they were just whipping each other," Slade says. "Jay would stare at Mike and Mike would stare back, and they'd make this unison roar. Jay reminded me a lot of Mascis, because he barely said a word between takes. I thought he didn't like me, until I realized he was like that with everyone—he wasn't saying anything to anyone. But when he had that guitar in his hands, there was a recklessness and looseness there that you never could have imagined."

The producers marveled at the hiccups in the band's arrangements, the stop-start, loud-soft peaks and valleys that came as naturally to the Tupelo clan as downing beers between takes. "Their whole thing was this rolling tumbleweed of sound," Kolderie says. "It reminded me of those cartoons where Popeye would get into a fight and there's a big cloud with arms and legs sticking out and unintelligible curse words flying out."

Sean Slade still marvels at the screwball tempos the trio had mastered. "The time signatures they were doing—you could sit down and get all music school on it if you wanted to," he says. "They were playing measures of 2/4 against 4/4, and they could switch to a waltz on a dime. But it wasn't like they had this plan mapped out. It was the product of three guys who knew each other really well playing music they innately felt, an unspoken communication that was unique to them."

Unique in execution, certainly, but not unique in its overall scope and vision. Ever since its release, and especially since Uncle Tupelo's demise in 1994, *No Depression* has attained a mythic stature within a small but significant slice of the indie-rock community that has emerged in the last decade. Posthumously the album became something of a blueprint in the emerging alternative-country movement and for the work of bands such as Whiskeytown, the Old 97's, Marah, and half the roster of Bloodshot Records (the Chicago-based home of "insurgent country"). By the mid-1990s, it had inspired the title of *No Depression* music magazine and an Internet message board devoted to all things alt-country. It could be argued that the rise of the Triple-A, or Adult Album Alternative, commercial radio format was also at least in part fueled by post-Tupelo roots rock.

But neither Tweedy nor Farrar sees the album as being worthy of pioneer status; to them, it's at best a solid link in a long chain of albums by bands that saw indie rock and hard-core country as inseparable. "We were a young band trying to put everything we knew on a record," Tweedy says, "which didn't necessarily work or strike any of us as being particularly original." Farrar concurs: "We were conscious of the juxtaposition of putting a loud electric guitar next to an acoustic folk-oriented song, but at the time we didn't feel like we were really doing anything that different. There were a lot of other bands out there at the time that were doing folk and country-oriented stuff. We just thought we were putting our own stamp on it, not starting anything new."

Tweedy laughs whenever the word "roots" comes up in conversation. "When we were waiting in line to see the Stray Cats or INXS in St. Louis," he says, "Jay and I weren't thinking we were country-rock visionaries."

That didn't stop Rockville from hyping the band as "Woody Guthrie meets Hüsker Dü." "It was typical record-company promotion, maybe a little over the top, and some of the hipsters took offense," Pachman says. Among them was Matador Records co-founder Gerard Cosloy, an astute talent scout and a notoriously acerbic tastemaker. Cosloy had just signed the Scottish pop rockers Teenage Fanclub, and they did a short tour with Uncle Tupelo, including a sold-out concert at CBGB in New York. "Oh yeah, Hüsker Dü meets Woody Guthrie, right?" Cosloy mocked. "I bet Uncle Tupelo doesn't know the first thing about Woody Guthrie." Standing unnoticed behind Cosloy was Tweedy, who tapped the bespectacled record exec on the shoulder: "Oh, hey, Gerard, I was wondering if you could name more than one Woody Guthrie song?" Cosloy, for once, was speechless.

Cosloy's skepticism wasn't unusual, however, especially in indie-rock circles, where even the slightest hint of artifice, gimmickry, or pretension could bring an instant backlash. Because they'd worked with Buffalo Tom producers Kolderie and Slade, Uncle Tupelo was nicknamed "Uncle Tom" by some members of the Boston rock underground. Country and folk had always had a tempestuous relationship with rock, falling in and out of favor through the decades, and Uncle Tupelo entered with its take on the tradition during one of the down periods. The early 1980s had brought a revival of interest in traditional country music within the underground rock community, whose members saw in it the kind of realism and honesty they were searching for in their own music. Bands such as the Mekons, Meat Puppets, Green on Red, Rank and File, the Long Ryders, Jason and the Scorchers, and X began threading honky-tonk rhythms and plainspoken lyrics in the tradition of Hank Williams and Merle Haggard through their songs. Some even resorted to donning cowboy hats and adopting southern twangs. More than a decade earlier, Gram Parsons had infiltrated the Byrds to create the landmark country-rock fusion on *Sweetheart of the Rodeo* and imparted his appreciation for honkytonk and Appalachian mountain-soul music to Keith Richards and the Rolling Stones, who began writing songs like "Dead Flowers" and "Sweet Virginia" in their twisted take on the tradition. Buffalo Springfield and Poco evinced deep appreciation for country in best-selling albums, and Bob Dylan forged lasting bonds with Johnny Cash and recorded some of his finest work with Nashville session players, including *Blonde on Blonde*.

Voracious record collectors that they were, Tweedy and Farrar were well aware of those predecessors and in the summer of 1990 even recorded a faithful cover of "Sin City," written by Parsons for his band the Flying Burrito Brothers. A more recent influence was *Blue Earth*, the second album by Minneapolis's Jayhawks, released in 1989. The Jayhawks' Mark Olson and Gary Louris were writing close-harmony ballads that hewed far closer to country traditions than anything Uncle Tupelo was creating at the time.

"I remember coming to work at the record store one day and Tony saying, 'You gotta hear this record. It's really great and it's kinda like what you guys are doing,'" Tweedy recalls. "And I'm thinking, 'Shit, I don't want to hear this.' But once I did, I felt okay, because I felt like it was really different than what we were doing, though it was unique to hear those influences on a record at that time. They weren't trying to write image into their music, the way some of these other bands working the same territory had done. Like Rank and File—they were a good band, but you never got the sense they were writing about themselves, but using hybrids of themes from other things, like coyotes and Westerns. Or Green on Red, where all of a sudden this psychedelic band had a country influence and started singing with a drawl. The Long Ryders were a total fashion statement, to the point where they even looked like the Byrds during *Sweetheart of the Rodeo*. So hearing that Jayhawks album was a real revelation; they were taking stuff from the past but still sounding like themselves. We were a lot different, mainly because I didn't think we were as good at doing the pretty stuff. If you put *Blue Earth* next to *No Depression*, I'd listen to *Blue Earth* every day of the week."

Gary Louris thinks the Jayhawks "were mining the same territory as Uncle Tupelo but from different sides. We'd all been involved in rock bands, and punk rock, which is fun to listen to but doesn't always age well. When we stumbled on country music, it sounded rebellious to us. It was definitely outsider music. We surely weren't doing it because we thought we could sell records— we'd send our demos to record companies, and they'd say stuff like, 'I love it, but don't know what to make of it.' I feel like we started something in a way, us and then Uncle Tupelo, because for whatever reason the whole alternative-country movement said we did. It's like they skipped a generation. I know the audience for our music was interested, and kind of confused. I remember playing a set in 1985 and the sound man coming up to us afterward, saying, 'You guys just played a country set and nobody knew it.' It's like we slipped one past them, because we were playing loud and kind of fast. But we also definitely had a twang, and twang wasn't really cool back then. We looked around, and we certainly didn't see anyone else doing it at the time."

No Depression came out on June 21, 1990, with a blurry black-and-white photo of the boys hanging out and playing songs. Based on the album cover alone, *No Depression* could easily have passed as a Folkways recording from the 1950s or 1960s.

"Pretentious? We didn't think of that, though we probably should have," Tony Margherita says. "We didn't know how to spell 'pretentious,' much less think that we were. It was not easy to get a consensus out of that group, but that was one of those things everyone agreed on."

The band celebrated the release in the usual fashion: on the dank stage of Cicero's for two nights. Opening the first show were the Hilltops, a roots-punk band that included their Oxford, Mississippi, pal John Stirratt; his twin sister, Laurie; and the singer-guitarist Cary Hudson. Heidorn was hoping for something a little more, some sense of camaraderie, a moment to acknowledge what they'd accomplished, a victory toast. "We didn't talk about our beliefs or what our band direction was, ever," the drummer says.

"It was one bummer of a thing. It should have been a big deal to get a record out, especially for a band from Belleville, but it wasn't a big deal to Tony, Jeff, and Jay. It was nothing special. There was no meeting, no dinner, no conversation."

The only socially acceptable outlet for emotions in Tupelo world was the music. After the show, Stirratt and the Hilltops went to the second-floor Eleventh Street apartment with Heidorn, Farrar, Tweedy, and Henneman, where a refrigerator stocked with cheap beer and a living room decorated with stringed instruments provided the ideal setting for a drunken blowout. George Jones's "Good Year for the Roses," Buck Owens's "Buckaroo," and a batch of Carter Family songs were gleefully desecrated.

John Stirratt remembers those early song-swapping days with fondness. "I've known a few painfully shy people in my life, and Jay Farrar definitely was one of them," he says. "Jeff was a lot more gregarious, and I bonded with him immediately. He was the guy I gravitated toward, and Mike was always wonderful. I loved them all. We had this hilarious, really loud country jam session. It got a little out of hand. The cops showed up and told us to shut it down. I thought that was really funny—turn down those acoustic guitars! I felt kind of proud."

Playing in these more informal contexts allowed Tweedy and Farrar to indulge themselves in ways that Tupelo would not. Between tours, Tweedy and Farrar would join Henneman and the drummer Mark Ortmann in a boozy honky-tonk cover band they dubbed Coffee Creek, banging out Merle Haggard's "Sing Me Back Home" and "The Bottle Let Me Down," Doug Sahm's "San Antone," John Anderson's "Wild and Blue," even Freddy Fender's "Wasted Days and Wasted Nights"—songs with themes of drinking and longing not all that far removed from Tupelo's originals but performed with a swagger that Henneman's mirthful presence encouraged and underlined.

Henneman was as good a musician as anyone in Uncle Tupelo, and a fine songwriter. But he was between bands and without a record deal, and when Tupelo invited him to hit the road with them, he eagerly jumped in the van to serve as the trio's glorified guitar tech, gear schlepper, driver, raconteur, sounding board, and instigator. More than anything, he became a buffer between the increasingly distant Farrar and Tweedy on the endless cross-country drives in Old Blue.

"There was a little golden era there, where it was still just this great boys club, a combination of drinking and camaraderie, when the whole thing was still fresh and touring was still an exciting thing," Henneman says. The band would break out the acoustic instruments at roadside rest stops and picnic grounds and transform themselves into the Dust Bowl Boys, devoted to playing songs exclusively from the pre-rock era. Here they once again indulged their fascination with folk and field recordings, only now they were playing it for laughs and as a way to blow off steam. In some ways, these little impromptu hootenannies came closer in spirit to the music they were trying to emulate than some of their more self-serious interpretations on *No Depression* and, looking ahead, the all-acoustic *March 16–20, 1992*.

After hustling to repair Farrar's never-ending streak of busted guitar strings during the shows, Henneman would jump onstage with a guitar of his own to join in on the encores: epic versions of Neil Young's "Down by the River" or "Cortez the Killer," Lynyrd Skynyrd's "Gimme Three Steps," or, on rare occasions, "Mike," a ribald tribute song to the band's beloved, Ringo-like talisman, drummer, and all-around nice guy. There were gut-busting waffle-eating contests at all-night diners that had everyone doubled over in laughter. Farrar and Heidorn were frequently paired against Tweedy and Henneman, who packed on the girth for the good of the team: the 180-pound Henneman ballooned to 213, while Tweedy earned the nickname "Old 196" in honor of his record-breaking bloatedness. One night, when Farrar ordered the chicken-and-eggs breakfast combo, Tweedy leaned over to Henneman and said, "Whichever Jay eats first will answer that question."

Tweedy fended off the migraines that had plagued him since boyhood—they'd caused him to miss forty days of elementary school one year alone—by ingesting diet Coke and M&M's. And he would drink, heavily. He often drove straight through the night after shows with a twelve-pack, his smokes, and Henneman's laughter for company, while Heidorn and Farrar were sacked out in back.

Tweedy was, in Steve Scariano's words, the "politician" of the group, the approachable ambassador who'd stay out till sunrise partying with the fans. Heidorn and Farrar were both in long-term relationships with women back home who would eventually become their wives, and they would inevitably cut off the drinking before it got out of hand. Tweedy didn't know when to stop, often greeting the next day with a pale green complexion, a hangover, and lurid memories of spitting up bile. He never blew off a gig, but his drinking began to deeply concern Margherita and the rest of the band. Once, while visiting Boston, the band lost track of him; he showed up late the next day covered in mud and reeking of booze. He was so sick he couldn't make it through a brief live performance at a local radio station, so Henneman had to sit in for him.

"Jay's face said it all: he was pissed. Pissed that Jeff was out there having a good time, then making everyone wait," Mike Heidorn says. "We were getting to the point where we were starting to live separate lives anyway, and stuff like that didn't help things between Jeff and Jay at all. I felt sometimes like I was the only communication between Jeff and Jay in a weird way. Jay wouldn't talk unless I was in the room, or Jeff would try to talk about a song and Jay wouldn't elaborate and I could see the frustration in Jeff's face."

Awaiting a late-night gig at CBGB, Farrar and Henneman strolled through the Lower East Side of New York buzzed on forty-ounce malt liquors. "I was running my mouth as usual," Henneman recalls, "and out of the blue Jay just says, 'I don't know about Jeff anymore. I don't know.' 'What's the matter?' 'He's getting too much into fashion.' I was so shocked I just let it drop. Fashion? Jeff? What the hell did that mean? I blew it off, but years later I began to realize these guys really weren't talking anymore, except through their music. It was Jay's way of saying that he and Jeff were going in opposite directions."

Mike Heidorn understands Henneman's reluctance to dig too deeply. "We didn't talk about shit like that," he says. "The only thing that mattered was the gig. Show up, play hard."

There was never any doubt about that. Tweedy and Farrar harmonized on Gang of Four's "I Found That Essence Rare" like a pair of rabid dogs. They made the Rouse Brothers' bluegrass classic

"Orange Blossom Special" sound like it was being interpreted by Black Flag, and turned Black Flag's "Gimme Gimme Gimme"—a song about restlessness, addiction, and runaway hormones—into a mournful country song. *No Depression* began to win rave reviews, and the audiences slowly increased as the band crisscrossed the country. Even mainstream publications such as *Rolling Stone* started to pay attention; the magazine highlighted Tupelo in a feature about rising stars, alongside the Black Crowes and Garth Brooks. "Back then, *Rolling Stone* was much more important to the overall perception of music than it is now," says the St. Louis musician Chris King. "Seeing Uncle Tupelo in there made a lot of people in St. Louis take notice of them. The attitude was like, 'Oh, wow, they must matter because *Rolling Stone* noticed them.'"

In March 1991, the band returned to St. Louis to headline not at Cicero's but at the one-thousand-capacity Mississippi Nights. Uncle Tupelo was finally welcome on the Landing. Even Pat Lacey, the club's manager at the time, seemed mildly surprised by the development. The *Belleville Journal* quoted her on the eve of the show: "They play with no synthesizers, and they're not overly produced. But they're good." "Jeff had this chip on his shoulder from the beginning," Heidorn says, "that his music was every bit as good as the Eyes' music, and that Uncle Tupelo deserved to be playing on the Landing as much as or more than those other bands. I don't think Jay ever cared about things like that, but for Jeff stuff like that was a big deal. He had the drive to get us there."

Not that it was paying off financially. Rockville had yet to pay the band a royalty from sales of *No Depression*, even though Pachman estimates the band had sold at least fifteen thousand copies, a major hit by indie standards and more than enough to recoup the label's thirty-five-hundred-dollar investment. But even though Pachman and Southwood-Smith were enthusiastically promoting the band, they had no control over the accounting and payments. It was the first sign of trouble in a deal that would end in acrimony and lawsuits years later; but for now the band had few other choices. Columbia Records paid the band to record additional tracks with Kolderie and Slade at Fort Apache in the summer of 1990, but nothing came of it. On their tax statements, Heidorn,

Tweedy, and Farrar each claimed less than six hundred dollars in income from their business partnership. Between tour dates, Heidorn returned to his production duties at the *Belleville Journal*, while Tweedy would drive to Chicago, where he had struck up a relationship with Sue Miller, co-owner of the indie-rock haven Lounge Ax.

Miller, born on August 12, 1957, in Chicago, was ten years older than Tweedy and a fixture in Chicago music for having brought bands such as the Replacements, Hüsker Dü, and the Red Hot Chili Peppers to various North Side clubs for some of their first concerts. In Tweedy's notebooks from the late 1980s, her name appears on several pages—"Call Sue Miller"—as he tried vainly to get his band booked at the Cubby Bear, then a major rock club across the street from Wrigley Field where Miller worked as the talent buyer. Finally she granted Tupelo a date on what was to be her last night at the Cubby Bear—August 12, 1989—before moving on to Lounge Ax. Tweedy was smitten when he met her, but Miller was pretty much oblivious to his interest in her until years later.

"It took me a real long time to tell Jeff and Jay apart," Miller says. "I thought they were twins: They both had hair in their eyes, head down, wouldn't say anything, shuffled their feet a lot. They were ridiculously shy. Every other band, backstage it would be like, 'Whoopee!' I've dealt with lots of rock bands, and it's usually pretty insane back there. But everytime I walked into the Uncle Tupelo dressing room, I thought I was walking into a funeral. There was not a lot of talking or camaraderie or goofing around."

Miller loved the band, though, and booked Uncle Tupelo for sixteen shows over four years at Lounge Ax. And she ended up falling in love with Jeff Tweedy. A long postshow conversation at her apartment in 1991 was the first step toward their eventual marriage four years later. Soon after he started dating Miller, Tweedy quit drinking, cold turkey. "I didn't have anything to do with it, though I was very happy he did," Miller says. "He wanted to nip it in the bud, to avoid having to deal with more serious issues down the road. He's a very emotional person anyway, and alcohol isn't a good thing for him to be around. I don't think I could be married to a drinking musician. Being married to a musician is enough, thanks."

David Dethrow, Tweedy's friend since the Primitives days, says it wasn't a decision Jeff agonized over: "His brothers and his father had their difficulties with drinking, and Jeff knew he had to be careful. He knew where he'd be heading if he kept it up, because he saw it in his own home. He didn't like being out of control. And if you keep drinking, you've got no control at all."

Tweedy also began stockpiling songs for the next album and slowly shaking off the awkwardness and sense of inferiority that had kept him in Farrar's artistic shadow. Before connecting with Miller, he'd broken up with the latest in a long string of girlfriends. The emotional fallout fed into Tweedy's expanding skills as a musician and songwriter. "Jeff wasn't as confident of his writing, but he was so hungry for people's feedback and opinions," says his St. Louis confidante Heather Crist. "I remember 'Black Eye' and 'Cold Shoulder,' because he would call me and sing them to me over the phone."

Chris King also was invited by Tweedy to hear his new songs. "I went out to his car, and we listened to the rough mixes for the second record," King says. "That's when I heard 'Gun' for the first time. I'm indifferent about a lot of Jeff's songwriting, but 'Gun' I think is a song for all time. I was like, 'God, what a fuckin' great song. What a terrific song.' It mattered to him to hear that because I think he was a fairly insecure guy; he may still be, but was certainly then and needed approval in a way that Jay never did."

Steve Scariano saw the song as a turning point. "Up until 'Gun,' Jay was always the artistic leader of the band, and Jeff was always the personality leader," he says. " 'Gun' changed all that. It was the most pop thing they'd ever done. All of Jeff's songs on that record were about a specific girl who had the nerve to break up with him. We were at a party after a gig at Cicero's, and Jeff was excited. 'I nailed it. I finally nailed it,' and he yelled the lyrics to 'Gun' in my ear. 'Wait until she hears this one.' So he came into his own, and that certainly changed the dynamic within the band. Nobody was looking at his songs yet, and now everyone had to pay attention. It was only positive at that time, but down the road it was going to cause problems."

Brian Henneman saw the dynamic change as well. "I kind of look at Uncle Tupelo's songwriting the same way I do Bruce Springsteen's," he says. "I love the guy; I love everything about him. My least favorite thing about him is his songwriting. He's so great at everything else that it makes up for the fact that sometimes the songs are just okay. But I remember when they played 'Gun' at a sound check in Atlanta, months before the second album came out. They played this song that I thought for sure was a cover of something great. I never asked those guys who did the covers they did, for fear of being labeled a hopeless dweeb. But this one was so entrenched in my head I had to ask, 'Why haven't I heard this before?' And it was because it was a song Jeff just wrote. When Jeff told me, I was blown away. I knew it was no longer President Farrar and Vice President Tweedy anymore. It was co-CEOs from then on. Lyrics, melody, power—it's like you take for granted the guys you're hanging out with, your buddies. And then all of a sudden one of them comes up with something that just makes you re-evaluate everything you ever thought about them."

"Gun" kicks off with an ominous rumble of guitars and tom drums before a big melody that wouldn't have sounded out of place on Hüsker Dü's *Flip Your Wig* barrels out of the noise. Indeed, it competes with it, the tune and the chaos fighting for supremacy. Farrar's sheets-of-sound guitar and Heidorn's lashing drums push Tweedy's voice past its comfort zone as the singer's stumblebum charm ("tripping on a wrinkle in the rug") melts into anger, anguish, and finally sadness as he picks through the wreckage of a love affair. The phrase "Don't bother" becomes a raging kiss-off just before the guitar solo, then a devastating good-bye as the song fades. It's a pop song, but it's played with a full-tilt intensity that commercial radio still wasn't ready for. (Nirvana's "Smells Like Teen Spirit" was still months away from breaking down commercial barriers for the rock underground.)

It would be the leadoff track and first single off the band's second album, *Still Feel Gone*, which would again be recorded with Slade and Kolderie, this time in more plush surroundings at Long View Farm in central Massachusetts, a recording and practice facility where the Stones had set up rock 'n' roll boot camp for one of their early-1980s North American tours. The recording budget had been bumped to a still ridiculously modest six thousand dollars, and the band was given an extra week, with the idea of making a more layered album than *No Depression*.

Long View had its own kitchen-equipped residences, but Kolderie quickly found out the Belleville contingent had no intention of using them: "I thought they'd dig the rural aspect of it, the chance to cook their own meals and hang out. So we go shopping, and it was like going out with a bunch of teenage boys. All they did was buy Golden Anniversary beer, noodles, presliced cold cuts—they had no concept of cooking. Even the idea of heating up spaghetti sauce seemed foreign to them."

Soon after, Kolderie had a run-in with one of the barn's resident felines and came down with cat scratch fever. The freak accident dimmed his energy and shortened his tolerance for what he saw as some of the band's indulgences. Both producers felt the band was distracted because they were simultaneously working on songs and recording after-hours demos with their friend Brian Henneman. They also noticed a more palpable tension within the band. "They definitely weren't having as good a time with each other," Sean Slade recalls. "At first I chalked it up to the fact that one guy was trying his damnedest to be clean and sober and the other guy didn't give a shit. When you suddenly swear off beer, it can make you more uptight, and Jeff definitely was. Plus, Jay seemed even more withdrawn, more distant. I realize now it probably had as much to do with Jeff's growth as a songwriter and basically that he wanted to be treated as an equal. And, in a lot of ways, Jay did treat Jeff as an equal, but it was just less of an organic, unified, we're-friends-from-high-school feel. Jeff was definitely writing songs that were a little more serious. Whereas on the first record he was the antidote to Jay's intensity, now it's like he was competing with him. He'd lost the more whimsical, offhand aspect of his singing, and it made for a more intense, serious album in a lot of ways."

The band and the producers compensated for the similar tone of many of the songs with more ambitious arrangements. By Uncle Tupelo's spartan standards, *Still Feel Gone* is their answer to the Beach Boys' *Pet Sounds*; no other album they ever recorded would be so layered. It's thickened by contributions from the guitarists Gary Louris and Henneman, Slade's keyboards, and a bit of accordion and piano from one Chris Bess, a bandmate of Chris King's in the St. Louis band Enormous Richard who crammed his 275-pound frame into a compact car and drove twenty hours halfway across the country to participate in the sessions.

For Tweedy's "If That's Alright," the Zulus' Rich Gilbert was enlisted again, this time to add some disorienting, psychedelic textures on an Optigan, which plays back instrumental sounds encoded on celluloid discs. The song is a clumsy stab at introspection, weighed down with pseudo-poetic lyrics in which the narrator compares his life to a blurry, upside-down slide show that, for some unexplained reason, is being presented on a carousel. What's more, the narrator says it's making him nod off. But the Optigan gives it an eerie, otherworldly vibe—the creaky soundtrack to an old black-and-white movie. "If you want to look ahead to what Wilco's doing in terms of creating sonic freak-outs," Slade says, "that's where Jeff started." It's doubtful Jay Farrar would have allowed one of his own songs to be so embellished.

Still Feel Gone contains some of Tupelo's finest moments: Tweedy's bittersweet yet hard-rocking anthems "Gun" and "Nothing," plus "D. Boon," a fiery expression of indie-rock solidarity with the late Minutemen guitarist ("Part of what he was is a part of me now . . . It's just me and Jay playing our guitars along with it all"); Farrar's "Postcard," which expertly compresses Tupelo's countrified twang and electric bang into a thrilling three-and-a-half-minute roller-coaster ride; and the elegiac "Still Be Around," the longing-for-home response to the trapped, claustrophobic vignettes of *No Depression*.

But the mood of the album is perhaps best understood by a song that didn't make it: a flamethrower interpretation of the Soft Boys' lost 1980 classic "I Wanna Destroy You." Slade was blown away by the performance and insisted that it belonged on the album. "It's an amazing version of a great song," he says. "They didn't write it, but the song lyrically and musically is a Tupelo song. It wasn't just a random cover. It's an obscurity that they'd been playing in their sets for years, and their version is better than the original. But they just wouldn't have it. I actually got so angry I was stomping my feet, yelling, 'No, you've got to put it on. You've got to put it on.' Then I realized I was going over the top and they were looking at me like I was crazy. I realized, 'Okay, you just lost.' "

"I Wanna Destroy You" was eventually released, but only as the B side to the "Gun" single. The band didn't want any covers on the album and was put off by the stacked harmonies Slade and Kolderie had punched up for the chorus. Subsequently, they gave interviews slagging what they felt was the overproduction and Dinosaur Jr.–like heavy-guitar sound of the first two albums, particularly *Still Feel Gone*. After reading one of the interviews, Slade hurled the magazine across the room and dialed the band's Belleville apartment. He left an angry voicemail message: "C'mon, guys! You were the ones who asked for more production on the second record. You were the guys with the Dinosaur Jr. tapes in your car. What gives?"

Years later, Kolderie visited Tweedy backstage after a solo concert in Boston. Tweedy hadn't spoken to the producer in nearly a decade, but after the two exchanged hugs, he couldn't help but ask: "Is Slade still mad at me?"

Slade laughed when Kolderie told him the story. "Yeah, well, I still love those guys," he says, "and I still think we made two great albums with them. *No Depression* still ranks right up there with anything we worked on. And, luckily, we didn't have to deal with songs about being a coal miner."

That would come next.

CHAPTER 5

"THE LOUDEST RECORD WE HAD EVER MADE"

On the way to recording their third album at the home of
R.E.M.'s Peter Buck in Athens, Georgia, Uncle Tupelo
decided to discard a few of the crutches that had served
them, and their fans, so well: volume, speed, power chords, feedback.

Uncle Tupelo's previous albums, *No Depression* and *Still Feel
Gone*, were made in the safety zone of the familiar. These albums
allowed the band to reprise what it had been doing in front of
audiences for several years, and then embellish it slightly in the
recording studio. Now that people in the world outside Belleville
were paying attention, the stakes were raised for what was to be
March 16–20, 1992. But instead of turning it up and beckoning a
broader audience, Uncle Tupelo unplugged. Just as loud rock was
coming back in vogue, the Belleville boys decided to make an
album of acoustic songs, split between rustic originals and a batch
of folk and country tunes that predated the rock 'n' roll era.

"We had definitely made the connection that folk and country
music was as direct and as raw as punk rock, but we respected it to
the point that we didn't feel comfortable playing it," Jeff Tweedy
says. "We felt like we had to earn the right to play it. The only way

to do that record was to not overthink it, to let it be what folk music was, as much a moment in a field recording as it could be. The only reason that a bunch of twenty-two-year-old kids could approach that music and have the audacity to play some of these songs that are eighty years old and have it sound at all sincere or real is that (a) we really believed it and (b) we didn't go back and change it. We didn't grow up in the hills; we weren't removed from the mainstream society like someone sitting out on a porch singing the 'Old Holler.' But we felt pretty cut off from what everybody else was doing anyway."

More than a decade after its release, the audacity of *March 16–20, 1992* resonates. "By the third day I thought, 'This is going to be a really great record that about eighty people are going to buy,'" Peter Buck recalls. "I thought it would be a record that people would have to discover, but once they did, it would be regarded as a classic."

Buck knew the timing couldn't have been worse for a band supposedly on the verge of bigger things: an acoustic record at a time when Nirvana's era-defining *Nevermind* was riding high on the charts, when the sound of overdriven guitars and Seattle grunge was all the rage, when indie rock had gone mainstream, when anything seemed possible. Even veteran underground acts such as the Butthole Surfers, the Melvins, and Bad Religion had signed or were about to sign major-label deals. Uncle Tupelo was in the right place at the right time to cash in, if they made the "right" record. Buck knew in his heart that *March 16–20, 1992* wasn't going to be that record, but that didn't mean it couldn't be great, and he believed so strongly in the band that he donated his home and his time to the project.

Buck knew all about misunderstood records. Long before he founded what would become one of the most commercially successful and aesthetically accomplished rock bands of all time, the guitarist was a discriminating music fan who worked in record stores and scrutinized music magazines in an endless search for the good stuff. He knew that worthy music didn't always filter into the popular consciousness right away, if ever, in part because the very things that make a piece of music timeless sometimes also make it

alien to the culture around it. Buck was championing obscure talents such as Robyn Hitchcock, Alex Chilton, and Nick Drake long
before they became fashionable cult artists for hipsters to name-
check, and he maintained his enthusiasm for discovering unsung
talents even as R.E.M. grew from indie-rock trailblazers into a
multimillion-selling arena act.

In 1990 he was still living in the college enclave Athens, Georgia, from which R.E.M. had emerged a decade earlier. After being
tipped to Uncle Tupelo's *No Depression* album, he wanted to check
them out when they came through town at the 40 Watt Club, and
he was not disappointed. The Belleville trio opened their set with
the Louvin Brothers' mountain-soul vision of nuclear-age apoca-
lypse, "Great Atomic Power," and Buck had a new favorite band.
He sought out the trio after the show.

"The chemistry at the time was like they were brothers," Buck
says. "They were drinking together, and it was obvious they'd
known each other for what seemed like a million years. So the first
thing I say to them is, 'God, that's pretty cool opening with a Louvin Brothers song,' and Jay and Jeff just looked at each other. Then
Jeff says, 'You know, we've been playing that song for two years
and no one ever recognized it.' We talked for maybe an hour about
our favorite bluegrass duos: the Monroe Brothers, the Stanley
Brothers, the Delmore Brothers. The Louvins are probably the
most melodramatic of the lot, and there was something cool about
these guys from the Midwest not just tapping into that but making
it their own, where it felt so natural that nobody in the audience
could tell they were doing this mountain ballad from another era.
They already had the idea of doing an acoustic record, and it was
just a matter of figuring out when we could get together to do it."

The dates are etched in the title of *March 16–20, 1992,* a five-
day string-band blowout that Buck didn't so much produce or
orchestrate as facilitate and encourage; he played cheerleader for
what would turn out to be the trio's breakthrough. At a time when
"Gun" and their cover of "I Wanna Destroy You" suggested they
were just a song away from joining the alternative-rock gold rush,
Uncle Tupelo swung hard in the opposite direction with *March.*
No more smash-your-face-in sonics, no more bumper-car dynam-

ics; in their place were a parched sparseness and a renewed focus
on lyrics as unsettling and unsentimental as a Flannery O'Connor
short story.

In an interview with Daniel Durchholz of the *St. Louis Post-
Dispatch* after the album was completed, Jay Farrar mustered about
as much bravado as he ever has in discussing his music: "This
should insulate us from that industry bullshit, people looking for
the next Nirvana. I don't think anybody is the next Nirvana, certainly not us. People will always talk about the next Beatles, the
next Elvis. You can't predict that stuff. The next Nirvana isn't
going to be Nirvana; they're going to be who they are. Those
'next' people never make it."

By Farrar's standards, that response was practically a manifesto,
and it spoke to the band's increasing skepticism about the business
it was participating in. The royalty checks weren't coming in from
Rockville, even though Tupelo continued to sell albums, and the
idea of working with producers who could broaden their sound
was becoming an increasingly less palatable option after the mixed
experience of *Still Feel Gone*. So in that nothing-to-lose context,
why not turn down the amplifiers and record an album that
sounded like a long-lost if slightly wayward response to *High
Atmosphere*, a collection of 1965 field recordings by John Cohen of
the New Lost City Ramblers that had become a band favorite?

As usual, the decision to go left when the rest of the music
world was going right was a matter less of strategy than of intu-
ition. It may have been the wrong move from a career-growth
standpoint, but it just felt right. Tweedy and Farrar had been stocking up on folk records for years and working songs like "Great
Atomic Power" into their late-night apartment jams, their Dust
Bowl Boys roadside respites, and their rock-club sets.

Brian Henneman, the wild-card multi-instrumentalist, would
become their secret weapon on *March 16–20, 1992*. He would
find out about his new responsibilities in typical Tupelo fashion. "I
first heard about it on tour after the *Still Feel Gone* record came
out, and, of course, it wasn't from the guys in the band," Henneman says. "It was from somebody in the crowd at Maxwell's [in
Hoboken, New Jersey], who came up to me and said, 'I hear

they're making a folk record and you're going to play on it.' 'Oh, really? I don't know anything about it.' "

Henneman wouldn't know much more a few months later when he jumped in the van and drove to Athens with Heidorn, Farrar, and Tweedy for the sessions. The musicians stayed at Buck's three-story Victorian house in a residential section of town, a few minutes' walk from the recording studio. Buck was the perfect host in many ways; he worked for free, so the entire $13,500 budget went to rent the recording studio and to the engineers John Keane and David Barbe.

Buck loaded up on beer before his guests arrived, only to find that the band had pretty much forsaken booze and was subsisting primarily on Mountain Dew and chewing tobacco. Each session was preceded the night before by a homework assignment from Buck, who asked them to prepare a certain number of songs. Though Farrar and Tweedy had several songs in mind that they wanted to record, they were still working out arrangements until the last minute. Bedroom prep sessions rolled till two or three in the morning on the second floor of Buck's house, and then continued the next day on the porch outside John Keane's studio.

Henneman taught himself to play mandolin—the same one Buck used on R.E.M.'s biggest hit, "Losing My Religion"—and bouzouki, a long-necked eastern European stringed instrument that sounds like a cross between a sitar and a mandolin. He also added banjo and slide guitar to the songs, which weren't so much studio productions as musical snapshots, moments captured on tape, field recordings in which the "field" happened to be a room equipped with high-fidelity recording equipment. In the studio, Buck and Keane dashed around moving microphones as the musicians settled in and began strumming, so as not to lose a single precious first take. There wasn't enough time or money in the Uncle Tupelo budget for fussing over bum notes or missed cues.

"Jeff and I had gone through some of the songs in Belleville before we left, but we didn't have a chance to introduce them to Brian," Jay Farrar says. "When we got there, we'd teach the songs to Brian, and then record them. It was a case of let's dive in and see what happens. Fear? Yes, there was that. I found over the years that when a song is new and fresh, it can have a shaky quality until you play it ten times or so and find a groove. But a lot of the *March* songs never got to that stage. I finished writing the song 'Criminals' the morning we recorded it. I had it partly done but didn't figure out where the bridge would go, and what the lyrics for the bridge would be, until ten in the morning. At 1 p.m. we recorded it, and that's the song you hear on the album."

"Criminals" is one of Farrar's angriest songs, and one of his finest contributions to the album, in large part because it makes a contemporary statement out of its old-fashioned acoustic foundation. "We're all criminals waiting to be called," he sings, then paraphrases a campaign promise by then-President George Bush: "They want us kinder and gentler at their feet."

Amid the murder ballads, union songs, and fire-and-brimstone spirituals from old-time country's leading metaphysicians, Farrar's "Grindstone" and Tweedy's "Black Eye" stand tall. "Grindstone" adopts the push-pull of the electric Tupelo to fashion a wide-screen blue-collar cry of protest. "Black Eye" goes in the opposite direction; it takes a Tweedy loss-of-innocence lament to the haunted interior universe of Leonard Cohen. It's the story of a young man growing old before his time, a theme that Tweedy would return to persistently thereafter.

A few of the cover songs mention Jesus and the afterlife, but the context isn't religious devotion so much as the madness and fear that would drive men to wish for such redemption in the first place. The stark arrangement provides no escape from the horrors described in Dillard Chandler's "I Wish My Baby Was Born," sung by Tweedy, in which the narrator wrestles with the love he feels for his unborn child and the murderous hate he aims at the expectant mother. Farrar and the band slow "Lilli Schull" to a crawl, as if to savor every nuance of this bloody tale of repentance gleaned from a 1939 field recording.

"We didn't flatter ourselves to think that we could possibly sing or perform those songs as well as the originals," Jay Farrar acknowledges. "In a way, we played them all the wrong way, but we'd been doing that since the first record with songs like 'No Depression' and 'John Hardy.' We didn't care what anyone else thought. We knew there was a contrary element to what we were doing, that we weren't part of the pack of bands that was coalescing into this grunge-rock phenomenon. I felt then and now that we were sticking our necks out for something that was important for us to do."

Farrar's neck has never been more exposed than it is when he assumes the voice of a downtrodden coal miner or hillbilly on several *March* songs. It's difficult not to become incredulous when a twenty-two-year-old kid who once worked at a bookstore sings a ballad like "Moonshiner" in the first person:

> *And I go to some hollow*
> *And set up my still*
> *If whiskey don't kill me*
> *Lord, I don't know what will.*

Nick Sakes of the angular post-punk band Dazzling Killmen, a fan of Farrar and Tweedy's since the Primitives days, was taken aback: "We would occasionally imitate Jay's singing and insert our own words: 'It gets real hot working down at my mom's bookstore.' It was a little too much to hear these songs about coal miners coming from regular dudes that worked in record stores and bought SST albums and went to Black Flag shows."

Darin Gray, Sakes's old bandmate, says that reaction was typical of musical hipsters at the time, including himself. But the daring of *March* eventually couldn't be denied. "It seemed kind of retro to me at the time, like a step back," he says. "Now, though, it seems like a leap forward. I was playing in a band that was all about pushing the envelope, and it was my own inability that didn't allow me to realize that they were pushing the envelope, too, except they were pushing through from the other side."

In a sense, reaction to *March* among the band's most ardent listeners was reminiscent of the debate that once raged over early Rolling Stones or Led Zeppelin albums, when these middle-class British bands dared to cover, reinterpret, or otherwise appropriate old Chicago blues songs. For every fan who saw in those records more than a whiff of how-dare-they? exploitation, another ten were likely introduced to worthy artists they might not otherwise have heard. "They had a young, mostly under-thirty audience,"

Gray says of Uncle Tupelo. "Most of those fans had no idea where this music was coming from, and *March* exposed them to it in a context they could understand."

For those with a rooting interest in the band's fortunes, *March* represented a major crossroads. The band had pulled a Neil Young: it had followed its version of the commercially accessible *After the Goldrush* with a record nearly as stark and challenging as *Tonight's the Night*. It upset expectations, including those of one of their biggest cheerleaders, *The Riverfront Times*'s Richard Byrne. "I thought they fucked up big time," he says. "The track for them was really clear when you look at 1992 and what was happening in rock at that point. It was clear what they were supposed to do, and they just didn't do it. I give Tony [Margherita] a lot of credit for not only not talking them out of it but actually aiding and abetting it, making it happen. Some folks couldn't stomach those songs, and they saw the band as frauds, poseurs for attempting to sing them. Those songs nurtured them for a long time before they recorded them, so I could understand why they would want to record them. But I also wanted them to be massively successful, and I knew this wasn't going to take them there. It was just a remarkably self-indulgent album, in the best sense of the word. There was a sense that they let the alt-rock team down, that twelve-year-olds weren't going to ever buy this album. But it's also the reason that people still revere that record today."

Tony Margherita understood the implications of putting out an acoustic album as grunge mania was peaking. "Basically, it was a big 'fuck you' to the rock scene, and we knew it would cost us," he says. "The irony of that is, we started having some pretty serious discussions with record labels soon after. The record was a turning point in a lot of ways. It's like before you can make an abstract painting, you have to demonstrate that you can draw really well. They'd been doing this countryish indie-rock thing before, and now they made a record true to the music on which all that was based."

The band also stepped away from *March* with a glimpse of how it could be done, with Peter Buck as a role model. They enjoyed his easygoing company and investigated his record collection; Tweedy in particular found his world rearranged when he listened

to Buck's copy of Nick Drake's *Pink Moon*, an album of such profound intimacy that it made *March* sound like Black Sabbath. But
just as important was the idea of Buck as a rock star who had been
able to succeed on his own terms. "We saw what it could be like,"
Margherita says, "that you didn't have to sell your soul to succeed."

For Tweedy, after the misgivings that lingered over *Still Feel
Gone*, *March* felt like a breakthrough: "The performances were
way more in keeping with the way the songs were actually written than the rock-band material was. It felt like something to build
on, as opposed to the other records that raised the question of how
do we continue this? Where else can we go?"

It's a feeling intertwined with his belief that music is as much
or more about the listener's response to it as it is about the artist's
intent. "I felt with *March* we made the loudest record we had ever
made," Tweedy says. "It was the feeling I got from other people
who heard the record, even the ones who didn't like it. It was the
feeling that it spoke much, much louder and more directly than
anything we'd done before, when we were banging away on stuff.
That made it a watershed record for us, and for me personally. It is
definitely my favorite Uncle Tupelo record, because of all the rev-
elations it provided about music making. The main thing I learned
is that the more I can forget about being embarrassed when I make
something, the more it is going to mean something to somebody
else. I can't anticipate what it's going to be or how it's going to be
perceived, so the quicker I let go of something I make, the better."

CHAPTER 6

"SOLITUDE IS WHERE I'M BOUND"

March 16–20, 1992 was both Uncle Tupelo's great leap forward and the beginning of the band's end.

"I was working with Jeff one day at the record store, and he said, 'You know Mike is hardly on this one?' " says the St. Louis record-store manager and indie-rock scenester Steve Scariano. "And then after they got back from recording *March*, I was at a show at Mississippi Nights and one of the big fans, one of the original fans, says, 'Hey, did you hear Mike is quitting? This is his last show.' They were on the encore. 'What are you talking about? I work with those guys. Nobody said anything.'"

Scariano, like many Tupelo fans, was stunned by Heidorn's departure: "It was never the same after that in my eyes."

Mike Heidorn had added brush-stroke percussion to a handful of *March* tracks. His presence was welcome, as usual, but bittersweet. Before the sessions even began, he told the band that he wanted out. The drummer had been torn for months about Tupelo's increasingly busy schedule. This was no longer a band of high-school friends jamming for their friends in Cicero's basement, subsisting on pizza and draft beer. It had become a mini-corporation almost in spite of itself, sought after by bigger corporations with bigger plans. Heidorn had been dating Sandra Lynn Melahn, the mother of two children, ages three and seven, from a previous marriage. The longer stretches away from home and his steady-paying newspaper job were starting to wear on him. Tupelo, meanwhile, was about to spend even more time away from Belleville. Offers were coming in from a handful of major labels, and when Margherita drove in from St. Louis to consult with the band at their Eleventh Street apartment about a fall tour of Europe, Heidorn knew what he had to do. "I told them I'd be honored to do the record with Peter Buck, but if they wanted to get somebody else to play drums, it would be okay with me," Heidorn says. "They wanted me to play on it anyway, and they tried to talk me out of quitting. 'What about Europe? Don't you want to go to Europe?' Jay said. But I just said, 'Jay, I'll go to Europe with my own family sometime. I don't have to go right now.' "

For the music critic Richard Byrne this was disastrous news. "Mike is just one of the sunniest personalities you could ever meet," Byrne says. "And he doesn't take a lot of shit; if you're moping, he wouldn't stand for it. He just refused to indulge in that, and that was incredibly helpful for Jay and Jeff to be around someone like that. You can definitely date a lot of the trouble with Uncle Tupelo to his leaving."

Tony Margherita didn't presume to think it could ever be like the good old days again with Heidorn gone. "Mike was crucial to the way things worked," he says. "He's a funny, loose, laid-back guy. He was the buffer. You couldn't take anything too seriously with Mike around. When he left, things got weird pretty quickly. Everybody was disappointed when he left, but we accepted it. Mike had a relationship that was suffering, and he was tired of being on the road all the time and not making any money. It was a totally logical move. Being in a rock band at that level is not a logical thing for any human being to do. And that eventually dawned on Mike."

The economics of indie rock could dispirit even the most optimistic personality. Tupelo was playing clubs nationwide for guarantees that ranged from one hundred to two hundred dollars.

"Maybe one hundred people would show up at the gigs, and thirty would buy T-shirts," Margherita says. "We survived on T-shirt money. We were really moving up: some nights we could afford to get two rooms at the Red Roof Inn."

Bob Andrews joined the band as tour manager in the summer of 1992 and was appalled at the condition of their gear. "There was a huge stack of junk sitting by the kitchen door in their apartment, and I said, 'This is what you guys tour with?' " he recalls. "Everything had something wrong with it. Knobs broken, frayed strings, duct tape holding things together. Everything was broken that could be broken on every instrument. They had a running joke at the expense of bands who had new stuff: 'Must've spent all their money on this gear instead of writing songs.' But they were basically making a living off playing on the road, and their stuff was pretty sad."

Rockville Records was of little help, even though the label executive Jeff Pachman says that combined sales of the first two albums had already pushed past forty thousand. Pachman and Debbie Southwood-Smith had trouble persuading their bosses to pay them in a timely manner, let alone their bands. "Rockville Records was remiss in giving the band proper royalties," Pachman says. "I was walking upstairs to talk to the owners and always hearing the same thing: 'There's a long list of people to pay and you're at the bottom of it.' They bounced paychecks to me, and I was running up credit-card bills, and I let my phone bill bounce a few times. It was starting to wear on me, and I know it had to be wearing on the bands. My dream was to find another A&R job, and then try to buy Uncle Tupelo out of their contract and bring them with me, but Joe McEwen beat me to the punch."

In indie-rock circles, Joe McEwen represented the "bad guys," the major labels that had been viewed skeptically in the underground ever since the Sex Pistols ranted about the evils of EMI at the dawn of the punk era. But McEwen was also part of the last golden age in Warner Brothers music, one of a dwindling breed of die-hard music connoisseurs in a business increasingly manned by executives who measured a band's worth strictly by units sold. McEwen was the antithesis of the stereotypical industry smarmtalker. On the contrary, his diffident demeanor often suggested he was much less of an enthusiast than he actually was; Warner staffers referred to him as "Mr. Excitement." But his track record for identifying and cultivating talent was impeccable.

Born on August 10, 1950, in Philadelphia, McEwen was a rock journalist and the host of a soul radio show in Boston before joining Columbia Records in 1978 as a junior talent scout. Among his signings were the brilliantly skewed jazz guitarist James Blood Ulmer, Parliament-Funkadelic's Walter "Junie" Morrison, New Orleans's Dirty Dozen Brass Band, and the future folk-pop star Shawn Colvin. In 1989 McEwen moved over to Sire Records, a Warner Brothers subsidiary, and recruited a bevy of cutting-edge bands for the label: My Bloody Valentine, Dinosaur Jr., Ride, Primal Scream. He also signed idiosyncratic talents such as the jazz singer Jimmy Scott to his Blue Horizon boutique imprint. McEwen knew his stuff, and he had been keeping tabs on Uncle Tupelo since their 1989 demo, *Not Forever, Just for Now*, landed on his desk. He was a regular at their Maxwell's concerts in Hoboken, New Jersey, just a few miles south of his home in Montclair.

He was impressed by the way the band cut against prevailing trends; they didn't quite fit in with alternative rock or grunge, and though there were country elements in their sound, it wasn't the kind of country that Nashville was selling in the age of Garth Brooks. Jay Farrar's voice "sounded like it came from 1949, an alternative to the alternative," McEwen says. "They didn't fit with Dinosaur Jr., Sonic Youth, Nirvana. So where do they fit? Maybe nowhere—the best I could come up with is that they reminded me a bit of Buffalo Springfield or the Band," groups with multiple singers and songwriters whose image and personality were subservient to the songs.

For some talent scouts, that would've been enough to turn them off. It's possible to divide major-label A&R execs into two camps: those who worry about how to sell a band before signing it, and those who put the music ahead of everything else, confident that the economics will eventually catch up with the art. McEwen fit into the latter camp, and Uncle Tupelo's grand "fuck you" to business as usual, *March 16–20, 1992*, convinced him that he had to have this band. It was an easy sell: Sire was run by Seymour Stein, who had previously launched genre-busting talents such as the Ramones and Talking Heads.

"Gary Louris of the Jayhawks was in my office one day, and he says, 'You know, you really should sign Uncle Tupelo,' " McEwen says. "That was it really—it was like a lightbulb went off in my head."

The band met with McEwen over dinner in St. Louis. They were wary, but McEwen's interest in them since the early days carried weight. Plus, what did they have to lose? "We didn't have any money to take Rockville to court for not paying us. That's how a lot of indie labels get away with not paying bands," Margherita says. "It's probably easier to control your own destiny artistically on an indie, but getting paid is no easier. How could we not be getting paid for a record [*No Depression*] that cost thirty-five hundred dollars to make?"

That question would finally be put before a judge in May 2000, when Farrar and Tweedy sued Rockville Records and Barry Tenenbaum in U.S. district court for unpaid royalties. They won an undisclosed settlement from Tenenbaum and rights to the master recordings for *No Depression, Still Feel Gone,* and *March 16–20, 1992,* which were reissued on CD with bonus tracks in 2003. At the time of the suit, it was estimated that the three albums had sold more than 200,000 copies, for which the band hadn't received a penny in royalties from Rockville.

Though being ripped off didn't sit well with Farrar and Tweedy, they were more concerned about their freedom to cut exactly the type of records they wanted to make, without the label's interference. McEwen understood this instinctively; he knew that talented artists do their best work when the business people stay out of their way. He promised to leave Uncle Tupelo alone if they signed to Sire—and he proved true to his word. Plus, Margherita had introduced an escape clause into the band's contract with Rockville, allowing Tupelo to be bought out of its deal at any time for fifty thousand dollars—chump change by major-label standards.

In 1992 Tupelo signed a seven-record deal with Warner Brothers, which guaranteed at least two albums and a $150,000 recording budget for the first album. Mike Heidorn's departure from the band was of no consequence to Joe McEwen, but it probably should have been. Heidorn and Sandra Lynn Melahn were married on August 22, 1992, in Belleville. Tweedy and Farrar were the groomsmen. Three months later, they began their first tour of Europe, with a boyish-looking Kansas City funk drummer named Bill Belzer as Heidorn's replacement.

Belzer beat out two dozen candidates for the job, including the guy that Farrar and Tweedy agreed was the flat-out best drummer among all those trying out: Ken Coomer. "I knew the songs better than they did, but I'm six four, I'm loud, and I had dreadlocks," Coomer says.

"You scared Jay to death," Tweedy told him.

"I thought he was the greatest drummer I'd ever heard in my life," Tweedy says. "When you play with a drummer like Mike for such a long time, it was very obvious he was never gonna be a technically proficient drummer. I'm amazed when I listen back to those records with Mike how cool the drumming actually is. He is totally self-taught and idiosyncratic, but his feel was dead-on. That's the recording. But working out the nuts and bolts in rehearsal, his drumming could be like a shoe in a dryer. It was work sometimes to hear the kick drum, because Mike wouldn't play loud. And then Ken comes in and is just a powerhouse: tons of experience, tons of chops, and yet not so flashy that he can't come down and play a country beat. As a bass player, I could finally relax. With Mike, I was playing and singing and hoping that I was playing somewhere near where the bass drum was. With Coomer there was no doubt where the bass drum is: it's right up my fucking ass. I couldn't deny it. He was also overwhelmingly loud in the rehearsal space. Ken left, and I looked at Jay and said, 'That's the guy, huh?' And Jay said, 'He's really loud.' I think there was a certain amount of discrimination against Ken at the time because he had dreadlocks down to his ass. I don't think my concerns or Jay's concerns were ever so pure that we didn't have some vanity about how we pictured our band to be like; everybody does it. It was as simple as he didn't look like our drummer."

Belzer was slender, bespectacled, and competent, but lasted only six months.

"In some ways anyone who came after Mike wasn't going to feel right, because we played with him so long and we were so used to his idiosyncrasies," Tweedy says. "We wanted to hear things in weird places, and in a lot of ways whatever guy we hired was never going to get it right. We had Bill in the band for six months. I want to believe it was purely musical, and I honestly believe that it wasn't working musically. I also believe we weren't emotionally mature enough to be close friends with a gay person at that point in our lives. We come from a really small town and definitely grew up feeling threatened by things like that. We grew up not even being exposed to that many gay people. And Bill was and is a very proud and righteous gay person, very open and demonstrative of his homosexuality. Maybe it was hard to separate the comfort of people, the intimacy, from the music. Over time I felt really bad over the way he was treated, and was really happy that he was above it, and was friends with us."

Belzer hung on through the European tour, on which Uncle Tupelo opened for Bob Mould's first post–Hüsker Dü band, Sugar. Reviews of the new three-piece lineup were ecstatic, even though Tupelo was playing lots of acoustic songs that contrasted sharply with the loud, lacerating headliner. "Tupelo are hard and right-eous. Their songs have as much in common with John Steinbeck or Raymond Carver as they do with Crazy Horse, the Replace-ments, the Minutemen or the young R.E.M.," the *New Musical Express* raved in its review of the band's December 15, 1992, show in London. The U.K. critics were unusually forgiving of the trio's earnest stabs at channeling Depression-era characters via the *March 16–20, 1992* songs. Only *Melody Maker* offered a hint of derision: "Present this stuff without irony, as fresh as back when it meant something, and the longing and hurt of some grizzled old boot-legger taste almost tangible. Christ, it does sound laughable. Uncle Tupelo are anything but. Maybe you just had to be there."

When Farrar and Tweedy got back to Belleville, they said good-bye to Belzer and called Coomer. Born in 1960, the Nashville native is the son of Don Coomer, an accomplished country guitarist who once shared a band with Pat Boone, before the crooner found fame neutering rock 'n' roll songs such as Lit-tle Richard's "Tutti Frutti." By the early 1990s, Ken Coomer had recorded a handful of albums with Clockhammer, a jagged-edged progressive-rock band that was a distant musical kin to anarchic post-punk outfits such as Fishbone, Gone, and the Minutemen.

When Coomer finally made his belated Tupelo debut in January 1993, Tweedy and Farrar were already in the midst of a full-scale expansion of the band's lineup. They'd met Max Johnston on a brief, ill-fated tour the preceding autumn with his sister, the folk singer Michelle Shocked. Johnston, born in Dallas in 1969, is a multi-instrumentalist steeped in bluegrass. He began jamming with Tweedy and Farrar in hotel rooms and eventually was invited to add violin and mandolin solos onstage.

"I was really nervous because I was wondering if I could even play in a rock band, but Jay and Jeff knew the music I knew and a lot of music that I should have known," Johnston says. "I hadn't really listened to the Louvin Brothers, or even Loretta Lynn and Ernest Tubb. They turned me on to all of that stuff within the first few weeks, and I started getting more comfortable with the idea of playing with them."

John Stirratt, Tupelo's old friend from Mississippi, was on board as a guitar technician, taking over for Henneman, who was beginning to get his new band, the Bottle Rockets, off the ground. Stirratt, born in 1967 in New Orleans, had seen his roots-punk band the Hilltops disintegrate after a gig in Chicago in the summer of 1990; his sister, the bassist Laurie Stirratt, and the singer-guitarist Cary Hudson drove off to Los Angeles, got married, and went on to form the acclaimed country-flavored rock band Blue Mountain. Bringing in John Stirratt to play bass and guitar made Tupelo more versatile and freed up Tweedy to play guitar on the songs he wrote—a small but important step in the singer's maturation as a songwriter and musician capable of fronting his own band someday.

The new additions soon became privy to the unspoken complexities of the fragile Farrar-Tweedy union. "Jay would get interviewed at these radio stations, and his answers were just classic Jay: 'Uh-huh,' 'Nope,' 'Yup,' " Coomer says. "At that point Jay really had Jeff under his thumb, so they'd both clam up, and the deejays would just be squirming while these two guys are sitting there nodding in response to their questions."

In early 1993, the band was back in Europe, preparing for a concert at the Borderline in London. The set usually opened with Tweedy, Farrar, and Coomer playing acoustic *March* material, and then gradually expanded into an electric lineup with Johnston and then Stirratt. But on the eve of the London show, Coomer came down with food poisoning and collapsed in the back of the old hospital X-ray van the band was using to tour England.

"Jeff was telling Jay that we should do an all-acoustic show, because I wouldn't be able to play," Coomer says. "And Jay just turned around and said, 'No, we're going to do it all electric.' I was so groggy and sick I hadn't eaten in twenty-four hours, and I was as weak as I'd ever been. I remember thinking, 'Is Jay evil?' I played the show, I got through it, but to this day I would love to pull Jay aside and ask him why."

Excitement over the possibilities opened up by the new five-piece lineup glossed over the ill will, at least temporarily. When Uncle Tupelo rolled into Cedar Creek studio in Austin, Texas, to record *Anodyne*, the band was playing at a higher level than ever. Tweedy in particular found himself energized and inspired by his new bandmates; whereas on previous albums he had contributed one or at best two standout tracks, for *Anodyne* he was unusually prolific, bringing a half-dozen songs that equaled anything he'd submitted previously.

"For a long time, I felt like it was Jay's band, and I was writing things that I felt would sound good in contrast to Jay's songs," Tweedy says. "I definitely didn't just write what I felt like writing. I didn't just present anything that I dug. I really scrutinized things, and I didn't present anything that I didn't think he would like, which was a very narrow thing in my mind, maybe even narrower than Jay actually is. But because of the tension I felt trying to communicate with him, it really narrowed everything down to things I felt would hit home with him.

"But around the time of *Anodyne*, I felt like I had slipped some things through that were more open about me. I think when Mike left the band, a parade of different people came into our lives that disrupted this insulated world we had lived in for a long, long time. A lot of people came into the band that didn't know the rules of engagement about dealing with Jay. 'You're gonna say stuff to Jay,

aren't you? Oh, dear.' And I'd see him react to it like a normal person, because there wasn't that dynamic that built up over time. You
never talk about sex with Jay—that wasn't something you'd share
with Jay. And somebody else like Ken would bring it up, and I'd
feel horrified about what he was getting himself into, then be
amazed that it went off okay. Because I never allowed myself to
have that kind of freedom. That emboldened me in a lot of ways.
If everybody else can be relaxed and normal around Jay, why can't
I be relaxed and normal around Jay? Or, at the very least, stop
spending so much time thinking he was judging every single thing
I was doing."

But Tweedy's increasing sense of freedom only disrupted the
band's emotional equilibrium even further. "I spent a lot of time
hanging out with the new guys, because it was relaxed," Tweedy
says. "And with them it was like, 'Hey, I'm working on this song,'
and try it out on them, because that's more how I really am. Jay
interpreted that as arrogance. It bothered him. Around this time, I
would say something into a microphone onstage, and afterward
he'd pull me aside and say, 'Don't you ever fucking talk into that
microphone again.' He would misconstrue me talking into the
microphone as more evidence of my out-of-control, rampant ego,
more evidence of me feeling like I didn't have to be so fucking
afraid anymore. And I guess that is ego out of control, in some
ways. But I didn't think that was the kind of ego that you malign;
I think that's the kind of ego you cherish in your friends, that you
hope your friends care enough about themselves to be themselves."

That tension made for one last burst of creativity, an album on
which the songs of Farrar and Tweedy seemed to talk to each other
in ways the two bandmates couldn't outside the recording studio.
It's not a stretch to wonder if Farrar's "Slate" addresses his grave
doubts about Uncle Tupelo's increasing ties with the corporate
record business ("working in the halls of shame"), and if "Chickamauga," named after one of the bloodiest battles of the Civil War,
could be the first draft of a breakup letter to Tweedy and the rest
of the band ("the time is right for getting out while we still can . . .
solitude is where I'm bound"). And what of the dire warnings
contained in the title song: "No sign of reconciliation, it's a quar-
ter past the end"? In response, Tweedy's songs sound like eleventh-

hour pleas for a truce: "The Long Cut" acknowledges that "we've been in a deep rut, and it's been killing me . . . [but] we'll get there eventually," and "No Sense in Lovin'" pronounces, "You might think that I don't care, but I do."

Tweedy's songs move with a spring in their step and a fraternal camaraderie in the vocals that suggest the *Sweetheart of the Rodeo*–era Byrds, especially on "New Madrid" and "No Sense in Lovin'." His "Acuff-Rose," an homage to the revered country songwriting duo, sounds like the twang-pop companion piece to Tweedy's earlier tribute to the Minutemen's D. Boon. Even the cynicism of "We've Been Had" is redeemed by a buoyantly irreverent guitar riff, as if a schoolkid were teasing the tortured-artist rock star described in the song. Farrar's songs continue to walk the dark side of the road, brooding, inconsolable meditations that cry ("High Water"), crash ("Chickamauga"), and mourn ("Fifteen Keys"). They're balanced by an ebullient duet with one of his heroes, Doug Sahm, on the Texas maverick's "Give Back the Key to My Heart."

The grizzled singer had been invited to the recording session by Farrar, who once drove from Belleville to Nashville with Henneman to see a reunion of Sahm's Sir Douglas Quintet; the two rock 'n' roll pilgrims ended up in front of the stage at the sparsely attended concert, shouting requests at the amused singer. Sahm swept into the Austin recording sessions wearing a house robe, swigging carrot juice, and trailing dust from a 1974 Lincoln Town Car, his personality so effervescent that it instantly shrank everyone else in the room to the status of valets, gofers, and acolytes.

"We're playing a song, and Doug turns to me and says, 'Play it like Cosmo,' " Ken Coomer says. "My jaw drops, because he's talking about Doug Clifford [of Creedence Clearwater Revival]. He wants me to play like Doug Clifford! I was nervous. I dropped a beat so far back it's in another song, and I wanted to do it again, but the answer was no. The whole album was like that—all live takes with the band playing together, slowing down, speeding up, bum notes all over the place. But it was real, and it worked because of that."

Johnston and another Texas musician, the pedal-steel guitarist Lloyd Maines, embroidered the melodies, giving *Anodyne* a textural richness that previous Uncle Tupelo albums only hinted at. "There was more of a pop element or a buoyancy that just didn't seem to be a part of Uncle Tupelo before," Tweedy says. "But through John's playing and Ken's playing and my songs at the time, it was just more tuneful and less contrived arrangement-wise. I felt like we had done all these really elaborate start-stop arrangements in emulation of the Minutemen and really worked hard to make things obtuse, and that was getting to be a drag to me over time. Being able to concentrate on playing acoustic guitar was liberating, because the songs sounded like extensions of the way I wrote them on the couch at home."

It was highly unusual for any major-label rock band in 1993 to turn in an album that was essentially recorded live in the studio, without a single overdub. But the response at Sire was favorable. "The philosophy at the label was that you sign things, and plant grass so the grass would grow over time," Joe McEwen says. "That was the history of bands like the Ramones, Talking Heads, Depeche Mode. There was enthusiasm at the label for the record. We didn't consider it a record that radio might play, but everybody considered it a step up from what they'd done before."

The *Anodyne* tour climaxed with a December 1993 show at Tramps in New York, a club several times larger than any the band had ever played before in town. "Advance ticket sales were really slow, and we wondered if we'd made a mistake booking them there," McEwen says. "The club owner was nervous, the booking agent was nervous; they were calling me days before the show saying, 'Did we blow it?' I was worried this was going to be a disaster. But I walk up that night, and there's a line down the block. We'd sold it out, and the place was going crazy for them. They looked like little stars up there, and it felt like this great American band was flowering. We all felt that way."

A week later, McEwen had the band over to his house in Montclair, New Jersey, for a Christmas party, where they were schmoozed by Sire and Warner Brothers executives. "I was still pretty ecstatic about the show. It's like everyone could feel that the band had hit this next level," McEwen recalls.

"Everything built to that show in New York," Tony Margherita says. "It got a great review in *The New York Times*. I remember coming back from that trip and thinking when we go back on the road next year, it's going to be great. Everybody in the label felt that way, like we were on the cusp of something."

Bill Bentley, a label executive who would later work closely with Wilco at Reprise Records, says Uncle Tupelo was viewed as Sire's next big band. *Anodyne* sold more than respectably, despite a lack of radio or MTV support; it would eventually surpass 150,000 sales. On the road the band was building the type of steady audience most bands could only imagine. "They were selling a thousand to twelve hundred tickets to shows in some of the bigger markets around the country," Bentley says. "We had bands on the label who couldn't sell ten tickets. People here thought we were going to have platinum records from Uncle Tupelo."

But in January 1994, Warner Brothers' platinum dream came crashing down with a phone call from Margherita to McEwen. "I've got some news," Margherita said. "They're breaking up."

CHAPTER 7

"THERE WAS A TIME, THAT TIME IS GONE"

With one phone call to his manager, Jay Farrar hit the tri-
fecta: pissed off Jeff Tweedy, torpedoed a band on the
rise, and ruined Christmas. It would not make Farrar a
particularly popular figure in Tupelo world, but it was a prescient
decision: it was time to move on.

In the first hot flash of incredulity, tears, and anger, however,
that was apparent only to Farrar. "I got the call from Jay and said,
'You're kidding, right?' I knew he wasn't kidding. Jay didn't kid
around," Tony Margherita says. "We had a drink the next day to
talk it over. Jay said he wasn't having any fun, that he wasn't getting along with Jeff. I told him to think about it over the holidays.
'If we need to make some changes that will make you happy, let
me know.' "

Jeff Tweedy was stunned. "I made Tony tell me over the phone
what was so heavy that he wanted me to come over to his office
in St. Louis and tell me face-to-face," Tweedy says. "I knew it
could be only one thing. It was still a surprise. I still took it hard.
I freaked out, basically."

"He was fucking furious," Margherita says. "He was pissed that

Jay not only broke up the band, but that Jay had told me and not him."

Tweedy and Margherita hung out in St. Louis later that night, and the singer vented. The two tried to hash out a plan to salvage the band but soon began turning their attention to life after Tupelo. "We talked ourselves into the idea that it was really going to be fun and great not to have to deal with all of the rules, with everything always being so difficult—even if it wasn't at the level we hoped it would be," Tweedy says.

When Farrar and Tweedy finally confronted each other in their Belleville apartment a day later, emotions and misgivings that had been suppressed for the good of the band, for the sake of the music, came undone. Voices were raised until these two soft-spoken roommates were screaming at close range.

"Tell me to my face . . . Why do you hate me?"

Farrar squared up with the person he'd been playing in bands with for twelve years. "You don't know what it's like to stand onstage with somebody every night who loves themselves as much as you do."

Tweedy was taken aback. "You're right, I don't have any idea."

Over the holidays, Jay Farrar and his future wife, Monica Groth, showed up unannounced at Brian Henneman's apartment in Festus, Missouri, thirty miles south of St. Louis. They drank beers and downed Rice Krispies Treats in Henneman's kitchen. "Wow, this is wonderful," Henneman thought. "Odd, but nice." Farrar never once mentioned that he was quitting Uncle Tupelo. "Jay seemed like the happiest guy in the world, especially by his standards. Maybe he came down to hide out from phone calls. It was weird, man, fucking weird. Talk about a guy who plays his cards close to his vest."

Jay and Monica also visited Stirratt in New Orleans, and they went out for drinks and had a few laughs as if nothing had happened. Farrar looked relaxed, like the weight he'd been dragging around for the last few years had suddenly been lifted.

Out of loyalty to Margherita, Farrar agreed to give the band one more shot on a North American tour. The band was several thousand dollars in debt to their manager, who had piled up personal credit-card and phone bills to keep Tupelo running. Uncle

Tupelo would tour for the first time in a bus instead of a van, and it had gotten successful enough that the band members could share hotel rooms instead of crashing on the couches and floors of sympathetic fans. Perhaps the less claustrophobic conditions would ease the tension and somehow keep Tupelo rolling.

But two weeks into the 1994 tour, the wheels came off. In North Carolina, Farrar and Tweedy had it out again, this time in the parking lot of a club after a concert, a face-to-face war of words and spit. Coomer and the road manager, Bob Andrews, had to pull the two apart. "Jay wasn't singing harmonies on Jeff's songs, and Jeff called him on that," Coomer says. "Jeff had a point. There was definitely some of that going on." Stirratt knew the score as well. "Jay had become disinterested in Jeff's songs," he explains. "Just wouldn't play on them."

Andrews tried to play peacemaker and called a band meeting back at the hotel. "A bad decision," he says. The year before, the sum of his experience in the music business had been working at a music store in Nashville. Now he was trying to broker a truce between two heavyweight singer-songwriters who were finding that Uncle Tupelo wasn't big enough for both of them. What happened next affirmed that Tupelo was history.

"I don't want to put you on the spot, man, but what's up?" Andrews asked Farrar. "Everything's going great. The band sounds great. What's wrong?"

"I don't have a problem with anyone in here but you," Farrar said, and pointed at Tweedy.

At that moment, Michael Praytor, the band's sound man, passed out and hit his head on a coffee table. "It's like Keystone Kops in there," Coomer recalls. "And all I wanna do is get out of there."

"It was like the bad family meeting, like when everyone wants to talk about why Uncle Jimmy is a drunk, and then Uncle Jimmy turns the tables on everyone," Andrews says. "I thought everyone needed to know what was going on, that we needed to clear the air. Because even though we knew Jay wanted out, he had never told any of us directly. Up until then, it had all been through Tony. After that, there wasn't any doubt."

The rest of the tour was a sullen affair, the band broken into two camps, with Farrar hanging in the front of the bus and Tweedy in the back. The singers had stopped communicating about everything, even the set list for each show, which Andrews had to draw up by shuttling between the two feuding Tupelo fiefdoms. Even the band's first appearance on network television, on *Conan O'Brien*, was a cause for friction rather than celebration. At the behest of the label and the late-night talk show, Tupelo played Tweedy's "The Long Cut" instead of one of Farrar's songs. The song couldn't have been timelier. "We've been in a deep rut," Tweedy sang, "and it's been killing me."

"You think Jay wanted to do 'Long Cut' on *Conan*?" Coomer says. "I don't think he wanted to do any song on any TV show, ever, let alone one of Jeff's songs. When we got the rented tour bus, it was one of these deals with the airbrushed paintings on the side that another rock band had used, and Jay was just horrified. The aesthetics of any kind of rock stardom just freaked him out. Jay went through with it, but reluctantly."

Opening the tour for Uncle Tupelo was the North Carolina singer-songwriter Joe Henry. His band included the Minneapolis multi-instrumentalist Jim Boquist, who later that year would join Farrar in his first post-Tupelo band, Son Volt. Meanwhile, Tweedy was rallying the rest of the troops around him. Everyone was worried about his job, his next paycheck, but Tweedy assured Stirratt, Coomer, and Johnston that they could continue making music together. "It was a relief to all of us to hear Jeff say that," Johnston says. "We were all vaguely replaceable, and that made me think our little honeymoon wasn't going to end."

McEwen had tried to repair the damage, but after meeting with Farrar and Tweedy before a March show at Lounge Ax in Chicago, he knew the band was heading in two directions and adjusted his plans for a follow-up album accordingly. "It was like two brothers, and the younger one catches up with the older guy," McEwen says. "The dynamic had been cast years before with Jay as the older brother, but Jeff wanted to break out of the mold. Jay wanted the relationship to stay as it had been, and Jeff didn't. There was nowhere to go with it except to have bitterness and resentment toward each other."

The A&R man put a positive spin on this potentially dire news for Warner Brothers. "He said we're losing a great band, but we're gaining two great songwriters and two great bands," says Gary Briggs, then working in radio promotion at Warner. "And everybody just nodded and said, 'Great!' It says a lot about what kind of respect Joe McEwen had that he was able to pull that off so smoothly, to lay the groundwork for two careers."

By the time Uncle Tupelo played its final shows, two sold-out concerts on April 30 and May 1, 1994, at Mississippi Nights in St. Louis, it had become common knowledge that the band was breaking up, though there had been no official announcement. There was a certain irony in Tupelo's playing its final shows on "enemy" turf—on the dreaded Landing that had been host to so many of the fashion-conscious bands they had loathed only a few years before. They wryly noted their continuing unworthiness in the posters for the final shows, proclaiming their status as "St. Louis' 4th Best Country Band," as voted in a *Riverfront Times* readers' poll.

Opening the first night was Steve Scariano's band Blown, whose live sound was mixed by a couple of friends from Champaign, Illinois: Adam Schmitt, who had overseen one of Uncle Tupelo's pre–*No Depression* demos; and a hotshot guitarist named Jay Bennett, who in a few months would find himself playing with Jeff Tweedy.

The final show was a fairly sober affair, the band efficiently and professionally dispatching eighteen songs, with Tweedy and Farrar splitting the lead vocals so evenly it was as if a lawyer had brokered the set list. "It was really depressing," says Heather Crist, a longtime fan from Tupelo's days as Cicero's house band. "There were people crying in the audience. Hearing all those songs from *Anodyne*, it became very apparent what all those lyrics were about. Jeff and Jay weren't looking at each other. It was just like they wanted to get it over with."

But the encore was a different story. Joined by Heidorn, who stepped behind the drums for the first time in two years to a huge ovation, Tupelo found the bittersweet core of "Looking for a Way Out." Farrar's small-town blues became something of a farewell: "There was a time, that time is gone."

Jay's brother Wade was now more a fan than an insider, and the show brought a decade's worth of memories flooding back. "It was a relief to see Mike get up there; it popped the tension. To me it was never the same band after he left," he says. "Why'd they break up? I had no better idea than anyone else. When Jay and I were in the Primitives together, we talked a lot, but once I left, he talks to me about as much as he talks to anybody else."

Henneman and his new band, the Bottle Rockets, then helped close the Tupelo era with hell-raising vocals on Lynyrd Skynyrd's "Gimme Three Steps," a buoyant finale for a night of mixed emotions. While Farrar walked off, Tweedy hugged Henneman and waved to the cheering audience. "That's got to be it."

The finality settled in only afterward. Tweedy and his girlfriend, Sue Miller, joined Henneman for a postconcert meal at Steak n Shake, then drove over to Margherita's home for a band party that tried to put an upbeat spin on what was essentially a wake. But the parting, like the band's final months, was painfully awkward. Tweedy and Farrar's girlfriend, Monica Groth, hugged. Her last words to him were "You smell like grease."

"I walked to my car, and I see Jay and Jeff," Coomer says. "I watched Jay walk by Jeff and Jay just give him a nod, like 'See ya.' Jeff is an emotional guy; he probably wanted to at least hug the guy. But that's how it ended. With a nod."

Tweedy drove to his parents' house on Fortieth Street in Belleville, sat down on the footstool in the living room, and sobbed.

Brian Henneman didn't feel much better. "They were set to pop; they were doing good work and getting good results from it," the former Tupelo roadie says. "They were in a position that any band would love to be in. I had no personal stake in it at that point, but I was pissed at Jay for a long time, because he derailed it. Jeff was hurt, and why shouldn't he be? His band was destroyed. And for what? Some internal fashion-related shit boiling underneath the surface for years? I still don't really know why he did it. No one does."

Jay Farrar's execution may have been lacking, but his instincts were positively visionary. No one else saw the future as clearly as he did at Christmas of 1993, and the phone call he placed to Tony Margherita should have immediately closed the book on the band.

Instead, nobody—Margherita, Tweedy, the record label—really wanted to believe that Farrar was pulling the plug. And so the band dragged through another four miserable months on the road, though not without benefit. After the final St. Louis shows, Margherita and Andrews walked to a bank near their office with a brown paper bag holding ten thousand dollars in small bills. Most of the post-*Anodyne* shows were sellouts, and the band was hauling in three hundred to four hundred dollars a night in T-shirt revenue alone.

For Farrar none of that mattered. "Commercial success wasn't the reason that we started the band," he says, "so that wasn't any reason to keep it going forward. That's the wrong reason to start a band, and the wrong reason to continue a band. It had run its course."

Uncle Tupelo never recovered from Mike Heidorn's departure. They no longer could be the three boys from Belleville, a unified front against the world. Songwriting credits had been split three ways, and the revenue split evenly in the original band. But once Heidorn left, the songwriting partnership officially died, and Farrar and Tweedy began taking individual credits on songs. R.E.M.'s bassist, Mike Mills, doesn't hesitate when asked to pinpoint the key to his band's two-decade longevity: "We split the songwriting four ways from the beginning, and that headed off any jealousy or ego intruding on the creative process. Any time there is competition in a band, there is bound to be friction."

Major-label demands divided the band further, the journalist Richard Byrne says. "With Uncle Tupelo, it was turning into more like the Beatles, where Paul McCartney, John Lennon, and George Harrison were all bringing in their songs at the end and competing for space on the albums. It's harder to sustain a band dynamic in that situation. Especially when you have the record-company machinery saying, 'I like his song better,' and making it the single. To someone like Jay, who is suspicious of record-label politics anyway, that's going to be the sound of fingernails on the chalkboard. Jay didn't like what he saw coming down the road, and I think Jeff loved it. Jeff could see this band selling a lot of records and being on tour—and how can you not look at that and think that's not the greatest thing in the world if you're in a band?

To Jay, that wasn't fun. And he wasn't going to explain why it wasn't fun either. He wasn't going to sit down with Barbara Walters and say, 'Well, I just didn't want to be a rock star.' He just left."

For Tweedy, living in the cocoon of a boyhood dream come true, it was a wake-up call. "I was happy to do anything to make the band work," Tweedy says. "I was ambitious, more than Jay was. I felt like I was ready to make a record the first time I played an E chord the right way—completely naive ambition. Jay had this really natural, God-given voice, this big sonorous gift, and I had this squeaky nasal thing that it took me years and years to figure out how to use. I realize now that before Uncle Tupelo, I sang in my bedroom like I sing now. It took a long time for that to come out. I listen to those early records now, and they sound really affected, like we wanted to be Homer and Jethro. But I thought it could go on for a long time, with each of us contributing our six best songs to an album, and I would have been happy to continue on that way. I was naive."

Daniel Corrigan, a Minneapolis photographer who has snapped many rock bands behind the scenes over two decades, spent several months on the road with Uncle Tupelo in its final year. His beautiful black-and-white images adorn the *Anodyne* album, including its prophetic cover portrait. Here, the band's ghostlike images are barely visible from behind a stack of guitars and amplifiers, a poignant evocation of disintegration, of personality subsumed by music. He was impressed with Tupelo's commitment to their music, that the band literally seemed to go to bed playing their instruments, huddled in acoustic hotel-room jam sessions. In the end, it was the one common pleasure they all had.

"Yeah, there was tension in that band," the photographer says. "There seemed to be tension between Jay and pretty much the rest of the world. I don't know why. I do know that it's hard to be in a band. It's hard to be in any sort of relationship where you have to be around somebody all the time, in close quarters. Jay and Jeff were together since high school, right?"

Thirteen years.

"Thirteen? Most marriages I know don't last that long. They had a good run."

CHAPTER 8

"IT WAS LIKE WATCHING A PRIZE FIGHT"

Fear was hurrying Jeff Tweedy toward his next destination—fear of being forgotten, fear of losing Uncle Tupelo's audience, fear of being left in the dust by Jay Farrar.

"Five or ten minutes after the last Uncle Tupelo show, it felt like we were back in the recording studio" is how Max Johnston describes it. Within weeks of Jay Farrar's surprise Christmas announcement, Tweedy was polishing new songs and rounding up his new band. Tweedy, Johnston, Ken Coomer, and John Stirratt morphed into Wilco ("roger, wilco, okay" trucker lingo), but only after some serious consideration was given to the name "National Dust." That idea was shot down by the band's closest advisers. "The womenfolk weren't havin' it," Coomer says.

Only days after Uncle Tupelo waved good-bye at Mississippi Nights, Wilco was rehearsing songs through tiny amplifiers in Margherita's St. Louis office. In June they were recording demos at Easley studio in Memphis, and in August they were laying down finished tracks at the same studio for their first album, *A.M.* The producer was Brian Paulson, who had overseen the recording of *Anodyne* with no-fuss efficiency.

It was all too much too soon.

"A band becomes who you are to a large extent, and Jeff had been in a band with Jay Farrar since he was in high school," says Darin Gray, Tweedy's friend since the Primitives days. "And when that's taken away from you, it's a scary, scary time. Who are you when there's no Uncle Tupelo? *A.M.* definitely seemed like a panic move on Jeff's part."

"I was fearful about a lot of things, and one of them was that I would psych myself out the longer we waited," Tweedy says. "I didn't want to lose any momentum. We were playing in front of more people, and more people were paying attention to the band, and I was having more fun than ever with the rest of the band. I wanted to get back on the road and play, but I had to make a record first in order to do that."

Though Warner Brothers was outwardly accepting of the Uncle Tupelo breakup and the prospect of separate projects fronted by Tweedy and Jay Farrar, the smart money was on Farrar, the singer with the once-in-a-lifetime voice and the songwriter who brought the gravity, the blue-eyed soul heaviness, to Uncle Tupelo. Now he was assembling a new band, Son Volt. He recruited Jim Boquist from Joe Henry's band, added his brother Dave Boquist, and persuaded Mike Heidorn to come out of retirement to play drums. By November, the quartet had started bashing out the songs for the *Trace* album in a Minneapolis studio with Brian Paulson. The close ties between Tweedy and Farrar that had suddenly been severed, and the fact that they used the same producer to record their debut albums only weeks apart, ensured that their work would be compared, dissected, and played off against each other by fans, critics, even their own record company.

"When Joe McEwen told me Uncle Tupelo was breaking up, it was not good news," says Bill Bentley, a Warner executive who ended up being Wilco's press representative. "I thought it wouldn't work, that losing the chemistry of the two songwriters was bad news. Doug Sahm would call me to give me stick. He'd always be saying stuff like 'Jay's the guy,' that 'Son Volt's the band.' And, let's face it, after their first albums came out, a lot of people thought that Doug was right. *A.M.* didn't make that big a dent in the Jay Farrar mystique. If anything, after *Trace* came out, it was enhanced."

When McEwen heard the demos for both *A.M.* and *Trace*, he couldn't suppress similar feelings. "Seymour Stein heard a few of Jay's songs—'Drown,' 'Windfall'—and said, 'This will be the greatest signing ever,' " McEwen recalls.

Even Margherita was briefly caught in the middle. "There were people telling me to manage Jay rather than Jeff," he says. "Jay's voice was something that anyone would've wanted to hitch their wagon to, and people told me I'd be crazy to stick with Jeff." But Margherita's ties ran deeper with Tweedy, and he offered to help Farrar find a new manager. "I don't have to do a lot of mind reading with Jeff," Margherita says.

Based on the Memphis song demos, Tweedy was signed to a deal with Reprise Records, another Warner subsidiary, while Farrar signed with Warner Brothers itself. Though Tweedy talked to the other band members about taking a more collective approach to the band, his was the only name on the label contract. Tweedy wanted a band rather than a solo project, and he envisioned a more collaborative situation than existed in the latter days of Uncle Tupelo. But when the paperwork was signed, there was no doubt that it would be his band.

"We were all in a room, and Jeff talked about having an equal band," Ken Coomer says. "But when we brought up the idea of being in on the deal [with Reprise], that's when the equality ended."

"I remember conversations where Jeff presented this as a full-partnership band when they first started, but it never really became that," says Bob Andrews, Wilco's first tour manager. "Everybody was complaining: 'We're salaried employees making five hundred dollars a week on the road while Jeff has the record deal, he has the publishing.' That was always a point with Ken: Why aren't we getting paid equal shares on everything? And that's because it was Jeff's band. He wrote the songs, which isn't easy to do. But it was never made clear to the other guys that's how it really was. It was presented as one thing and became this other thing. So Ken got looked upon as the squeaky wheel. He was the older guy, the guy who would take the money complaints to Tony Margherita. But John and Jay [Bennett] were right behind him, complaining just as loud."

The band did have a partnership deal when it came to splitting record royalties, but Wilco never sold enough records to make any. Tweedy let everyone in the band share in a percentage of his publishing income, whether they contributed to the songwriting or not—an unusually generous move for any songwriter to make. He also solicited songs from the other band members and even briefly held open the possibility of having them sing some lead vocals. But only Stirratt came through with contributions for the first album. The bassist submitted three songs that reached the demo stage for *A.M.*, and one—the gorgeous country lament "It's Just That Simple"—made it onto the finished album. The track is so strong, caressed by sighing pedal steel guitar from the *Anodyne* holdover Lloyd Maines and Johnston's mandolin, it suggests one possible alternative direction for Wilco, with Stirratt as a strong secondary songwriting and singing voice. But it was a road not taken. From that point on, Tweedy's voice and songs would dominate the albums and concerts.

"One of the reasons I went with Jeff instead of Jay is I thought I might have a better shot to break into the songwriting," Stirratt says. "But the album was done almost before I knew it. I was back in New Orleans when I got a copy of the master recording, and it had only one of my songs on it. I was hoping for at least two. I felt like we'd rushed into something, made the record too soon. If we'd taken more time to develop some of the songs that were out there, both Jeff's and mine, it would have been a stronger record."

That *A.M.* was recorded relatively quickly suited Brian Henneman just fine; he was brought in expressly to play lead guitar. "I think Jeff was a little shook doing it all on his own," Henneman says. "Think about it: he had to prove himself to the record company. They wouldn't take anyone's word that he could make great records on his own. I certainly wouldn't have handled that pressure as well as he did."

Henneman provided just what Tweedy and *A.M.* needed: a rock edge to balance the Johnston-Maines country voicings. His riffs don't just color the songs, they define several of them: it's impossible to imagine "Casino Queen" without Henneman's finger-wagging, rooster-strutting riff; "That's Not the Issue" without his bluegrass picking alongside Johnston's banjo; or "Too Far Apart" without his stoned-country fills. "He completely saved our asses," Stirratt says.

Henneman was on an artistic roll, fresh off recording the second Bottle Rockets album, *The Brooklyn Side*, a blend of southern rock, Stones boogie, and tragicomic lyricism. He held nothing back during the Wilco recording sessions, perhaps because he had the least to lose. "I was in the slam-bam mode and thrilled to be there," he says. "We ended up using a lot of the demos on the finished album. During the actual recording session, there was some weirdness, because I was going through a dysfunctional relationship at the time. It involved a rendezvous with a woman in Memphis that backfired, so when you hear the bottles clinking on 'Casino Queen,' that wasn't staged. That was out of necessity. I was too fucked-up to play that day, too belligerent and drunk, because I drank two bottles of gin. Literally the only thing I could do was to clack those two empties together while the contents were being processed by my liver."

Even though they may have been marinated in gin, the final mixes sounded muddy, and the recording was not enthusiastically received by Tony Margherita or Joe McEwen. "I called Jeff and Tony and told them that we needed to make a really competitive record and that this didn't sound as good as *Anodyne*," McEwen says. "I thought that it was a step back, like they were making an indie record. I wanted a more seasoned person to take a crack at mixing it."

The seasoned pro was Richard Dodd, who had most recently worked on Tom Petty's *Wildflowers* album. He pushed Tweedy's vocals up front, giving the album a punchier pop feel, the type of mix that a radio programmer wouldn't dismiss out of hand.

A.M. holds several fine songs: "Box Full of Letters," with its Byrds-like chime, sounds like Tweedy's farewell to Farrar ("I got a lotta your records / In a separate stack / Some things that I might like to hear / But I guess I'll give them back"). Deceptively dark undercurrents course through the drunk-driving sing-along "Passenger Side" and the equally cynical "Casino Queen." But overall it was a tentative first step toward establishing an identity outside of Uncle Tupelo. Tweedy's voice and personality are as modest as the arrangements; there's little sense of drama, and virtually no hint of risk.

It's little wonder: the sessions were hurried, and Wilco's lineup was still in flux. Henneman would've made a fine addition to the band, but he was in no position to stick around; the Bottle Rockets' *Brooklyn Side* would be released on November 1, and he was going on tour.

To fill the guitar gap, the road manager, Bob Andrews, and Steve Scariano, Margherita's old record-store companion, both pointed Wilco toward Jay Bennett, a bespectacled, frazzle-haired guitarist with a radio announcer's foghorn baritone, a mathematician's intellect, and a penchant for flamboyant thrift-shop clothes. Born on November 15, 1963, in the Chicago suburb Rolling Meadows, Bennett came on like a mad professor who had never met an instrument or musical gadget he couldn't tame. Scariano had run across Bennett while playing in bands during the mid-1980s in Champaign, Illinois, where Bennett was attending school when he wasn't strumming his guitar playing Bruce Springsteen's "Johnny 99" or Nick Lowe's "(What's So Funny 'bout) Peace, Love, and Understanding?" at parties or on the porch of his apartment. Andrews met Bennett behind the sound board at the final Uncle Tupelo shows, and they hit it off. Bennett had a reputation as a formidable guitarist. He was versatile enough to play twang rock with the band Steve Pride and His Blood Kin, and Replacements-style power pop with Titanic Love Affair. It sounded like the perfect combination for Wilco, and, best of all, Bennett was very much available. Titanic Love Affair had been dropped from its label deal, and Bennett—who has multiple degrees, in secondary education, mathematics, and political studies—was scraping up rent money by working at a VCR repair shop in Champaign.

"Jeff sent me a tape of the *A.M.* mixes and a few old Uncle Tupelo songs," Bennett says, "and it sounded a helluva lot better than anything I was doing at the time."

On November 27, 1994, Wilco made its live debut at Uncle Tupelo's old basement hangout in St. Louis, Cicero's. Even though the quintet was billed as Black Shampoo, a name culled from

Coomer's stash of trashy cult-classic movies, the place was packed to a Tupelo-like level of claustrophobia. Tweedy's voice cracked and wobbled, and the band sounded unsure and sluggish. Besides dutifully replicating Henneman's meaty riffs, Bennett threw a lifetime's worth of chops into the performance, evoking a junior version of the Byrd's Clarence White or an apprentice to the British-born country guitarist extraordinaire Albert Lee. He's clearly the standout performer in an otherwise-shaky debut concert, but he hadn't really figured out how to mesh with the band or the songs. "We weren't playing as a unit yet," Ken Coomer says. "Everyone was concerned about his own part. Jay was shredding on guitar, but the songs were buried by the solos. Jay is a fabulous musician, but he hadn't figured out less is more quite yet."

Bennett's enthusiasm for his new role was undeniable, however, and that energized Tweedy. A month later, Tweedy and Bennett played an acoustic show at Lounge Ax in Chicago and began cementing a partnership that would expand over the next half-dozen years. It was a bond that extended well beyond music.

Two weeks before the release of *A.M.* in March 1995, Wilco was to play the South by Southwest Music Conference in Austin, Texas, a major annual gathering of industry executives, bands, and critics. Bennett and Tweedy decided to drive down to the festival from Chicago with road manager Daniel Herbst and sound man Michael Praytor.

"Jeff made a bunch of pot cookies," Bennett recalls. "After quitting drinking, Jeff had become a big pot smoker. He put way too much pot in the mix, and when it was digested, it took on hallucinogenic properties. We're listening to Television on the cassette player, so imagine these two psychedelic interweaving guitars getting more and more intense and Jeff's having the equivalent of a bad trip, an anxiety attack times ten. I'd been having anxiety attacks since I was in fifth grade, ones that would last for hours, so I understood what he was going through. It's the equivalent of feeling you're in a foreign country and something horrible is happening; me being there was like bumping into another person from your own country. You're not just going to pass that guy on the street. You're going to bond a little bit. Jeff's stuck in a van in the middle of nowhere with two guys up front who aren't particularly sympathetic with someone who's having a bad trip—'Ride it out, dude.' So I'm hugging him, holding him, and he's shivering. He had something really important to do the next day. When you're having an anxiety attack, there are moments of clarity where you're realizing, 'I just lost my mind.' He thought he was gone. I think he would have literally thrown himself out of the van or something if I wasn't there holding him. He lost it and he got through it. We decided not to tell anybody. But it changed a lot of things: Jeff's personality, the way Jeff wrote songs, our relationship."

Soon after, Tweedy quit smoking pot, and his songs turned introspective as he began writing what would be Wilco's breakthrough album, *Being There*. There were other reasons his life was turning a corner. He had been living with Sue Miller in Chicago, and on August 6 they would be married. Four months later, their first son, Spencer, was born. And then there was the matter of Jay Farrar. Son Volt debuted in September with *Trace* and was greeted with rave reviews and brisk sales.

"The first Son Volt record was pretty fucking good," Brian Henneman says. "It was like watching a prize fight at that point. Wow! He slammed him there! Ouch! What a counterpunch! It was exciting being on the sidelines watching these guys. It's like Jay had something to prove with that first album, an urgency to it that none of his albums since have had. I felt he had a chip on his shoulder, and it shows up in the music. It was stunning. It was humbling. I think that kicked Jeff in the ass."

"Absolutely there was competitiveness between Jeff and Jay," Sue Miller says. "How could there not be? They might say there wasn't, but I can't imagine them not feeling that way. It would be only natural. They wouldn't wish each other ill, but they had their eyes open. And if they didn't, the press certainly did. They couldn't do anything without being compared to the other person, which was irritating to both of them. Jeff handled everything fine, but I know it was annoying to him. With the Internet getting the way it did and all those message boards talking about them, fomenting these wars between them, he couldn't avoid it."

When John Stirratt first heard *Trace*, he saw it as an unspoken challenge. "There was a certain element of failure around *A.M.*," he says. "As the tour went on, we were playing to fewer people the second time through certain towns, which is the first and only time that's happened to a band Jeff was in. Then *Trace* came out, and it was eye-opening. Just classic Farrar songs. It was definitely daunting, and I felt we had something to prove after that."

With *Trace*, Farrar didn't so much try to shake off or reinvent his old approach as deepen it. Opening with a chorus like a blessing—"May the wind take your troubles away"—Farrar plunges into an album stacked with one instant classic after another. Gorged with melody and ornamented with banjo, fiddle, and pedal steel, "Windfall," "Tear Stained Eye," and the elegiac "Too Early" sound like long-lost mountain-soul hymns, while even the heavy guitars on "Route," "Drown," and "Loose String" can't blow the sure, stately tempos off course: "When in doubt, move on / No need to sort it out."

It was the assured work of a major artist, and its arrival was heralded with prosaic pieces of music journalism by *Newsweek*'s Karen Schoemer, *The Philadelphia Inquirer*'s Tom Moon, and *The Village Voice*'s Ann Powers, among others, most of them concurring with Schoemer's assessment that *Trace* proved "that the soul of Uncle Tupelo rested with Farrar." Most significant of all, *Trace* and Son Volt were the subjects of a cover story in the debut issue of *No Depression*, a magazine that proclaimed itself "the alternative country quarterly."

Not only was the magazine named after Uncle Tupelo's first album; it would include recurring sections named after Tupelo songs: "Postcard" and "Screen Door." In death, Uncle Tupelo had been adopted as the poster boys for a movement.

To a new generation of listeners, Uncle Tupelo may as well have been pioneers; their blend of folk, country, mountain soul, punk, and Crazy Horse–style classic rock had little to do with the arena-ready alternative rock of Nirvana, Pearl Jam, Smashing Pumpkins, the Red Hot Chili Peppers, and Stone Temple Pilots. But it was anything but new, as Farrar and Tweedy went out of their way to point out whenever they were interviewed, and there were at least a handful of fine indie bands and artists playing in a similar roots-punk style: Blue Mountain, the Gear Daddies, Freakwater. Rather than dimming their appeal, however, the sense that Tupelo had emerged from a deep American tradition only enhanced their status as "serious" artists within a core group of committed fans, writers, and record labels.

Farrar and Tweedy were among the latest wave of rock 'n' roll kids inspired by hard-core country's enduring virtues: a stripped-down instrumental attack, devastatingly direct lyricism, whiskey-and-cigarette-fueled emotion. Their emergence anticipated the rise of Bloodshot Records, an indie label specializing in what it called "insurgent country."

Bloodshot was based in Chicago and run by a couple of ex-punk rockers, hardly a promising bedrock for reaffirming honky-tonk's verities. Yet that's exactly what it accomplished. Compared with the music coming out of 1990s Nashville in the guise of suburban cowboys and cowgirls such as Garth Brooks and Shania Twain who mimicked the mainstream rock and pop of the 1970s, the bands and record labels lumped into the alt-country bin sounded like the second coming of Hank Sr. and *White Lightning*–era George Jones.

"When I was a kid, country was 'The Gambler' or '9 to 5,' appalling dreck that had a bad mainstream stigma attached to it," Bloodshot's co-owner Rob Miller says. But while he was attending college in Ann Arbor, Michigan, in the mid-1980s, he discovered a terrific happy-hour country band whose ferocious versions of Commander Cody and Tammy Wynette songs triggered a psychic connection with rootsier punk bands such as the Gun Club and the Cramps.

Miller's label partner, Nan Warshaw, went to college in Olympia, Washington—riot-grrrl central in the underground punk scene—but took a liking to then-new neotraditionalist country acts such as Dwight Yoakam and Steve Earle. Miller and Warshaw ended up in Chicago and began deejaying country nights for jackbooted punks at the Crash Palace, later Delilah's, on North Lincoln Avenue with such other unlikely honky-tonk fans as Ministry's Al Jourgensen.

"About a year later we started talking about putting together a compilation of all these cool little bands around town," Miller says. "The talent was there . . ."

"But nobody identified it," Warshaw adds. "We realized there were about twenty underground country bands primarily playing rock clubs in Chicago."

The debut Bloodshot release, *For a Life of Sin*, came out in 1994 and documented the then-nascent Chicago scene: Freakwater, the Texas Rubies, the Handsome Family, the British punk-rock expatriate Jon Langford, and Robbie Fulks.

"Most of these bands were like us, discovering the music as they were creating it," Miller says. "Terms like 'alternative country' are now standard critical fare, but back then no one had any idea of what to do with it. Bands were struggling with their identities, and club owners were saying, 'Country music? In a rock club? No, we don't do that.' You got blank stares or overt hostility doing this stuff."

All that changed after *For a Life of Sin* took off, quickly selling out its first pressing of one thousand copies and inspiring two sequels. "We heard from people around the country, 'Hey, there are great bands like this in Dallas,' like the Old 97's, or in San Francisco, where they had Tarnation," Miller says. "It just spiderwebbed. We didn't know what we were doing, but we tapped into something."

Within a year, *For a Life of Sin*–like compilations documenting local alternative-country scenes emerged out of Austin (*True Sounds of the New West*; *Austin Country Nights*), North Carolina (*Revival*), Atlanta (*Bubbapalooza*), and St. Louis (*Out of the Gate Again*). What united these scenes wasn't so much a sound as a healthy respect for the art of the song.

"The music of these artists doesn't have much in common," Robbie Fulks says. "But it's identified in my mind as this audience that is more broad-minded than your typical audience, a little more urban, an audience that likes to listen to words and think about words."

In celebrating a new generation of songwriters who crossed country's twang with punk's brashness, *No Depression* elevated Uncle Tupelo to icon status. The magazine was founded by two music writers, Grant Alden and Peter Blackstock; both were in their early thirties and had followed a career path similar to that of the bands they would profile in *No Depression*. They had both gravitated from covering rock and punk acts to country and roots artists. Alden had edited the Seattle weekly *The Rocket*, which covered the rise of grunge, and Blackstock had been writing about music for daily newspapers in Austin, Texas, and Seattle.

No Depression—the name of an Internet message board devoted to all things Uncle Tupelo—had sprung up on America Online soon after the band's demise in 1994. Blackstock had been a fan since interviewing Jay Farrar after Uncle Tupelo's first album was released, and through the message board found a community of listeners who shared his passion.

"Originally the message board was called 'Uncle Tupelo,' but by the time I started posting on it in the fall of '94, it was called 'No Depression' and the term 'alternative country' was being used," Blackstock says. "A lot of people on there were coming from more of a rock background certainly than the country one. Grant and I were at a Bad Livers show in Seattle the next spring and hatched the idea for a magazine that was coming at rock music from a roots perspective. Grant was running a folk-art gallery that was failing miserably, and looking for something else to do. He was the one who suggested taking the idea of this discussion that was happening on the Internet and turning it into a print magazine covering the same area. The first issue fell in line with Son Volt's first album, which was a pretty ideal time to launch it."

In his Son Volt cover story, Blackstock deified Tupelo: "a great American rock band"; "the launching pad for what has now become a bona fide movement"; "[Farrar] may well be the best songwriter of his generation."

R.E.M.'s Peter Buck could understand Blackstock's enthusiasm. "They were the right band at the right time, and, maybe just as important, they broke up at the right time," he says. "Just when a lot of stuff that was influenced by them was starting to break through to the mainstream, and older artists doing the same thing—like Steve Earle and Lucinda Williams—were starting to get recognized, the bright young hope called it quits. It reminds me a lot of bands like the Velvet Underground and Big Star, who made great music and were playing to audiences of like eighty people, and it was only years later that a larger audience figured out how great they were."

With the rise of the Internet, it didn't take years for Uncle

Tupelo to pass into posthumous legend, to find a nationwide community of fans starting magazines, Web sites, and bands in their name. Their figurehead status arrived just as Tweedy and Farrar were launching Wilco and Son Volt. Just as Tupelo was breaking up, a number of bands and artists with Tupelo-like characteristics were signed to major-label deals: Whiskeytown and Ryan Adams, the Old 97's, Marah, the Geraldine Fibbers, the Bottle Rockets, Gillian Welch.

But there were other tangible offshoots of Tupelo's legacy. Like punk bands before them that toured relentlessly—Naked Raygun, the Minutemen, Black Flag—Tupelo set an example simply by playing just about everywhere that would have them. To the kids who saw them play, they weren't a myth, and they weren't remote rock stars lost in the spectacle of a hockey arena. They were people much like their audience, midwestern guys who set up their gear and loaded it out, then had drinks with the fans afterward and sometimes slept on their floors. That made an impact on everyone from Ryan Adams, who saw Uncle Tupelo play in North Carolina, to Nick Sakes and Darin Gray of the Dazzling Killmen.

"I point to those Uncle Tupelo guys as directly getting me into this whole music thing," Sakes says. "I was in bands because they showed me how it was done. I saw how they got the shows, how they got paid at the end of the night, and how many times they practiced—little things that you don't appreciate until you hang around a band."

That single-mindedness is why the band originally appealed to Joe McEwen, and why he became one of their greatest champions in the music industry. "You can't underestimate that alt-country was pretty unfashionable when Uncle Tupelo picked it up," McEwen says, "and they were from the mid-Midwest, which also was pretty unfashionable. When was the last time a band from that area had made any kind of national impact?"

Tupelo knew they were from nowhere and sometimes got stick about it from the hometown press because they sounded ambivalent about it, at best. But by writing and talking about a nondescript place in such specific terms, they also ennobled it in some strange way. "Uncle Tupelo talked about being from Belleville and wrote about it in their songs," says Darin Gray, who still lives in nearby Edwardsville, Illinois. "Before that, if you were from one of the communities outside St. Louis, you just naturally deferred to St. Louis, because it wasn't cool to be from Edwardsville or southwestern Illinois. So them talking about Belleville gave other bands—not just bands that wanted to sound like Uncle Tupelo, but countless punk bands, bands that wanted to sound like R.E.M., or whatever—the license to be proud about where they were from, too."

Peter Blackstock has continued to chronicle the careers of Farrar and Tweedy with poetic insight. His original enthusiasm for Uncle Tupelo remains undimmed. "Uncle Tupelo's influence wasn't as musical innovators, like they were doing something that hadn't been done before, but they were very influential in galvanizing a fan base and a base of artists interested in this kind of music," he says. "A lot of people who are listening to a lot of these bands now did so by starting with Uncle Tupelo, or the first Wilco or Son Volt albums. It's a smaller version of what R.E.M. did for alternative rock in the '80s."

The attention was all too much for some of the locals who had known Tupelo since the Primitives days. "A magazine called *No Depression*?" Tweedy's friend David Dethrow says. "We thought it was hilarious. It's like they were building a huge myth around something they didn't really understand. The level of scrutiny was weird for a band that had broken up."

Tweedy remains bemused by the importance now attached to his old band. He sees in it parallels to the way previous generations of rock critics had mythologized the work of Bob Dylan and the Band, in acclaimed books such as Greil Marcus's *Invisible Republic: Bob Dylan's Basement Tapes*. "With Dylan and the Band, it comes down to this: it was a bunch of guys who got together to drink coffee and smoke pot and make tapes in their basement," Tweedy says. "They're really good musicians and one of them is one of the most incredible songwriters of any generation, but it's still basically a bunch of guys who liked to get together and play music. It was something social and functional in their lives. It was something that they enjoyed doing together, so they just went and did it. That to me is more amazing than any insight any number of books on the subject could come up with."

Uncle Tupelo, Tweedy suggests, got together for many of the same reasons: hanging out, having fun, and nothing better to do. "I honestly think so," Tweedy says. "There's an enormous amount of revisionist history that has gone into the idea of what Uncle Tupelo was, and I'm grateful for it. It's given the band's music a life it might not otherwise have had. But at the same time, the collective idea of Uncle Tupelo that has grown in people's minds over time doesn't have a lot to do with why the music came about in the first place."

Tweedy speaks from the perspective of the indie-rock 1980s, a kid who pored over albums like the Minutemen's *Double Nickels on the Dime* and Hüsker Dü's *Zen Arcade* and discovered they were made for dirt cheap by people who lived in remote towns, people who were not that much different from him and his Belleville roommates. From those do-it-yourselfers he learned a valuable lesson: that the creative act is not the province of remote oracles or rarefied geniuses but a transparent process that is open to everyone. Without that belief, it's doubtful Jeff Tweedy would ever have set foot onstage.

In debunking the idea that he or Uncle Tupelo walked on water, Jeff Tweedy had a few allies, especially among an older generation of music critics and listeners. Their attitude toward the Tupelo legacy was epitomized by *The Village Voice*'s longtime critic Robert Christgau. In his review of Son Volt's *Trace* for the *Voice*, Christgau acknowledged that he "never gave two shits about Uncle Tupelo" and now he had figured out why: Farrar didn't write actual songs, he claimed, because he was too busy "mourning an American past too atmospheric to translate into mere words." The critic dismissed Son Volt by saying Farrar "never met a detail he couldn't fuzz over with his achy breaky drawl and, er, evocative country-rock—and needn't trouble with the concrete at all now that that smart-ass Jeff Tweedy is Wilco over-and-out." He was nearly as contemptuous of *A.M.*: "realist defiance grinding sadly down into realist bathos."

It would be a recurring theme in Christgau's reviews of both Son Volt and Wilco: the seductive aroma of nostalgia and sentimentality, a lack of concreteness, an over-reliance on "atmosphere." And he's got a point. Both Farrar and Tweedy began writing in concrete terms about what they knew best; early Tupelo songs such as "Whiskey Bottle" and "Screen Door" couldn't be more plain in their use of language and their depiction of a particular time and place. But they began moving toward a more abstract, poetic language in their post–Tupelo releases. In 1995, when *A.M.* came out, Jeff Tweedy might even have agreed with parts of Christgau's unkind assessment. If *Trace* was in many ways Jay Farrar's pinnacle, Tweedy knew that *A.M.* was for him just a starting point.

"There are lots of things not fleshed out on that record, lyrically or musically," Tweedy says. "They're more like sketches. Something like 'Passenger Side' is probably one of the more coherent and linear things I've written, a song that I could hear someone else singing. But as I started to write the next album, I started getting more excited about writing songs that nobody in their right mind would want to sing except me."

CHAPTER 9

"I WANT TO THANK YOU ALL FOR NOTHIN', NOTHIN' AT ALL"

The call couldn't have been better timed. Jeff Tweedy had just finished recording Wilco's *A.M.* album to fill the vacuum left by Uncle Tupelo's sudden demise, and he was still finding his way as a band leader and songwriter.

"Jeff, it's Dan Murphy." The Soul Asylum guitarist was riding high. His band was coming off a multimillion-selling album, and a few months earlier he'd been hanging out at Uncle Tupelo gigs, buying shots for the band and the crew. Despite Soul Asylum's long-in-coming success, he was still not far removed from the punk rocker a teenage Jeff Tweedy had interviewed for *Jet Lag* magazine in the mid-1980s. Back then, Murphy had drunk Tweedy's beer and sweet-talked his girlfriend.

Now Murphy was calling Tweedy as a peer, a fellow songwriter. Murphy invited Tweedy to Minneapolis to write songs with him. The visit culminated in a hastily organized concert with Murphy and a loose collection of Minneapolis musicians who had been calling themselves Golden Smog: Gary Louris and Marc Perlman from the Jayhawks, Kraig Johnson of Run Westy Run, Noah Levy of the Honeydogs.

The group gathered primarily to play covers of their favorite

1970s songs: AM-radio pop staples such as Three Dog Night's "Easy to Be Hard," the bluesy classic rock of Bad Company's "Shooting Star," Thin Lizzy's "Cowboy Song." It was a way of blowing off steam, a vacation from their regular, higher-profile bands. With Tweedy now in the mix, they decided to reconvene at Minnesota's Pachyderm Studio to record original songs for a Golden Smog album.

"They reached out to Jeff and made him feel like he had some talent," Tweedy's mother, Jo Ann, says. "Only a few weeks before, I saw him sobbing in my living room, heartbroken because his band broke up. At that moment, I don't think he thought of himself as talented or capable."

The ad hoc band gathered for a five-day recording session in 1994 that was the equivalent of a party where songs, smokes, and drinks are passed around, tall stories are told, and in-jokes abound. The band borrowed its name from the *Flintstones* character known as the Golden Smog, Bedrock's answer to the Velvet Fog, a.k.a. lounge crooner Mel Tormé. The band adopted fake names— Tweedy was "Scott Summit," Louris "Michael Macklyn," Johnson "Jarret Decatur"—that were combinations of their middle name and a hometown street, so as not to violate the terms of their deals with various record labels. They created an elaborate fictional history that reads like the *Spinal Tap* of rock biographies and released a make-believe box set of fancifully packaged and titled albums (*Swingin' Smog People*, *America's Newest Shitmakers*). The album they did actually record, *Down by the Old Mainstream*, is a casually ingratiating collection that, almost in spite of itself, eclipses some of the more earnest recent work of the participants.

"It was a boost when I needed it most," Jeff Tweedy says. "I was really beaten down. I always had a lot of confidence, and there is no chance I would have given up. But it was really nice to be in an environment where I didn't have any baggage at all, among these real demonstrative guys. 'Man, that tune rocks!' I had never experienced that in my life. With Wilco, we were still deer in the headlights when we made *A.M.*, and all the changes were really fast. Wilco was a lot more vocal about liking or disliking things, but there was still a lot of the Uncle Tupelo–dynamic residue. There was still a certain tension. But the Golden Smog guys, there is this totally midwestern humor, which can be vicious, but it's so out in the open you just have to laugh: 'You call that a guitar solo?' And they were also demonstratively positive about things. With Dan, it was this earnest, almost macho sensitivity: 'Dude, I don't know how to tell you this, but that song made me fucking cry.' At that point in my life, I needed to hear something like that."

Gary Louris could relate. "A musician is a strange balance of being really cocky and being completely insecure at the same time," he says. "You can think you're the shit, but there's also something in the back of your mind going, 'You suck.' Jeff has that exact mixture: he's really confident, really felt like he had some great music and probably could do it, and yet there was this nagging doubt. 'Can I do this? Am I crazy? Will anybody like this? Can I do it without Jay?' Just like I felt when Mark Olson left the Jayhawks: 'Can I do it without Mark?' For about a week after Mark quit the band, I was pretty convinced we were done. So it was good for all of us, the idea of friends hanging out and sort of inventing this cool band, without the other pressures that go along with it, that all of us were experiencing in our main bands."

The mini-vacation produced two albums spread over three years, and despite its informality it provided an outlet for some of Tweedy's finest songs. On "Radio King," co-written with Louris, Tweedy evokes the innocence of Uncle Tupelo's "Screen Door" a few years further down the road. In the understated poetry, there are the pull of memory and the comfort offered by small pleasures:

> Your music fills my car
> And your voice breaks every time
> I'm still wonderin' if I know who you are
> I hang on every line.

The musicians would convene again two years later to record a second album, *Weird Tales*, a darker, more serious exercise that lacks the first disc's charm. But it also contains Tweedy's "Please Tell My Brother," a song about distance, travel, and late-night phone calls—as literal a song as he has ever written about his family, and all the more moving because of it.

"Some of the songs I brought to those Golden Smog records

sounded obviously whimsical or not quite as fleshed out lyrically; the material I considered best went to Wilco," Tweedy says. "But there are things on those Golden Smog records I like a lot. I don't think I would have put 'Please Tell My Brother' on a Wilco record. At the time, I was trying to write stuff that sounded like folk songs, without resorting to recycling folk themes. I wanted the same melancholy feel as a Carter Family song, but with lyrics talking about phone bills as opposed to Mother's grave.'"

The instant camaraderie that Tweedy found among his peers in Golden Smog was not as easily achieved in Wilco. But on the endless 1995 tour for *A.M.*, Tweedy, John Stirratt, Ken Coomer, Max Johnston, and Jay Bennett became a band. "We had a lot of practice—they were called shows," Coomer says. "We went on the road for three hundred days on *A.M.* Either a band is going to break up after that or we're going to get a helluva lot better."

Bennett's prowess on guitar made a difference in lifting Wilco's confidence, but the real breakthrough came on an instrument he barely knew how to play. While the band was in Los Angeles for a performance at KCRW on May 12, 1995, a baby grand piano in the public radio station's studio caught Bennett's eye. Perhaps out of boredom, he wondered aloud what "Passenger Side" might sound like with him playing piano instead of guitar.

"Jeff's response was, 'I didn't even know you played piano,' " Bennett says. "We gave it a shot. He played acoustic, I played piano, and I sort of faked my way through it, but it turned out beautifully. He says, 'Next album, you're playing keyboards.' "

Bennett may not have been the most technically accomplished keyboardist, but his academic background in mathematics combined with his intuitive ability to play just about any instrument opened up chord structures and harmonic possibilities to which Tweedy and the rest of the band could respond. Bennett had dabbled in piano since junior high school, and he wouldn't play keyboards again on the *A.M.* tour, but once the band began recording its next album, *Being There*, he immersed himself in the new toys he found at the Chicago Recording Company studio in downtown Chicago: Clavinets, Wurlitzer organs, Rhodes electric pianos.

"I was a little intimidated by these guys at first," Bennett says. "They already had a sound that people really liked. But they also wanted to make pop records—*A.M.* was supposed to be a pop record, but it didn't really come across. Unlike the rest of Wilco, I didn't have a mold that I wanted to break out of, and so I was a good fit for them. When we did *Being There*, I began to suggest parts on keyboards that weren't part of the song as originally written on guitar. And once that happened, the door was kicked open to another way of making a record."

There also was a new energy in Tweedy's songwriting because his personal life had changed radically. Marriage, fatherhood, and a mortgage—in 1996, he and Miller bought a $246,000 frame bungalow in Chicago—were a sudden introduction to adulthood for a twenty-eight-year-old musician who for four years had basically been living with his two high-school buddies in a rock 'n' roll clubhouse that always had plenty of beer and never enough toilet paper. As Tweedy tried to assess it all, doubt began invading his songwriting. The next two albums—*Being There* and *Summerteeth*—he would describe as "basically crisis situations about growing up."

"I was a late bloomer," Tweedy says. "I was in my thirties before I even came to terms with the idea that I was making a living as a recording artist. I was in a punk band for a long time and thought it was my life. I was a bass player in a band making fifty dollars a night, paying eighty dollars a month in rent, making indie records and not getting paid for them, and having this naive sense of well-being that I would always do this and never have much more responsibility than that. I went from that to being a dad and a major-label recording artist who had the pressure of supporting a family and also making something I felt good about artistically. Those albums were basically an extreme reaction to feeling change, resisting it, and assessing it. To be honest, I didn't know if I loved having a house, a kid, and a wife. And I didn't know if I could reconcile having that with making music. I didn't know if music could mean as much to me ever again, and that scared the shit out of me. Everybody goes through that, whether they play music or not: reevaluating things they love and wondering, 'Am I holding on to this too tightly? And if I let go of this, will I care about it anymore?'"

Being There was Tweedy's response. Whereas *A.M.* aspired to be little more than a collection of recent songs bashed out by an uneasy new band in the studio, *Being There* aimed higher from the start. Tweedy had been writing songs from the road, a world of inflated egos and deflated dreams, artifice and reality. He always saw himself as not just an artist but a fan; on *Being There* he identifies with both, and the songs often blur the lines between the two perspectives. The album would become an extended dialogue between musician and listener, a critique and commentary on the creative process, one which tacitly states that no piece of music is finished until the listener makes it his own, that a recording is only as brilliant and realized as the person hearing it: fan and artist as uneasy confidants, subject to the same doubts, ecstasies, and betrayals that invade only the most intimate relationships.

"Misunderstood" opens the album immersed in chaos: haphazard drums, tortured guitar strings, screeching violin. Relief arrives with a handful of lovely piano chords, over which Tweedy's voice drifts like exhaled cigarette smoke. The music continues to morph between these extremes, an amalgam of three distinct versions of "Misunderstood" culled from three reels of tape, including a sixteen-minute noise deconstruction with everyone hacking away on unfamiliar instruments (Coomer on guitar, Stirratt on violin, Johnston on bass, Bennett on drums). The narrator's self-pity ("You're so misunderstood") dissolves into a fragment from the 1977 song "Amphetamine" by the late Pere Ubu guitarist Peter Laughner:

> *Take the guitar player for a ride*
> *'Cause he ain't never been satisfied*
> *He thinks he owes some kind of debt*
> *It'll be years before he gets over it.*

The tortured artist sees his reflection in a compact disc as a fan might, and mocks himself with the same words Jay Farrar said to Tweedy the day Uncle Tupelo broke up: "You're just a mama's boy." By the end, the narrator has lashed back—"I want to thank you all for nothin', nothin' at all"—with increasing vehemence.

"Misunderstood"—not really a song at all, but six and a half minutes of ebb-and-flow extremes climaxing in a rant against the listener—leads off the album for more than just thematic reasons.

"I was joking with Jeff when I heard it," the Reprise executive Gary Briggs says. "I said, 'You know, you're going to piss off a lot of people who liked your music before.' He got a big smile on his face."

The song bowled over longtime fans such as David Dethrow. Love it or hate it, the song carried weight that Tweedy's previous songs lacked. "People would talk at the shows, and some of them were convinced that 'Misunderstood' was heroin-induced, that he's writing about heroin," Dethrow says. "When my wife saw them do it the first time, we had a really long talk afterward. Her first reaction was, 'Why does he even play that song?' It opens the record, and that's the kind of reaction it got. He was challenging people who thought they had him pegged after *A.M.*, which was laid-back in the way Gram Parsons or the Jayhawks might be. *Being There* was his way of rebelling against that. It was the start of Jeff's rebellion."

Steve Scariano heard anger in the music. "Belleville was being turned into the alt-country mecca after *No Depression* wrote about Son Volt, like we were the Appalachia of the Midwest," he says. "It was out of control. Then *Being There* came out, and it was basically Jeff saying 'fuck you' to all that."

Ken Coomer, as usual, had to laugh about it. "The whole *No Depression* thing was funny to us because people seemed to forget that Jeff was a bigger punk-rock fan than a country fan," he says. "It led to things like us all switching instruments on songs like 'Misunderstood,' where I'm playing guitar."

The camaraderie gained by a year on the road manifested itself in an album that was recorded not just with a sense of duty to play the individual parts as expertly as possible but with a sense of urgency and responsibility toward the overall sound. Songs weren't just performed; they were shaped by an ensemble thinking as one. The band set itself the task of recording and mixing each song in a single day, no do-overs. It forced the issue in ways even Tweedy couldn't have envisioned. "Sunken Treasure" was unlike any song Tweedy had previously written, a collage of lyrics and half-remembered sounds that Tweedy used as a shaky foundation for a dreamlike meditation on disconnection: "I am so out of tune with you"—out of tune with a lover, with a listener, with music itself. It's a stream of consciousness, both in the way the lyric took shape and in the way it was recorded in the studio. It ends with the mantra of a fifteen-year-old Belleville kid in thrall to the sound of an electric guitar, this time from the perspective of a man nearly twice as old and half as confident, desperate for renewal: "I was maimed by rock 'n' roll, I was tamed by rock 'n' roll, I got my name from rock 'n' roll." It was a mature realization of the themes broached in earlier Tweedy songs such as "Gun" and "Black Eye," the music feeding off the lyric, creating an emotional atmosphere that immersed the listener.

"That was a turning point," Coomer says. "It was a looser structure than anything we'd done previously. *A.M.* was basically us trying to finish a bunch of songs, based on what Jeff played us. On *Being There*, songs weren't finished, but tape was rolling. 'Sunken Treasure' was never 'arranged.' We didn't know where the finish line was, so we took different routes to get there."

The song was also a turning point for Tweedy as a songwriter. *Being There* is split between songs that represent Tweedy making the transition from a writer of would-be standards ("Far, Far Away," "Forget the Flowers," "Someday Soon," "The Lonely 1") toward a more personal language ("Misunderstood," "Hotel Arizona," "Sunken Treasure"). It was not unlike the transition Bob Dylan worked through on *Another Side of Bob Dylan* and *Bringing It All Back Home* that took him from the plainspoken verse of "The Times They Are a-Changin'" to the surrealism of "Visions of Johanna."

"I ran out of things that I was confident in that I could express in terms of someone else," Tweedy says. "I was left with material like 'Sunken Treasure.' That actually really messed with me, to sing those songs in front of people. But the idea during *Being There* was to learn, record, and mix a song a day, so I had to keep the wheel rolling. By the time it was happening, it really felt like the way I was recording on my cassette recorder. I could see it coming, I could see what it was supposed to be, and it went that way. One of the things that's really hard to not do in a rock band is to have references. It's a lot easier to communicate musically when you're not using sheet music and you're not well versed in music theory and explaining things. It's a shorthand that critics use, or everybody uses: 'Let's try to sound like Big Star,' or, 'This is a Roy Orbison thing.' I ran out of songs that I could express that with. Like 'Monday' is kind of an upbeat Stones stomp. But I didn't know how to describe 'Sunken Treasure' ahead of time. So I loosely mapped it out. I'd play it once for everybody, and let them write down the chords, and then I'd show them the alternate parts that might happen: an atonal chord progression in the middle of the song, but I'm not sure if that's going to happen, or when, or if it'll happen more than once."

For Tweedy, the revelation was that he had a band that would think along with him, five heads melding into one piece of semi-improvised music. The notion that writing songs was about leaving enough space for the unexpected to happen took hold. *A.M.* never once sounded like an accident—save for Brian Henneman's clinking gin bottles on "Casino Queen"—whereas *Being There* was packed with spontaneous moments caught on tape.

For years, Tweedy would sit down and write songs in his room by pressing the "record" button on his tape player and improvising. He developed the ability to see what might happen next seconds before he played the chords or sang the lyric. It was as if he were hearing the sound of his own record as he was making it. "It's a skill that I think everybody has," he says, "just like everybody has the ability to improvise a conversation. You don't sit down and rehearse a conversation. Playing the guitar is the same way with me. There are little bits of building blocks from previous conversations that you have rehearsed, but you just put them together in a different way. Those are the chords of a guitar, the notes of a scale, you know those little things over time the more you do it, so it's almost impossible to think about it if you're doing it in a spontaneous or exciting way. I'd listen back to five minutes of that, and sometimes it's shit, but sometimes something happens that I didn't expect. And then from there the writing starts. The brain kicks in, and I shape it."

Now he was shaping the songs in the band's presence. Tweedy's overarching vision of what the album should be and how it should be recorded was abetted and embellished by Bennett's knowledge of the recording studio: not only playing guitars and keyboards, but arranging background vocals and adding overdubs that took the album well outside the boundaries of the No Depression world. As Bennett tweaked the arrangements, he took glee in playfully chastising the others. "Y'all are forgettin' your roots!" he cackled as he filtered more distortion into the mixes. The band was thrilled to bury those preconceptions.

"There was an attitude somewhere between having something to prove after the Son Volt record came out and not giving a fuck," Stirratt says. "We had *A.M.* mixed to make it more radio-friendly, and that just failed miserably. So we went into *Being There* with absolutely no aspirations about getting on the radio. Let's not worry about any of that."

Stirratt's bass playing took on orchestral colors as he developed lines that complemented melodies instead of simply anchoring them, and his background harmonies add a pop exuberance to songs such as "Outta Mind (Outta Sight)." "The songs were pretty straight the way Jeff brought them in," Stirratt says. "Jay opened the door to us thinking about countermelody, harmonies, and overdubs. But we were all thinking more in terms of making a pop record, as opposed to a country-sounding kind of record."

Jay Bennett's versatility opened up the possibilities. "I can honestly say that I personally didn't give a rat's ass if we made the twangiest record in the world or if we made *London Calling*," Bennett says. "I didn't feel the weight of that tradition like Jeff might have. It was more a case of me and the rest of the band learning stuff from each other. Those guys were used to going in, recording a song, and in the past that would be pretty much it. Maybe they'd overdub a solo or fix a bad note or something. But nothing too complicated. I'd been a recording engineer and working in recording studios professionally since 1984. I happened to be in a band [Titanic Love Affair] that overdubbed a lot, because we sucked live. That weakness helped me develop another skill. So I learned a lot about the confidence of playing live in the studio, because Jeff, John, and Ken were great at that, and they learned a lot about taking things to the next level in the overdub area from me. It was the pinnacle of us learning from each other."

Bob Egan became a part of the *Being There* sessions almost by accident. Tweedy had met the pedal-steel player when Uncle Tupelo shared a few bills with Egan's country-punk band Freakwater, and the singer later invited him to play during one of his solo concerts at Lounge Ax.

Tweedy and the rest of the band extended cryptic invitations to come down and "party" at the *Being There* sessions. Egan blew them off because he was tied up running a music store in Chicago. Finally he showed up, thinking he was going to share a few beers and perhaps listen to a few finished takes. "So I walk in and the first thing they say is, 'Where's your gear, man?'" Egan says. He ended up playing on two tracks, the luminous country ballad "Far, Far Away" and the bash-and-crash closing track, "Dreamer in My Dreams."

"I took a pass through 'Far, Far Away' with Jeff standing over my shoulder," Egan says. "He basically orchestrated my part by saying, 'I like that, play this, not that.' I was trying things, and he knew what he wanted exactly. I'd never worked that way before, and it was a little nerve-racking. But he knew exactly what he wanted."

"Dreamer in My Dreams" was the live blowout that put a capstone on the recording session, a shot of Faces-style rock 'n' roll that ends with Tweedy tossing his guitar to the floor, coughing and sputtering, the song collapsing, only to revive it for one more charge by singing through a piano microphone while Bennett ad-libs blues chords. "That's it!" Bennett declares, slamming the piano lid closed.

That was it for Max Johnston as well. He was going through a tough time in his marriage that would end in divorce, and though he was an accomplished bluegrass musician, he was lost in the forest of overdubs and studio manipulation. "Jay Bennett was just taking over—through strength of personality he just took over from me—and it was a depressing record for me to make," he says. "I was no longer playing solos, because Jay was getting all of them, so I became this background-color kind of guy. I felt like we were all as replaceable as sink washers, because it was basically the Jeff Tweedy Band, and Jay was telling him, 'Well, you really don't need Max anymore.'"

At one point, as Johnston sweated through take after failed take of one song, he threw up his hands in the isolation booth and said, "I do what I do." Another violinist, Jesse Greene, was brought in to play a part on "The Lonely I" that Johnston never quite mastered to Bennett's and Tweedy's satisfaction. Johnston limped home to his wife in Lexington, Kentucky.

A few weeks later, relief came in the form of a phone call from Chicago while Johnston was pulling weeds in his garden. "Jeff was nervous, so I just tried to make it comfortable for him to fire me," Johnston says. "It was tough not to have a job anymore, but I felt like I'd gotten out from under a big black cloud. That was the last time I ever spoke to him."

There was more business for Tweedy to take care of. *Being There* had mushroomed into a nineteen-song, seventy-seven-minute monster. He envisioned a double CD, and, what's more, he wanted the record company to sell it at a single-CD price.

When Tweedy broke the news to his record label, Joe McEwen was stunned. " 'You can't do that!' " McEwen says he told him. "That was my first reaction. But Jeff was insistent, and persuasive. He laid out his case. He wanted to make a statement and he wanted to open it with 'Misunderstood,' and he wanted to present these songs in this particular order, sequenced over two CDs."

But Tweedy had to take money out of his own pocket to make it happen. He agreed to take a steep royalty cut so that *Being There* would end up reaching retail shelves priced at $17.98 or less, instead of $30 or more. The former Reprise product manager Gary Briggs estimates that Wilco lost about two dollars against future royalties for every album sold—nearly $600,000 by 2003. But to Tweedy the price was a small one to pay. "I had twelve songs that I had sequenced as a single record, but we kept recording, and the further it went, the more fun it got," Tweedy says. "We had thirty songs that we could have split off into any number of single albums: we could have made a real pop record out of this material, or a record with more country leanings, or a weirder record using just the six- and seven-minute songs. But none of those edited versions felt like an honest representation of what we had gone through."

It turned out to be an artistic, it not financial, coup. By spreading the nineteen songs that made the final cut over two CDs, Tweedy divided the listening experience into two easily digested halves; each could be absorbed in a single sitting, a throwback to the vinyl-album era. At a time when artists were going overboard to pad CDs with seventy-five minutes of music whether or not they had the songs to justify it, *Being There* offered a mid-1990s response to sprawling but multifaceted double albums of earlier eras: the Rolling Stones' *Exile on Main Street*, the Clash's *London Calling*, Dylan's *Blonde on Blonde*.

"Pretentious? Yeah, probably," Tweedy says with a laugh.

But Tweedy had had enough of modesty. He'd played the affable, underestimated sidekick to Jay Farrar long enough, and now he was in danger of being typecast as an alt-country songwriter by a bunch of boo-hooing Uncle Tupelo acolytes. It was time to show some new moves. With *Being There* he would lay out the full expanse of his musical ambition by juxtaposing pop, rock, country, and experimental elements. There were nods to his heroes: the Clavinet in "Kingpin" evoked the Band's Garth Hudson, the disorienting swirl of "Hotel Arizona" conjured Big Star's "Holocaust," the cavernous reverb of "Someday Soon" came straight out of Sun Studios in Memphis, circa a 1955 Johnny Cash session. And there were bold moves designed not to comfort and reassure but to disorient and challenge: "I want to thank you all for nothin', nothin' at all."

Being There takes its title from a 1979 movie, a surreal comedy starring Peter Sellers, who plays a simple-minded gardener. Sellers's character, Chance, is oblivious to the mayhem in the world outside his inner-city sanctuary. When the master of the house dies and Chance finally ventures out, his simpleton utterances are interpreted as insightful truisms. In a review praising the film, Roger Ebert called it "basically one joke told for two hours." In much the same way, *Being There* takes one idea—rock 'n' roll—and turns it inside out, celebrating it, disparaging it, and finally—in the last song, "Dreamer in My Dreams"—embodying its essence with ramshackle glee. It's one of the few tracks on the album without a single overdub, captured on two room microphones, a bunch of kids bashing it out in their garage.

"Most bands, and rock 'n' roll in general, have a lot in common with Chance," Tweedy contends. "When you're in a band, you end up in a position where people want to know what you think. The best ones intuitively can say something about everything, but for the most part they probably know less than everyone else. I've always had this skepticism about rock, because I worshiped it and believed in it for so long, the mythology of rock 'n' roll, and I got to a certain point in my life where there are people making stuff up about me and what I supposedly did as a singer in some band. I'm not saying there is the same amount of mythology about Uncle Tupelo as there is about Dylan or some icon, but there's certainly more than I would ever have expected. And it makes me really question the validity of it all. If it can happen to someone like me, who really didn't matter in the grand scheme of rock 'n' roll, what does that say about the bands that I worshiped? And being in the industry now and seeing the other side of it and knowing how the machinery can twist things around only made me question it more. None of that matters to a fifteen-year-old kid, and that's how I was. I'm not so much condemning that this is going on. It's more that I'm wishing I was still fifteen and didn't know anything about a record except whether or not it rocked."

CHAPTER 10

"A JOYOUS FUCK YOU"

Tears welled in the eyes of Jeff Tweedy and Bob Egan as
they stood beside the stage and watched Johnny Cash go
to work. The barrel-chested man in black strummed an
acoustic guitar over a clickety-clack train beat, and all was right
with the world. Cash's baritone cut through the smoke and chat-
ter at Irving Plaza, a casually commanding performance at one of
the year's more prestigious music-industry events: the annual College Music Journal conference in New York City. It was September 1996, the start of a new school year, and the students in the
audience looked up in awe as Cash sang, many of them seeing the
country legend for the first time.

Egan's aspirations as a pedal-steel guitarist had been limited to
occasional tours with the indie-country duo Freakwater. He was
thirty-eight years old and the owner of a guitar repair shop in
Chicago, and he was thrilled to be watching Cash perform from
such a privileged vantage point. What's more, his night was about
to get even better: Tweedy was about to give him the red pearl-
snap cowboy shirt off his back.

"In the middle of the show," Egan says, "I looked at Jeff and
Jeff looked at me and we were both kind of misty-eyed over

watching Johnny play, and he said, 'Are you going to join this fuckin' band now?' It was a pretty big moment for me, so I told him that in honor of this, we had to trade shirts. So we stood there and stripped down like high-school kids on the last day of school."

Egan took the stage with Wilco that night for the first time, and it was a performance he wouldn't soon forget. This was the night Wilco began breaking from the alternative-country parade it was supposed to be leading, the night the poster children for No Depression guitar strumming went wilding for the first time, an image-shattering spree that left the band's die-hard fans, its record company, even the band itself shaken.

Wilco was following Cash onstage not by choice but because the country legend said he wasn't feeling well and wanted to play earlier so he could get back to his hotel and rest. "I remember Johnny walking down those rickety-ass stairs by the stage at Irving Plaza, and I thought he was gonna plummet to his death," says drummer Ken Coomer, who got the skinny on the night's behind-the-scenes shenanigans when he later did a recording session with Cash's bass player. "It wasn't the original plan for us to follow Johnny Cash, but Johnny pulled a fast one. Johnny's road manager pulled us aside and told us Johnny is tired and not feeling too good, but it was all bullshit—he wanted to go on ahead of us because he wanted to go on at the primo moment, when the crowd was fresh. So he starts singing, and it's the greatest thing you've ever heard in your life, and it's kinda like we're all mesmerized watching it. And then it dawns on us that we have to follow that."

Wilco's set began with a raucous roadhouse twist on "Casino Queen" that wouldn't have sounded out of place on Bob Dylan's *Highway 61 Revisited*: Coomer battered the trap kit, guitars built to shattering crescendos between verses and then retreated, and Tweedy smashed the melody beneath the boot heel of his contempt. Gone were the song's mighty, unifying guitar lick and good-time barn-dance vibe. In their place were a new emphasis on the lyrics' sour view of legalized gambling, and a new verse specially added for the occasion: "I'm gonna sing this song till the cows come home, I'm gonna sing this song till you loooosers leave me alone, leave me alone."

"You cannot follow Johnny Cash," Tweedy said to the audience,

Jeff Tweedy, in the days before his
parents bought him his first guitar.
(Sue Miller archive)

Spiffed up for the Belleville Township
High School West prom, 1985.
(Bob and Jo Ann Tweedy family archive)

A Tweedy family Christmas in Belleville: Bob Tweedy, Jeff, Sue Miller,
Jo Ann Tweedy, brother Steve, and brother Greg (kneeling).
(Bob and Jo Ann Tweedy family archive)

The Primitives,
lords of the Belleville
garage-rock scene, circa
1984–87:
Wade Farrar and
Mike Heidorn
(top), Jeff Tweedy
and Jay Farrar.
*(Bob and Jo Ann Tweedy
family archive)*

A handmade flyer announces
one of the many all-ages gigs
the Primitives—sometimes known
as the "Primatives"—played at
the Liederkranz Hall in Millstadt,
Illinois, in the mid-'80s.
(Bob and Jo Ann Tweedy family archive)

Uncle Tupelo's founding lineup—Jay Farrar, Jeff Tweedy, and Mike Heidorn—towers over the nonexistent Belleville skyline, 1990. *(Bob and Jo Ann Tweedy family archive)*

Swilling beer and wearing house slippers, Elvis in his "Uncle Tupelo" guise invites fans to a 1988 show in Belleville. *(Bob and Jo Ann Tweedy family archive)*

Tweedy in Uncle Tupelo: a straw hat and the smile of a songwriter who had taken a step up on "Anodyne," 1993. *(Daniel Corrigan)*

Uncle Tupelo in their big-band glory, 1993: Max Johnston, Jay Farrar, Ken Coomer, Jeff Tweedy, and John Stirratt.
(Daniel Corrigan)

John Stirratt, soon after joining Uncle Tupelo in 1993.
(Bob and Jo Ann Tweedy family archive)

Jeff and Sue present their first son,
Spencer Tweedy, born 1995.
(Sue Miller family archive)

Jeff, Sue, and Spencer
at the Wilco recording
loft in Chicago, 1997.
(Sue Miller family archive)

Tweedy demonstrates
that he lives by the DIY
(do-it-yourself) credo.
(Sue Miller family archive)

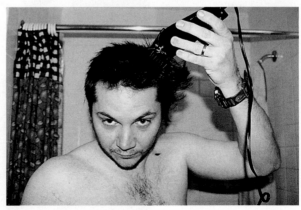

Jay Bennett, Wilco 1994–2001:
specializing in dreadlocks
and guitar solos.
(Marty Perez)

Tweedy in May 1999,
leaping into the
Summerteeth tour.
(John Bartley, Chicago Tribune)

Tweedy and Wilco stand triumphant before 25,000 fans at Grant Park in Chicago, July 2001; only days before, Reprise Records had told the band that it had rejected *Yankee Hotel Foxtrot*. (*John Lee,* Chicago Tribune)

"Tweedy and Popp," a.k.a. Scott McCaughey of the Minus 5, Young Fresh Fellows, and R.E.M. (*Sue Miller family archive*)

Wilco in the aftermath of Jay Bennett's dismissal, fall of 2001: Stirratt, Glenn Kotche, Tweedy, and Leroy Bach.
(Marty Perez)

Wilco's lineup, 2002–04:
Mikael Jorgensen, Bach, Tweedy, Stirratt, and Kotche.
(Stacey Wescott)

and then set out to prove himself wrong in the most abrasive fashion possible. Soon he was steering the band through a thick patch of songs from Wilco's forthcoming album, *Being There*, which wouldn't be released for another six weeks. Nine of the set's fifteen songs came from the new album. It was Wilco's first gig in a couple months; rehearsal time had been minimal with the four core band members living in different cities and a rookie sitting in on pedal steel. The new tunes not only weren't broken in; they didn't sound much like the old stuff. Combine that with more downtime backstage for the band to guzzle a few extra beers during Cash's set, and the stars were aligned for weirdness. About one-third of the way into the set, when it became clear that this wasn't going to be Wilco as usual, the fans' discomfort became palpable. Some drifted toward the exit; some called out in desperation for more familiar tunes. Their applause, if it came at all, was tepid. What the hell was going on? Tweedy did nothing to dispel the bad vibes. Instead, he reveled in them. *You think that last one made you uncomfortable? Try this!*

Seven years later, Jay Bennett still isn't sure what triggered Tweedy's response. "But I knew it was real and kind of joyous: a joyous fuck you," he says.

Tweedy and the band were of one ornery mind on this night, keen to test their far-from-perfected new material, consequences be damned. The new songs were no longer just ditties to be strummed on guitars with instantly inviting choruses. They now flashed denser, more forbidding keyboard-augmented architecture. How exactly to sing along with "Hotel Arizona," with its slow build toward the moment when the song's infrastructure begins to collapse in on itself? Or what to make of "Sunken Treasure," which concludes with the singer staggering off like some war casualty while muttering, "I was maimed by rock 'n' roll"?

Following a beautiful, if nearly unrecognizable, country-ballad take on what should have been one of the night's few slam-dunk applause winners, "Box Full of Letters," Tweedy got into it with a restless fan.

"Rock the house!"

"Rock the house?" the singer responded. "Thank you, sir. It's been done; it can't be done again. It's a rule. Follow Johnny Cash, there's no rockin' left in the building. We're just doing what we can, sir. I'll see you later."

Wilco had rarely ever been more out of tune with its audience than on this night, but it was just a prelude to the riotous year of touring to follow. What started as a coming-out party for the next Wilco album ended up a disaster, at least in the record company's eyes. "The crowd's reaction was very mixed," Stirratt recalls. "Some were kind of stunned, others left, but we were having a blast. That was the whole tone of that era that started with *Being There*. What Jeff could not stand is any kind of passive response. I mean, he could accept people hating it, but the reaction he couldn't stand was people just standing there, arms folded, judging him."

Joe McEwen, the band's A&R representative, was doing exactly that. Arms folded, brow furrowed, he was not pleased. McEwen didn't mishear much in his two-decade career as one of the most respected talent scouts in the industry. Tweedy and Tony Margherita respected his judgment. Unlike that of most members of the record industry, McEwen's opinion mattered to them, so what happened that night had telling repercussions.

McEwen had been thrilled with the way Tweedy was developing as a singer and stage presence: "Here's this guy that barely looked up when I met him, and now he was not just playing his songs but entertaining the audience with his humor, his charisma." But that vanished at Irving Plaza. "Jeff came out and was completely intimidated having to follow Cash, and it just wasn't happening," McEwen says. "It was one of the few times, maybe the only time ever, I felt like he gave less than his best, and I was upset. I remember standing there with [Wilco's booking agent] Frank Riley and saying, 'Boy, this is bad.' He just lost the audience, and there was only a few people left by the time he went off. To me it was a case of Jeff feeling the weight of the expectations: 'Okay, you're the new alt-country boy on the block, measure up to Johnny Cash!' "

Tweedy's self-awareness was expanding to the point where he was thinking deeply about how Wilco was being perceived and he wasn't happy about it. It was time to shed the alt-country baggage, and the quicker the better. He saw nothing to be gained from being the designated poster child for a musical movement he felt only marginally attuned to anyway. Let Jay Farrar, his old Uncle Tupelo sidekick, fly the alt-country flannel. Tweedy wanted out. And Irving Plaza was the first step toward emancipation.

It meant a confrontation with the very fans who had come to cheer him, who wanted nothing more than to hear "New Madrid" and "Passenger Side" and "Box Full of Letters," the old guitar-strumming two-steps with the straightforward lyrics and the sing-along choruses. At Irving Plaza, Tweedy fixed his sights on the diehards, the folks who saw Wilco as their roots-rock security blanket.

Looking back on that night, he still has blood in his eyes. "They were the ones who in my mind were our enemies; they were the ones who were not going to allow this to change, who were very married to what they thought we were," he says. "And the only songs we felt like playing were the new songs, and the songs that were going to be harder for them to accept. The reality is, once we got up there and saw the looks on their faces and saw the attitude, and were basically committed to doing this, it became a punk-rock show. There was no way around it. You stand up and you fucking own that stage, regardless of who went on before you, regardless of how good you're playing, regardless of anything. It's like, all right, here we are, and it was a very raw, fucking outrageous performance, and everything was twice as abrasive as the record. 'Sunken Treasure' was just a squalling noise fest."

Tweedy, Stirratt, Coomer, Bennett, and Egan bounced off smiling. "I came off the stage totally invigorated," the singer says. "I thought that was a big, bold step in the right direction. That we had sucked nobly, that we had gone up there and not backed down, hadn't just cowered under the pressure, and made the most of it."

But their mood changed as soon as they heard from McEwen. Stirratt bumped into the A&R man first as he headed backstage to vent.

"What'd you think, Joe?"

"I fuckin' hated it."

Stirratt chuckles at the memory. "He seemed a little tipsy, but there was no doubt how he felt. I remember thinking, 'Okay, this is going to be an interesting campaign.' That was the beginning of the end for Jeff and Reprise. They thought they had this nice countryish band that sang catchy little songs, and instead they got this polarizing thing that was very in-your-face. It was a way of bringing out the themes of the record, being confrontational, but it was also a cry for attention, which is exactly what we needed at that point. But Joe didn't hear it that way. He pushed us away."

Shortly after, McEwen confronted Tweedy in the dressing room.

"What happened?"

"Whaddya mean?"

"It was horrible! It was fucking horrible!"

Tony Margherita tried to slide McEwen out of the room so he could talk with the A&R man in private, but Tweedy wanted it straight from his closest link to the record company. What McEwen said next made Tweedy realize that no one at Reprise shared his vision of Wilco and what it wanted to be.

"The last time I saw you, you guys were on your way to being as good a band as the Heartbreakers!" McEwen said.

Tweedy was dumbstruck at the reference to Tom Petty's band of arena rockers. "And I'm thinking, 'Yeah, except we were like the real Heartbreakers tonight—the Johnny Thunders Heartbreakers.'"

"He meant it as a compliment," Tweedy says. "But that happened a lot to us in this business. People would make comparisons to try and figure out where they were steering things: 'It reminds me of Springsteen right before he hit.' It's like they were talking about somebody else's band."

"It may not have been the parting of the waters between Joe and Jeff, but it was definitely the first ripple in the pond," says Gary Briggs, the band's product manager at Reprise and one of McEwen's staunchest supporters. "In the early stage of his career, Jeff would have hung on every word Joe McEwen said, but not after this."

McEwen soon realized his bluntness after the show wasn't what Wilco needed to hear on the eve of releasing its second album. "I should have bit my tongue," the A&R man says. "It was the one thing I regret in my whole relationship with Jeff." But he's unwavering in his assessment of how Tweedy acted that night: "He came across like a little kid."

Coomer, the band's most vocal bullshit detector, doesn't see it that way. "Jeff went a bit overboard following Cash," he says. "I mean, to have to follow that would've been kinda weird for anybody. But instead of Jeff being crushed by what Joe said, his reaction was like, 'Fuck that guy.' He knew what he was doing."

Artists bitching, sometimes at nauseating length, about the cluelessness of their record label is a story with a century-long history. But when Tweedy signed with Reprise, he was joining a label that was still highly respected for the way it treated its artists, and he was still the boy wonder for many in the Burbank, California, corridors of Reprise and Warner Brothers.

Advance copies of *Being There* had circulated around the building, and the reaction was favorable. "People liked *A.M.*, and we figured we could do better than 100,000 sales with the next one," says Bill Bentley, Wilco's media representative at the label. "But when people heard *Being There*, we felt like, 'Wow, this is better than just all right. We're gonna at least double or triple our sales here.'"

The subsequent year of relentless touring would help Reprise nearly realize those expectations, with the sales of *Being There* eventually approaching 300,000, nearly double what *A.M.* achieved. But there was a sense that still more could have been accomplished, given how favorably it was received by the press. When *Being There* was released in October 1996, it was greeted with glowing reviews in most major music magazines and newspapers. "Welcome to the new Wilco," declared *No Depression* in praising the album's audacity while reassuring its alt-country constituency that Tweedy hadn't gone completely bonkers by including a half-dozen songs "that would've seemed at home on the band's 1995 debut *A.M.* or a latter-day Uncle Tupelo album." Brian Henneman was on the road with the Bottle Rockets when he first heard the album: "It mystified and confused me. It was almost like he should have had three more albums after *A.M.* to prepare me for *Being There*. How did he come up with this fully formed new thing in a year? To me, *A.M.* sounds like it was written in first gear, and *Being There* went straight to fourth."

Yet radio support was tepid at best. Reprise invested more than $100,000 in a video for "Outtasite (Outta Mind)," and the song won some airplay on Triple-A (Adult Album Alternative) radio stations, but little else. A second single was edited—or "butchered," in Tweedy's view—when the horns were removed from "Monday." Edited or not, "Monday" never made it to Tuesday as far as programmers were concerned.

Without radio to expose the band to a larger audience, Wilco had to win new fans the old-fashioned way: one at a time, at every pit stop in North America and Europe that would have them. For Egan, it was like running off with the circus. He went back to Chicago after the Cash show and put his business up for sale, then set foot on a tour bus for the first time. The tour opened on Halloween night in 1996 in Raleigh, North Carolina. After stocking up at a Salvation Army store, Wilco played in drag: Tweedy in fuzzy pajamas and a cowboy hat, Egan in a blue evening gown and a wig with red Robert Smith lipstick.

Afterward a couple of women in a passing car flashed the tour bus, and the driver pulled over. "We thought this was Waylon Jennings's bus," the women declared as they climbed aboard, only to encounter a dreadlocked Jay Bennett stumbling out of the back lounge wearing a tiara and a sundress adorned with a string of pearls, a long cigarette holder protruding from his listick-smeared mouth. "Those two girls couldn't get out of there fast enough," says Egan, who exited the bus himself to deposit the contents of his alcohol-saturated intestines on the roadside.

It set the tone for what would be Wilco's breakthrough tour, in more ways than one. The band stayed on the road so long it collectively lost its mind. "It was so over-the-top because we knew a few hours onstage wasn't going to be enough to redeem a day of sitting alone on a bus," Bennett says. "So we acted like rock stars. We thought we were fucking rock stars! And we were having a blast. We wanted to make good fucking rock 'n' roll, play in front of a lot of people, and have them enjoy it and be moved by it."

The band came unglued, with prankster grins: Tweedy tweaking a dinner-theater crowd outside Atlanta by jumping into a table setting of bread, wine, and cake; Bennett igniting food fights by emptying the contents of a backstage deli tray into the crowd night after night; Tweedy diving like a deranged Iggy Pop into the crowd and returning to the stage missing his shirt and a shoe; the roadie Jonathan Parker emerging for encores in capes and aluminum headdresses to sing bombastic versions of "Ziggy Stardust," "War Pigs," or "Immigrant Song" while the band members traded instruments, Replacements-style. "We were on the line that whole year," Ken Coomer says. "Fun onstage, bad vibes backstage."

Like Glenn Close's spurned knife-wielding lover in *Fatal Attraction*, Tweedy would not be ignored at any cost. "If the audience wasn't reacting, I saw him test them and scold them from the stage, and that kind of set me back, because here's this mild-mannered Clark Kent all of a sudden jumping into the phone booth and out comes this guy who felt invincible," says Gary Briggs. "It wasn't like he started believing his own hype in a Ryan Adams kind of way. It was more like he started to gain confidence in his songwriting, and as it became more personal, he invested more in it, and he wanted people to pay attention."

Matt Hickey, an employee in Margherita's management office at the time, was amazed at the transformation. "It was like he was trying on personas, almost a David Bowie thing," Hickey says. "People were incredulous. We would get letters from fans saying things like, 'You're up there out of your mind! Why? What happened?' It was like they were forcing their fans to reevaluate who Jeff was and what kind of band Wilco was."

The pinnacle—or, depending on one's perspective, the nadir—of that bullish attitude came at a much-hyped gig in London in April 1997. Wilco was getting showered with attention in the British media, and the show sold out in advance.

It was one of the longest nights of Bob Egan's life. "I know there was just a lot of tension in the air, because playing London's a big deal," Egan says. "Our manager had flown over and all the label people were there, and Jeff opens with a bunch of slow, quiet songs that got kind of a muted response. I got the sense that the crowd wanted to rock, but Jeff would just pile on one slow song after another."

Tweedy sensed the uneasiness from the stage. "Hey, loosen up a little bit, all right?" he said. A few songs later he glimpsed a concertgoer rustling through a newspaper.

"What the hell were you thinking? It's a Sunday! Sunday crowds are really ready to go home and read the newspaper. Fuck that."

"Passenger Side" was played at three times its normal speed. After a spirited run through "Monday," the grousing resumed.

"We don't care," Tweedy spat out. "We get to go home tomorrow. This is the last date of the worst tour of our lives."

Booooooo!!!!!

"What? Somebody said something that sounded kinda snotty. But then, I don't know, you always sound snotty when you're British people."

Fuck you!

"Come up and get me, all of ya! . . . What's that? I'll come out and get you later."

Silence.

"Tony Margherita is standing in the wings with no expression on his face," Bob Egan recalls, "and I'm thinking, 'This is fucked! We're fucked!' "

"Kingpin" stumbled to its feet punch-drunk. Bennett put things back in order with a ferocious guitar break. The song slid into its breakdown, where Tweedy normally improvised lyrics and interacted with the audience. But instead of mending the newly opened wounds, Tweedy added salt.

"Act like you're fucking excited, be a part of the show."

There was more halfhearted, a-rhythmic hand clapping.

"You don't know where to come in, do you? We'll get out of here a lot quicker . . . Clap on the one and three. Do you do that in England? . . . It's hopeless."

Tweedy came out for the encore and extended a feeble hand in reconciliation, then withdrew it.

"You know what? You're not all snobs. I don't know, maybe you're not used to people talking to you or something. But I'm gonna come out there. I'm gonna rub my Yankee ass all over you. I'll sit on your heads."

"Box Full of Letters" came out strutting like the heavy-metal son of Lou Reed's "Sweet Jane," circa *Rock 'n' Roll Animal*, and then Tweedy reached back to his Uncle Tupelo days for his cynical rant about rock 'n' roll celebrity, "We've Been Had." When the key line arrived—"And every star that hides on the back of the bus is just waiting for his cover to be blown!"—Tweedy punctuated it with a vicious scream. Jonathan Parker ran in from the wings to finish the show, taking the lead on bombastic versions of Black Sabbath's "War Pigs" and David Bowie's "Ziggy Stardust."

"I'd never seen him bait the crowd that much," Egan says. "I thought it was irredeemable. The audience almost didn't know what to say. I think they were just so shocked by his conviction and his audacity and the fact that he was finally rocking, which was what they were looking for. Afterward, I remember two things. I remember this very old doorman who had been there forever saying, 'I have never seen a show like this in my life. This is the best show I've ever seen!' And then I also remember saying to myself, 'Never, ever doubt Tweedy.' You think he's lost? Watch out, the guy will pull it off."

Tweedy's other bandmates weren't so forgiving. "Jeff's always had problems with English audiences, because they aren't as expressive as American crowds," Stirratt says. "But it got ridiculous that night, and I got really pissed. It was one of those nights where I had to ask him after the show what the problem was."

"I was embarrassed to be there," Coomer says. "And Jay felt the same way. I had a friend in the audience, and he asked me afterward, 'Does your singer really hate us all?' A lot of it was based on insecurity. We all thought we were in a big nightmare. We were just looking around, thinking it'll be over soon."

Richard Byrne, who had moved on from his gig as a St. Louis rock critic, happened to be in London at the time vacationing with his girlfriend. He was amazed to see Wilco's performance previewed in every newspaper and magazine he scanned. He bought tickets to the show, only to be appalled by what he witnessed. "Jeff was mocking the audience, and people were screaming, 'Fuck you, mate,'" Byrne recalls. "Billy Bragg is in the back with his head in his hands. People were walking out. And I turn to my girlfriend and say, 'You know, maybe it's not such a good idea to go backstage afterward and say hi to Tony and the guys.' Because it was a shambles. I've seen bands disintegrate onstage before. I saw the

Replacements countless times, and I'd seen Uncle Tupelo drink themselves into oblivion. But I'd never seen a band disintegrate *and* abuse an audience like that."

For Tweedy, it was a sign of growing pains: he was trying to figure out how to play the game on a larger scale. There isn't a school that teaches rising rock stars how to deal with record companies, radio stations, video networks. Tweedy had to figure it out for himself, just like everybody else; already a hardened skeptic about the ways of the record business, he had to fight to keep from slipping down a black hole of cynicism. He had just made an album that was, in large part, about the relationship between artist and fan, music and listener, and now he was boring through that world on a higher plane than ever: Wilco was getting more attention, playing to bigger crowds, and chewing up more column inches in newspapers and music magazines than ever before.

"Jeff was never, ever from day one good at playing 'industry' events," Gary Briggs says. "One time he stopped the show at a radio convention after the first song, and he says, 'Will you fucking guys stop talking about SoundScan and turn your fucking phones off for a minute and watch my show—or leave.' It's maybe 3 percent of the audience that isn't paying attention, but they just happen to be in the best seats, stage right, and they were all cackling, talking their little radio-industry and record-industry bullshit, and, God, he was never good about that kind of stuff. I mean, he would come onstage with his hand on the gun, just waiting to hear anything. You think he's not perceptive when he's onstage, that he's distracted and in his own world, but he could hear a conversation going on in the twentieth row and recite it back after singing two verses. He really does connect himself to his audience, and he really feeds off them. That's why I think he struggled so much in London initially because it's really hard for a lot of bands to go over there and play your ass off and have them clap seven times and stop. Tweedy is the kind of guy that just doesn't get that. 'How can they wait in line for three hours to be in front of the stage and then sit there with their hands coupled under their chins?' This guy is coming from an indie-rock, punk-rock world where the audience is pogoing with them and hanging on every word and really participating with the energy that was coming off the stage. I think those London shows really fucked up his head."

Tweedy's petulance didn't go over well in the Time Warner offices either. "On both sides of the pond, it freaked out a lot of people," Briggs says. "They just really didn't understand how a guy could piss on his own audience that way. It's like, you're the headliner now. These people came to see *you*. You're not opening for Sheryl Crow anymore. Come to think of it, he did that at a few Sheryl Crow shows too."

The show at Shepherd's Bush Empire in London was just the outer edge of deeper problems. Recurring migraines and anxiety attacks and long stretches away from home conspired to push Tweedy toward excesses that would test his relationships with all the things he loved most: his wife, his bandmates, his music. "Basically, I was very unhappy as a person," Tweedy says. "There was a period there, beginning with the *Being There* tour, where it wasn't so much a relationship with a chemical, although those were involved too, as what was going on inside me, a painful type of depression; it was debilitating. I was just hanging in there."

He pauses. There were days when Tweedy awoke hating what his life had become. But he hates using his health problems as an excuse even more. "I've seen many different types of people over the years, therapists, psychiatrists, to find out how crazy my reactions to the world are," Tweedy says. "I hate talking about it in a lot of ways, because I really don't buy it . . . There is a certain amount of vanity that goes into this self-preservation instinct. I despise the image of a drug-addled rock star. I despise the tortured-artist syndrome. I don't like talking about it. I like talking about music, people being interested in the dynamics of the band, and my life, a certain amount of history, but what I don't like contributing to, and I'm sure there are plenty of contradictions in this, is encouraging the belief in people that the musicians or artists they respect or respond to somehow suffer more than they do, or experience life in an extremely different way. I don't think that's a healthy thing for people to get in their head, because it displaces the ability of people to look at their own problems. They can look at *Behind the Music* and feel superior, like that's the trade-off they made for creativity."

It's a trade-off that goes back at least as far as Robert Johnson's deal with the devil at the crossroads. Jerry Lee Lewis and his producer Sam Phillips argued about it in Sun Studios just before Lewis cut "Great Balls of Fire." Lewis was sure that if he were to record such a salacious piece of sacrilege, he'd have to renounce God: sell his soul to have a hit. VH1's *Behind the Music* turned that attitude into a franchise, with its endless tales of rock stars who destroyed everything in the name of musical success. When I interviewed Billy Corgan at the height of the Smashing Pumpkins' success in the mid-1990s, he looked back on a few years where he'd lost his wife to divorce, his drummer to drug addiction, and very nearly his mind, and said, "I gave up everything for music."

"I believe Billy Corgan's being honest when he said that, but I think it's pathetic," Tweedy says. "It's a symptom of the same thing I'm talking about, and it's one step worse than a fan believing that there was no other way, or that it's a badge of honor somehow to have lived an unsatisfying life, to be a poor human, all in the name of art."

For Gary Briggs, watching his friend struggle on that 1997 tour was difficult, even as he bought into the myth that out of suffering comes great art. "As a selfish, self-serving record-company fucked executive, I could sit back and go, 'God, he's going to write some amazing songs about this shit,' however he comes out of this," Briggs says. "As a friend of Jeff and Sue's, and out of respect for their new family, it really scared me during that time. He and Sue were going through a very rough time, their marriage was really tested. It scared me to the point where I felt like I could wake up one day and read in the paper that Tweedy was gone, that he would have done something to end the pain. I know just about every day he was going through the worst migraines that you could imagine. You could see the pain in his face, and he would have to sneak off to the bathroom so he could puke just so he could come back and say, 'I feel a little better.' But within an hour he would have those pains again, so he was constantly trying to medicate that pain. He was doing it all to stop that pain."

The entire day of a show would be devoted to Tweedy's trying to find the right combination of painkillers, diet Cokes, and food so that he could perform at his best, so that he could be peaking at just the right moment, then go back to the hotel room and crash.

"What's different about Jeff is that if he's not a happy guy, he can't hide it," Briggs says. "He allowed the audience to come inside. I remember people saying, 'What's up with Jeff? Is Jeff in a bad mood tonight?' And I would think to myself, 'You think this is bad, you should have seen last night.' There was a period there where you could just see the pain pouring through his body every night. You could see it in his eyes, and I know he wasn't sleeping, I know he wasn't taking care of himself, I know his diet went to shit, where you could tell he didn't care about himself anymore. His physical appearance, the way he carried himself—he lost that sparkle and confidence that he had in his eyes. Whenever I would have a conversation with Jeff, there was just this unbridled passion and purity that he had in his eyes. I saw all of that disappear during that time. It was just dark in there. It was dark behind those eyes. This wasn't chemical driven. This was just deep personal issues. He wore it. He didn't hide it. He wore it. And then he wrote about it."

CHAPTER 11

"I WILL SING WHILE YOU CROAK"

The songs for *Summerteeth* started taking shape on the endless road after *Being There*. Bloodier-than-blood feeling, transformed into music in hotel rooms, the back of the tour bus, backstage.

"During the *Being There* tour, we had about four days off in Paris, and Jeff never left his hotel room, except to get food, a fish sandwich at McDonald's or whatever," Bob Egan says. "He had the room next to me, so I could hear *Summerteeth* through the walls as he was writing the songs. I went in one day to visit him in the back of the tour bus, and he looked at me, and he just started writing words on a sheet of paper. After about five minutes, he handed the paper to me. I read it, and it was 'She's a Jar.' It was heavier than the stuff we were playing on tour. A lot heavier."

Summerteeth, though largely written while in the midst of a tour notable for its raucous misbehavior and punk pillaging, is in many ways the antithesis of the classic rock road record, bereft of bravado. Its world is dreamlike and insular, a private struggle magnified by distance, drugs, loneliness, and late-night phone calls.

"In 1997, that's all we did—live on the road," Tweedy says. "When you come home, it's hard not to feel like you're in somebody else's house, to make that transition and feel integrated as a human being. There's Dad and there's this guy who gets a lot of attention—a rock star or whatever you want to call it—and that doesn't seem to make him feel any better. Being home and trying to get back in touch with your real self is almost impossible in the time span which you have to do it, which is usually only a few days."

Sue Miller acknowledges that "it was a weird, difficult year for both of us. There were things he was doing at those shows that he never did before or since. It was like a midlife crisis—one of many, but maybe the worst of them all. I would see what was happening and wonder, 'Who are you?' "

Gary Briggs had seen this sort of thing before. A band suddenly finds itself with a bigger audience and reaps the rewards—and the consequences. "He was being more recognized; he was starting to get hit on for the first time in his career," Briggs says of Tweedy. "He would go places and girls would pay attention to him; there were never pretty girls backstage at an Uncle Tupelo show, ever. It was always guys, well-read guys and guys in baseball caps. That all changed with *Being There*."

Despite rave reviews and the confidence that they were growing into a mighty live act, Wilco was pushed to the breaking point several times on the 1996–97 tour. Stirratt, Coomer, Egan, and Bennett were on the verge of mutiny while waiting to board a ferry in Scandinavia. They called Margherita from a pay phone, waking the groggy manager in the middle of the night back home in Chicago to vent their frustrations. Tweedy was in no better shape. He was breaking down more often, gripped by anxiety attacks minutes before he took the stage. The band would surround him with hugs and reassurance, and he'd somehow pull it together in time to play. "It was a wasted year emotionally," Coomer says. "The breakdowns right before we went onstage, it got out of hand."

"Thank God they had the shows," says Jonathan Parker, a guitar technician beginning a six-year relationship with the band. "By the time Jeff got to 'Misunderstood' and could do some straining, that was his way of letting it all out. Some nights I definitely wondered how he could get up there, knowing what state he was in or how depressed he was. But in some weird way, playing shows was Jeff's therapy. That was the one place where he could control things."

He got friendly with solitude and silence, on the road or at home. While his wife and child slept, he spent long hours hunched beneath a reading light, immersed in William H. Gass's *In the Heart of the Heart of the Country*, John Fante's *Ask the Dust*, and Henry Miller's classic novel of Parisian misadventure, *Tropic of Cancer*. Though Tweedy had always been an indifferent student, he had developed into a voracious reader, and his love of language began to transform him as a lyricist. *Summerteeth* would be far denser and more daring than anything he had attempted so far.

"I definitely wanted to get better at writing, and those things happened simultaneously with trying to read better," Tweedy says. "I would write tons of stuff in my head, and forget. Some songs on *Being There*, I don't think I ever wrote any lyrics down. I was from the school of thought that you carry everything around with you. I was inspired by folk musicians, and I wanted to be able to carry songs on my back. I wanted to exist in their world, this oral tradition, this free language. I would turn on the tape recorder and see what came out. Words would marry themselves to certain chords and wouldn't change, even when I thought of better words later on. To fight that, I started writing words on paper and making up melodies to go with them. By writing things down, and putting more words into my head, it put more words into my mouth when I turned on the tape recorder to sing. There was just more stuff to choose from. I didn't have to resort to the first thought: 'I'm sitting on the couch, and you hurt my feelings.' I worked harder at laying the groundwork to generate inspiration. The work is putting yourself in that position more often. Creating the environment is the work. Picking up the guitar, picking up the pen, making yourself do that every day, and resigning yourself to the idea that it won't happen every day, but realizing that it's more likely to happen if you have the pen in your hand than if you don't."

Tweedy began accumulating notebooks filled with random thoughts, poems, lyrical fragments, tiny drawings, and transcribed bits of conversation and carted them in a knapsack with his books everywhere he went. Now, instead of starting songs from scratch, he'd flip through the notebooks looking for a place to jump in. "I was inspired by people who brought rich lyric poems to music: Dylan, Patti Smith, Pavement, Jeff Mangum from Neutral Milk Hotel, Rennie Sparks [of the Handsome Family], Leonard Cohen," he explains. "It was another thing for me to get around, that I would never be as good as them, and hating myself for failing to live up to that, but still going at it and coming out not the same, but somehow improved, and maybe realizing I'm not that bad. I found myself writing songs that weren't as linear as 'Passenger Side' or 'Box Full of Letters,' songs that I couldn't necessarily figure out everything about what they were saying, but knowing that they stirred something inside me when I sang them in front of people, even if I wasn't sure what it was. That it would be revealed only through singing or playing it."

If *Being There* showed the first glimmer of that approach in songs such as "Sunken Treasure" and "Misunderstood," *Summerteeth* brought it all the way home. It was loaded with songs that piled up line after line of vivid but seemingly unrelated images, then let the ax fall:

> *She's a jar*
> *With a heavy lid*
> *My pop quiz kid*
> *A sleepy kisser*
> *A pretty war*
> *With feelings hid*
> *You know she begs me not to hit her*

Tweedy's allusiveness went only so far. His lyrics were fiction steeped in truth, beauty dipped in blood. Tweedy carried around Henry Miller's *Tropic of Cancer* for eight years, never reading it all the way through in sequence, but dipping into it daily, as if he were consulting a bible. *Summerteeth* wouldn't have happened without Henry Miller—or Sue Miller, for that matter.

"This is not a book," Henry Miller wrote in *Tropic of Cancer*. "This is libel, slander, defamation of character. This is not a book, in the ordinary sense of the word. No, this is a prolonged insult, a gob of spit in the face of Art, a kick in the pants to God, Man, Destiny, Time, Love, Beauty . . . what you will. I am going to sing for you, a little off key perhaps, but I will sing. I will sing while you croak, I will dance over your dirty corpse."

Tweedy would attempt to do much the same on *Summerteeth*, an album not unlike the "autobiographical novel" Miller defines in his literary guide *The Books in My Life*, one that offers "not the flimsy truth of facts . . . but the truth of emotion, reflection and understanding, truth digested and assimilated."

Tweedy's emotional truth came pouring out in a weeklong recording session at Willie Nelson's studio in Spicewood, Texas, outside Austin, at the end of the yearlong *Being There* tour. It was November 1997, the windup to a year in which he'd seen his wife for only a few weeks at a time and had experienced the months leading up to his son's second birthday mostly through phone calls and photographs.

"He was crying, a wreck, recording some of those songs," Coomer says. "There was a lot of self-medicating going on. He was pumping painkillers and going through a horrific time. His songwriting got more personal, introspective. It was great, but, holy hell, what a price to pay. Sometimes I wondered how ambiguous his lyrics were, and I'd see things pop up and realize it was more personal. You put a bunch of grown men in this giant tube that travels across the country, you create your own moral universe, and you live by your own rules, and, as good a person as I think I am, I ruined some relationships that way. I think we all did."

Among the tracks recorded at the session were "Via Chicago," "Pieholden Suite," "I'm Always in Love," "We're Just Friends," and "She's a Jar." The songs cycled through various vantage points on a deteriorating relationship, uncensored and wrenching. The William H. Gass–inspired cry "Maybe all I need is a shot in the arm, something in my veins, bloodier than blood" that punctuates "A Shot in the Arm" alludes to a transformation so extreme it verges on suicidal.

Wilco's performances on these demos are stark, autumnal cousins to the atmospheric "Sunken Treasure." The real excitement lies in Tweedy's razor-blade lyrics, with their echoes of Miller's "I will sing while you croak." "I dreamed about killing you again last night, and it felt alright to me," Tweedy sings on "Via Chicago." The detachment in his voice as he describes how his lover's "cold, hot blood ran away from me to the sea" is chilling.

When Tweedy sang the last line of "She's a Jar," the band was startled. "I heard that line for the first time when he sang it at the session," John Stirratt says. "The music stopped, we stopped. We were blown away by the boldness of it. It was like, 'Whoa. NOW is really going to love that.' And I actually think the National Organization for Women wrote us a protest letter."

Tweedy says even he didn't know exactly what would happen when he opened his mouth in front of the microphone. When words emerged that were beyond his expectation, he felt a rush of well-being that far exceeded what any pill could induce. "I kept being surprised by stuff coming out of my mouth," he says. "But regardless of how Sue would feel, or my parents, or anybody close to me, I also knew that I was getting closer to this place of free expression, almost selfless, giving myself permission to just let go, no matter how it's going to be perceived."

What sounded daring in the studio struck Tweedy as unredeemable outside it. "When I got home and listened to that session," he says, "I didn't want it to come out. I didn't want people to have to sit through this, because I couldn't sit through it."

As for Tweedy's relationship with his wife, the lyrics to *Summerteeth* left the band's burgeoning fan base to speculate wildly on myriad Internet sites devoted to Wilco's music. Though it would be wrong to perceive the album as a work of pure autobiography, it certainly suggests the "truth of emotion" of Henry Miller's "autobiographical novel."

"Ever since spending a lot of time with Bob Dylan's albums, I've taken it for granted that lyrics are an idealized version of any relationship," says René Saller, who has known Tweedy and Uncle Tupelo since the Cicero's basement days in St. Louis. "I think Jeff was singing lines like 'She begs me not to hit her' for shock value. I love the Rolling Stones, but, good God, a song like 'Stray Cat Blues' will test any feminist principles you have. I remember Jeff singing 'I Wanna Destroy You' and dedicating it to his old girlfriend. I'm sure Sue Miller pulls a lot more strings than people would assume. I'm sure she isn't some long-suffering hausfrau."

Jeff Tweedy says it doesn't take a mind reader to figure out that he was in turmoil: "All I have to say about the topic is in the grooves of *Summerteeth*. I don't think you could find a more direct record about a topic than that one. There are things written in that record directly through my wife. It's amazing we're still together in spite of those lyrics. It's like Richard and Linda Thompson [on their brutally direct breakup album, *Shoot Out the Lights*], only she doesn't get to make a record to respond."

Sue Miller is a blond, blue-eyed take-charge type. She has survived open-heart surgery and guided a rock club for more than a decade through the rough-and-tumble world of Chicago nightlife politics, a world of fire marshals, liquor licenses, noise complaints, and unruly bands and even unrulier patrons. In indie-rock circles she's something of a legend, a den mother to countless struggling bands far from home. A lifelong Chicagoan, she is a mixture of street toughness and maternal compassion.

"I have to be honest and say it hasn't been easy all the time," Sue Miller admits. "Even though in my intellectual mind, I know these are works of fiction. But as much as the fans want to read into this stuff, it happens to me, too. I'll say, 'What do you mean by that?' It affects me. The line 'she begs me not to hit her'—they still talk about that on the Internet. Obviously, Jeff has never hit me. And I know I have to give Jeff his creative license. And I have no way of knowing whether he could have written as cool and brilliant an album without having to go through everything he went through in that year. I think that's one of our most common myths, that artists have to be miserable to be creative. I don't think that's true. I hope it's not true. I don't wish that kind of misery on anyone."

The relationship that provides a subtext for *Summerteeth* is in a better state today than any of the album's series of narrators might've imagined. Since *Summerteeth* was written, Jeff Tweedy and Sue Miller have had a second child, Sam, born in December 1999, and prepared to celebrate their ninth anniversary in the summer of 2004.

Summerteeth would have a far more troubled fate. Tweedy wrestled with how to present lyrics that he considered bold but depressing. To arrive at a solution, he would lean more heavily than ever on Jay Bennett, who was eager to accept more responsibility. He was working with a gifted lyricist coming off an acclaimed album, and after more than a decade of scuffling—Bennett was still working at the VCR repair shop in Champaign between tours—he had the opportunity and the time to explore every possibility in the music like never before.

But before the studio reclamation of the *Summerteeth* demos began in earnest, Wilco had a date to keep with Woody Guthrie.

CHAPTER 12

WOODY, THE FREAK WEIRDO

Despite the debacle of a concert he had witnessed at Shepherd's Bush Empire in April 1997, Billy Bragg was sure that Wilco could do the job he had in mind. He wanted a rock band that could play folk music, and he wanted some ballsy songwriters who could help him stand up to the legend of the late Woody Guthrie and rearrange it a bit—not so much to demythologize Woody as to free him from irrelevance by stereotype.

He got more than he bargained for: two volumes of *Mermaid Avenue*, a pair of acclaimed albums named after the street where Guthrie and his family lived in Coney Island, Brooklyn; unprecedented recognition and sales; and a clash of egos that nearly scuttled the whole enterprise.

Before Bragg and Wilco took a shot at making music with him posthumously, Guthrie had become something of a caricature. Because of the degenerative effects of Huntington's chorea, he had pretty much ceased recording by 1947. By the time he died twenty years later, his artistic reputation had calcified: he was the "This Land Is Your Land" union-touting, train-hopping, guitar-strumming hobo. He was the dust-bowl troubadour whose cracked-earth yodel found its modern counterpart in the music of his greatest disciple,

Bob Dylan. He was a prolific songwriter and a social activist, and his music would surface intermittently in the form of a tribute album or as an influence in the work of Bruce Springsteen, Steve Earle, or Uncle Tupelo, who covered Dylan's "Song to Woody." But to many in the MTV generation, he was a relic.

His daughter Nora Guthrie knew better, and she had the songs to prove it: more than twenty-five hundred sets of lyrics stored alphabetically in twelve large boxes in a white-gloves-only archive in midtown Manhattan, many known only to Woody and his immediate family. These included songs Guthrie wrote in his final years, when he was too sick to sing or record but still clearheaded enough to write. They reveal an extraordinary poet who was still expanding his reach till he was literally too weak to grip a pencil, an artist who was far more introspective, romantic, lusty, and playful than anyone but Guthrie's closest friends and family could have imagined. "His personality or his icon thing really is holding him back," Nora Guthrie says, speaking of her father as if he were still alive. "And it really pisses me off."

Nora Guthrie first approached Bragg in the spring of 1995 about getting past the "icon thing" and bringing her father's unheard lyrics to a new audience. "He was the only singer I knew taking on the same issues as Woody," she says. "But I didn't want a tribute album to Woody; I wanted somebody to jam with the guy like a peer" and create an album with a unified sound. Though Bragg is British, his political sensibilities clearly stamped him as a Clash-era Guthrie descendant—a rabble-rousing, guitar-spanking punk with a Cockney accent that proudly broadcast his working-class roots but who also was capable of poetic relationship songs such as "Levi Stubbs' Tears."

As Bragg began writing music for some of the Guthrie lyrics and road testing the results, many of his fans mistook the songs for his originals. "I looked at the songs I had chosen, like 'Ingrid Bergman' and 'She Came Along to Me,' and realized those are the kinds of songs I might've written, and that in order to do Woody justice it would really help if there were a few more heads in on this," Bragg explains.

He first approached Jeff Tweedy and Jay Bennett when they were doing a promotional tour of Europe soon after *Being There* came out in the fall of 1996. Tweedy was noncommittal, but Bennett was eager. He idolized the Brit folkie, to the point of naming his old band Titanic Love Affair after a Bragg lyric. "I thought we would've been idiots not to do it," Bennett says.

Tweedy shrugged. "I didn't go into it a huge Billy Bragg fan," he says. "I didn't think Wilco in a million years would've backed up Billy Bragg on a record, or shared a record with him even. I felt like our approaches to music wouldn't work together."

Bragg was used to having things his way as well. But he loved *Being There* for its varied musical attack, which in his mind elevated Wilco above the rest of the more one-dimensional alternative-country bands emerging in America. "There's something about Wilco being from the Midwest—whatever they do comes from the middle," Bragg says. "It's important that Wilco are not from Los Angeles or New York or Boston. With a lot of American roots bands, it doesn't go back much beyond the 1950s, but Wilco gives you the feeling that they go back to the '30s and even into the last century." After the Shepherd's Bush Empire show, Bragg swooped in to close the deal, though he realized his timing couldn't have been worse: "The state they were in, I thought they easily could have thrown me down the back stairs."

He figured he could entice them by proposing Dublin as a neutral site between London and Chicago to record the album. But for Tweedy the issue was less about geography and more about content: What lyrics would be molded into songs and who would choose them? "It wasn't that appealing until it was made clear to me that we could go through the archives ourselves and pick out songs," he says. "I never would dismiss Woody Guthrie, because he's such a huge part of my musical life, but I definitely went into it with the idea that the stereotype that had been projected on him was not that appealing to me anymore. The left-leaning-hobo stereotype of Woody stood in contrast to what I hoped would be true: that Woody never would have marginalized himself like that. He would have preferred to reach a broad section of society than be packaged and sold to a tightly knit group of initiated people. I suspected there was this other Guthrie in there, from stuff I'd read about him, but I didn't know for sure until I saw the archive."

There Tweedy and Bennett surprised even Nora Guthrie with some of the lyrics to which they gravitated. " 'California Stars' didn't strike me as one of my father's great songs," she says. "It's not a song I would have picked out. It didn't strike me until I heard the music with it, and that was a good lesson for me. Jeff has an incredible musical way of bringing out the meaning of a lyric. He went way beyond what I thought was possible."

"After seeing some of those songs, my take on him was that he's more alive than ever," Tweedy says. "And that it would be a disservice to him to keep hammering home certain aspects of his social concerns, or whatever politics he had, as opposed to affirming the idiosyncrasies that made him a major American artist. I'm not into Woody the icon. I'm into Woody the freak weirdo."

In contrast, Bragg embraced Guthrie's politics. He insisted that the pro-union "I Guess I Planted" and the Mussolini-bashing "All You Fascists" be recorded, while Tweedy rolled his eyes.

Bragg was well aware of Tweedy's feelings, and even gently nudged his counterpart to have the argument with him on camera, part of which surfaced in the British Broadcasting Corporation's *Man in the Sand* documentary film. Tweedy began pumping out sit-ups and joking about their intractable differences: "We don't need any songs about fascists, because a bunch of fascists are already working on this record." Instead, he suggested an alternative album title: *Hard Feelings*.

Despite the head-butting, the music flowed when Wilco and Bragg first convened on December 12–18, 1997, at King Size studio in Chicago as a warm-up for the Dublin session in mid-January. These two sessions yielded most of the songs that appeared on *Mermaid Avenue* and *Mermaid Avenue Volume 2*, released in 1998 and 2000, respectively. Only weeks earlier Wilco had bled itself dry recording the tearstained end-of-tour demos for *Summerteeth* in Austin. Jamming on Woody Guthrie lyrics in a cozy, low-pressure environment on their home turf went down like a tonic.

Greil Marcus's *Invisible Republic*, about how Bob Dylan and the Band made *The Basement Tapes*, served as an unspoken blueprint for the sessions. Bragg had already read the book, and Tweedy was immersed in it as recording got under way. "Both of us were quietly nursing our Bob Dylan obsessions," Bragg says. At the Dublin sessions, Tweedy grew a beard and started wearing a wide-brimmed hat. "What's with the Bob Dylan beard?" Stirratt asked.

In Chicago, the musicians huddled around copies of Guthrie's handwritten lyrics spread on the floor, instruments in their laps. "It was a bit like going to the dressing-up trunk as kids and seeing who we wanted to be that day," Bragg says. "It wasn't daunting. It was fun. *The Basement Tapes* were basically a bunch of young guys getting together in a room and playing fifty-year-old songs, which isn't that far removed from what we were doing."

"What came out is how we left it on the finished recording," Tweedy says. "We didn't have the time or the energy to push this stuff anywhere else other than how it came out, and even if we had, it would've been inappropriate. Those lyrics demanded to be lightly adorned. They sang themselves. The instruments in the band should sound effortless. Any kind of thought you put into that would ruin everything."

Wilco ended up finishing most of its contributions to the *Mermaid Avenue* album in Chicago, and a few of Bragg's as well.

A take of "Eisler on the Go," about the exiled German composer Hanns Eisler, who was deported by the United States during the Red Scare, became something of a spaghetti-Western ballad, redolent more of Ennio Morricone than of a civil-rights anthem. The understated arrangement was built on little more than Bragg's National guitar and Bennett's Melodica, but it was enough. "That's it! You can't do anything more with that," exclaimed Jon Langford, the Mekons' singer-guitarist who walked in while the session was in progress.

Bennett banged out the three chords for "California Stars" in his girlfriend's kitchen so quickly he was sure he'd lifted them off Springsteen's *Nebraska* or some other cherished album. When Tweedy heard the demo, he did some tweaking; he accelerated the tempo and took the melody up an octave. In the studio, Coomer and Stirratt made it swing, and Wilco knocked out the finished version in two takes.

"It wasn't much of a lyric on paper—it's just a song about stars in California," Bragg marvels. "And then they brought this beautiful aching lilt to it."

"Hoodoo Voodoo"—a nonsensical children's song that sounds like it could've been a precursor of both Dr. Seuss's *The Cat in the Hat* and Dylan's "Subterranean Homesick Blues"—was transformed when Stirratt and Coomer began exaggerating the groove, goofing on its herky-jerky possibilities. Tweedy jumped on the microphone while Bennett rocked the organ and Bragg joined in on electric guitar, and a song that had been dead in the water suddenly sailed.

The crowning moment—not just of the Guthrie sessions at King Size but of this incarnation of Wilco—arrived on the final day, after Bragg had already flown back to London for the holidays. "One by One" emerged like a mirage, with Bob Egan's pedal steel purring alongside Bennett's piano while Stirratt's bass danced slowly with Coomer's mesmerizing drums. Subdued and jazzy, Coomer evoked the great Tennessee session drummer Kenny Buttrey, who played with Dylan on *Nashville Skyline*. Tweedy sounded like he was singing with his chin on Guthrie's stooped shoulder, his tone unhurried and confiding as night closed in. The song didn't build. Instead, it receded like a wave retreating from the shore, until, two-thirds of the way in, it was just barely a whisper of foam: "One by one the days are slipping up behind you." Guthrie's lyric is from the perspective of a man much older than his twenty-seven years at the time. Tweedy was only a few months past his thirtieth birthday when he stepped to the microphone on that December evening.

"I tried to match Jeff's vocal, to really listen to it as I was playing," Bob Egan says. "I thought it was an original, that it was autobiographical, because Jeff sang it with such conviction. Afterward I'm saying, 'Dude, I'm sorry, I didn't know that was going on in your life.' And he says, 'That was written by Woody Guthrie in 1939.' "

It was to be the final Wilco song Egan would play on. He had dropped into the Chicago sessions on the last day, invited as an afterthought, not even aware that the band was working on an album of Guthrie songs. On tour, his overamplified pedal-steel playing had become an irritant to the other band members; it got so bad that Jonathan Parker was instructed to sabotage Egan's volume knob, so that he couldn't crank it up. Tweedy would occasionally introduce Egan onstage with zingers that were less than good-natured: "This is Bob Egan. He used to be in Wilco." The other band members were rankled that Egan was making $1,350 a week to their $800; he'd negotiated a higher salary because he had left his music store behind. When the *Being There* tour ended, hints were dropped that his services were no longer required, but no one bothered to come out and say it directly. Then Margherita bought him a plane ticket to Dublin in January. There he was welcomed by Wilco's leader at the door of the condo where the band was staying.

Egan was crestfallen by his greeting, such as it was. "The first thing he says to me," Egan recalls, "is, 'I don't know why you're here. There is nothing for you to play on. The record's done.' I was like, 'Oh, thanks. How are ya?' So I hung out in the studio with my game face on, and I think Billy felt sorry for me and asked me to play on a couple of his things. The whole experience was one of the harder things I've ever had to do musically."

Ironically, Egan ended up in Bragg's touring band that summer, playing many of the *Mermaid Avenue* songs that Wilco had performed in the studio. He also served at least one other role in Dublin: as a drinking buddy for Wilco's bass player. John Stirratt and Jay Bennett had been inseparable during the *Being There* tour, egging each other on to greater heights of inebriation and onstage frivolity. But Bennett had three root-canal procedures and had his wisdom teeth pulled while in Chicago and was forced to swear off the booze. He didn't pick up another drink for four years. "I'm so glad Bob came over because I had someone to drink with," Stirratt says with a laugh. "Everyone else was into prescription drugs." As Bennett adjusted to alcohol-free life, Tweedy's migraines were becoming a daily impediment to emotional clarity. A daily diet of painkillers, antidepressants, and homesickness clouded Dublin.

"That was the start of the real weirdness in the band, a breaking point," Stirratt says. "I look back on that now and I'm really surprised I hung with it all. Jeff looked exhausted and Jay wasn't much better off; they had their arms around each other on the plane over to Dublin. They were bonding over their misery."

Jonathan Parker was taken aback by the emotional wreckage around him, even as he was uplifted by the music his friends were recording. "I've never really been around pill popping," he says, "so at first I was like, 'Why would you want to do that unless you were in pain?' I mean, wouldn't you rather be in Dublin making records than in Champaign fixing VCRs? But they *were* in pain. They were far from home, after being far from home for most of the last year, and they didn't want to be there."

Bragg found himself confused a few times as Tweedy and Bennett juggled *Summerteeth* songs with *Mermaid Avenue* material. "They'd walk around playing things, and sometimes I'd join in, only to find they were doing their own stuff," Bragg says. He wasn't the only one feeling out of it.

"Jay and Jeff would play this game of 'Hey, let's work on a song together,' and no one was ever in the mood," Parker says. "One time Jay had a song working, and he was following Jeff around in the condo with an Epiphone guitar trying to persuade him. And Jeff just finally snapped and went off on him. 'I have a fuckin' headache, and I don't want to work on your song. Will you leave me the fuck alone?' Unlike the other guys in the band, Jay was not afraid to push it."

Adding to the surrealism was a forty-by-fifteen-foot rustic American flag painted on one of the walls of the warehouse-like recording studio in Dublin. To Wilco, it showed how little Bragg really understood about them or their culture. "I'm thinking, 'Are you gonna paint a hammer and sickle on the other side? Are we gonna reenact the Cold War?' " Tweedy says. "To this day, I think he doesn't think we understand politics at all, that we're just rubes who could never understand the depths of Marxist philosophy." Bennett just laughed when he saw more than fifty stars clustered in the flag's left corner. "I thought they were including all our former and future colonies or something," he says.

The cultural differences cut both ways. "I thought someone was upset. All of a sudden everybody just puts their equipment down and walks out of the room, and me and my producer [Grant Showbiz] are left sitting there," Bragg says. "I found that everything stops every night at the same time for *The Simpsons*. They knew every single episode and said every single line before the characters did. I got used to that . . . after a while." Wilco grumbled about the presence of Showbiz, who was paid a five-figure producer's salary, even though, in the band's eyes, he did little more than serve as Bragg's security blanket.

Wilco essentially functioned as Bragg's backing band in Dublin, but they didn't confine themselves to background harmonies. When Bragg ran into a cul-de-sac while working on "She Came Along to Me," Tweedy wrote a new intro and the eight-bar bridge. "Tweedy has a great ear for arrangement, which was crucial for this record because the lyrics are so straightforward and the melodies are relatively simple," Bragg says. "They were a great band, malleable, and I felt I could lead them in many different directions."

It led to one of the "loosest, freest" records Bragg had ever made, according to his longtime manager, Peter Jenner. Bragg's performances had undeniable charm and heart, especially when he investigated the more personal side of Guthrie's song poetry on the lusty fantasy "Ingrid Bergman" or delivered a performance as off-hand as the one on "Eisler on the Go" or as buoyantly bawdy as "Walt Whitman's Niece." The singer recorded enough Guthrie music for two more *Mermaid Avenue* volumes and suggested at least a sequel to Tweedy, only to be met with the usual noncommittal shrug.

The arrival of Nora Guthrie during the third week of sessions brightened Dublin for everyone and was the catalyst for one last moment of spontaneous beauty. She had brought additional songs from the archive, including one called "Another Man's Done Gone." It consists of eleven lines, every one precious. They're the words of a dying man clinging to his last hope for immortality: "I don't know, I may go down or up or anywhere / But I feel like this scribbling might stay."

Bragg shaped three chords on guitar and showed them to Bennett, who was tinkering on a grand piano. When Bennett went to work in earnest on the eighty-eights, the chords expanded, and the skeleton of a song emerged. Tweedy was napping on a couch behind a drawn curtain and arose bleary-eyed but curious. Standing at the piano, he briefly studied the lyrics and began singing. Out of his lips came a sound as forlorn as Richard Manuel's ghost, a distant echo of the Band's "Unfaithful Servant." In ninety seconds the song drifted into the room, and then vanished, with only silence and tears to mark its passage. Nora Guthrie's eyes glimmered as Jeff Tweedy sang her father's words through her headphones. The engineer Jerry Boys, a veteran of recording sessions since the Beatles, dropped his head. Bragg felt the hairs on the back of his neck rise.

"Tweedy sang it," Jonathan Parker says, "and brought grown men to tears."

Billy Bragg felt it, too. "It was a moment, and then it was done," he says. "A true collaboration. Nora found the lyrics, I had written the music, Jay played it, and Jeff sang it in a way that was beyond personal. It's a song of despair, a man facing death wondering if anyone will remember him if he's gone. And that performance was the four of us sending a clear message out to Woody that his scribbling was immortal."

But for Jay Bennett the performance brings back sour memories. "Billy had the chords to James Taylor's 'Fire and Rain.' Real simple chords," Bennett says. "I said, 'Hey, Bill, this might be cooler with something other than D, G, C. So I threw some Burt Bacharach five-note compound chords in there, B-minor 7 with F-sharp on the bottom. Made it prettier, basically. The song was getting too high for him to sing comfortably. So Jeff came out and sang it. Billy got us about one-third of the way there, I wrote the chords, and Jeff came up with the vocal melody. But when the album came out, it was credited only to Billy."

Even more significant differences developed over how Bragg and Wilco wanted the album mixed. "I enjoyed working with Billy," Tweedy insists. "He had a good sense of humor, the ability to laugh at himself. And at the same time, I was always suspect of him as being somewhat full of shit. I never did understand why we were recording songs about brownshirted Fascists clobbering people in the streets of Italy during the '30s. He could get really angry if we pushed the wrong buttons, and Wilco as a whole was pretty adept at pushing those buttons. For Jay, it was an atrocity that some of Billy's mixes would make the record. Instead of balancing instruments and allowing it to be an environment where it sounds like a singer and a band, his was very much a vocal solo mix, with a very faraway, easily palatable band. So squishy and soft and perfect. To me, the recordings we did for volume 1 were very raw, almost crappy sounding. Whereas his didn't sound crappy, they sounded chintzy. This faux glitz was on them, and to us that was antithetical to the idea behind the record."

Bennett insisted that Wilco have a crack at mixing Bragg's songs. Tweedy placed a transatlantic call to London. Bragg heard Tweedy out, and then offered a succinct response: "You make your record, and I'll make mine, fucker."

"That's the point, Billy. It's not your record," Tweedy said. "It's not our record. It's Woody Guthrie's record. All I'm saying is if we had a different set of ears on the record, it would sound more coherent."

Bragg backed down and sent copies of his masters to Chicago. Bennett remixed them, but Bragg decided to stick with his mixes instead. "I like to be there for the mixing and everything else," Bragg says. "I don't want to hand it off to someone else. I hate that. I think neither one of us were used to working in a situation where we surrendered any control. So it did lead to a bit of sulking. Transatlantic sulking on everyone's part, but not to the extent where we fell out completely. They could have easily said, 'Let's just leave it at that, because we can't start working with you any-more, you big-nose bastard, you're so rotten to us.' They would have been quite within their rights to say something along those lines, but instead they agreed to do another album."

Mermaid Avenue went on to sell 277,000 copies—outselling all of Bragg's previous albums combined in North America and nearly equaling Wilco's *Being There* peak. It also earned a Grammy nom-ination for best contemporary folk album, losing out to Lucinda Williams's *Car Wheels on a Gravel Road*. (The band was quickly reminded it didn't belong at the glitzy Los Angeles ceremony for the Grammys when Tweedy stood in the aisle with a handful of programs while he waited for his bandmates and Sean "Puffy" Combs mistook him for an usher.) The reviews were the best of either artist's career. Even longtime Uncle Tupelo and Wilco skep-tics were won over: "This time you got it right," Greil Marcus raved in a four-star *Rolling Stone* review. "While the words are wonderful and unexpected . . . it's the music, especially Wilco's music, that transfigures the enterprise," Robert Christgau declared in *The Village Voice*, where the self-appointed dean of American rock critics handed out a rare A.

But Wilco and Bragg could never agree on a tour, and their joint success was short-lived. Quarrels ensued over everything from paying union fees for guest musicians to festival concert commitments, or the lack thereof. Because the two camps couldn't agree on doing anything together to support the album, conflicts cropped up over tour and promotional expenses, since these would count against future royalties that Bragg and Wilco were to share. Jenner and Margherita tussled daily in transatlantic screaming matches.

"There were three or four months there that every day Tony was throwing his phone," Jonathan Parker says, "and I thought he was going to have a heart attack. I thought he was going to lose it."

Jeff Tweedy has no regrets about the *Mermaid Avenue* tour that wasn't. "We don't have a killer instinct as a band," he says. "We never felt like we had to capitalize on something, to really push it home. The response *Mermaid Avenue* generated was gratifying. It was the most attention Billy had gotten in the press in a long time, especially in the United States, and he was gung ho, booking mutual shows for us without telling us about it. Then he threatened to sue us when we wouldn't come and play with him and he had to hire a band. I felt like I was watching a guy shoot himself in the foot. They had it in their heads all along that it was their record, and rightfully so, because Billy was asked to do it first, but they wanted to believe that the success of it had nothing to do with us, that the relationship hadn't evolved at all during the making of it, that we were Billy's backup band. We were in the midst of recording *Summerteeth*, but we were willing to set aside a few weeks to tour with him. It ended up completely backfiring."

Billy Bragg got over it. The artistic accomplishment of the two *Mermaid Avenue* albums, rather than the acrimony that arose in their wake, is how the singer-songwriter prefers to remember the occasion. "That would be my only regret in the entire project," he says. "It wasn't really anyone's fault. It's just that I was between albums and they were in the middle of making one, and they were also at the beginning of their career. It was crucial for them to keep focused on what they were doing. So I put a band together with Bob Egan, put 'California Stars' in my set, and just got on with it."

CHAPTER 13

"MAKING A GREAT RECORD DOESN'T MATTER"

Overdubbing once meant selling out—at least for the earnest young men in Uncle Tupelo. For them, the studio was nothing more than an extension of the living room or the stage: a facility for recording the interaction of a band, in real time. Any sort of tinkering—extra instruments, weird sound experiments, layered harmonies—was an inexcusable excess. The overdub-free *March 16–20, 1992* and *Anodyne* drew a line in the sand: on one side was Uncle Tupelo, guardians of the spontaneous act of creation; on the other were the philistines who used the studio to cover up the impurities and imperfections that made music worth listening to in the first place.

But in Wilco all that changed. *Being There* stepped over the line a few times. *Summerteeth* demolished it.

What began in Austin as a straightforward live-to-tape band recording ended up in Chicago as an elaborate two-man overdub extravaganza. It was Jeff Tweedy and Jay Bennett, a few cartons of cigarettes, and a Pro Tools computer cocooned in a studio as they transformed songs of wretched despair into cathedrals of sound. In the process, they shut out the world and even their own bandmates.

Summerteeth is widely perceived as the Jay and Jeff album rather than a true band effort, a perception that Jay Bennett wholeheartedly embraces. Jonathan Parker, who spent countless hours on the road with Bennett as his guitar technician, saw it unfold. "If you give Jay half a step, he'll take three steps," Parker says. "His talent, self-confidence, and competitiveness are just overwhelming. Jeff gave him a little freedom. It's like, here's the baton, and Jay ran with it."

For Tweedy, Bennett's studio talents were required to rescue what he initially saw as a nearly unbearable set of lyrics. "I came back from Austin and I thought we should start again from scratch," Tweedy says, "that I could never imagine myself traveling around singing these songs to people, because they were so depressing to me. So it became a distraction, a necessary distraction, to focus really intensely on the music and the production instead of this carnage in the lyrics. The task became: How to quiet the voice of despair that's in those songs? How to make it as small as it should be? Because an album shouldn't rub anyone's nose into one person's problems, shouldn't make those problems seem bigger than they really are. That's where Jay's expertise in the studio came in. I felt I needed to bury those lyrics safely under glass."

Joe McEwen almost didn't recognize his boys underneath all that production: "It's much more of a Beach Boys record, a Brian Wilson, *Pet Sounds* sort of thing." More accurately, it's the loss of innocence chronicled on *Pet Sounds* running headlong into the ornately orchestrated masochism of Lou Reed's *Berlin*. Strychnine lyrics surgarcoated by baroque arrangements, poison pop that's easy to taste but deadly to digest. "She begs me not to hit her"? "I dreamed about killing you again last night"? This was innocence not just lost but defiled.

"Via Chicago" sets the tone. It is driven more by narrative than by music; a trite chord progression and a nearly static, slow-moving melody provide a rickety foundation for a murderous confession. It was recorded in two distinct versions in Texas: one a somber reverie swaying in minor-key slow motion; the other a distorted guitar assault. Neither by itself cut it. But in Chicago at King Size, Pro Tools software on the studio's computerized mixing board enabled Bennett and Tweedy to effortlessly weave the two versions together, and let them fade in and out, as if fighting for supremacy in the narrator's twisted world of dominance and submission. It was a striking moment, and after it there was no going back. Everything else on *Summerteeth* would have to sound at least as elaborate.

So Bennett and Tweedy thumbed through their personal dictionary of pop. "Pieholden Suite" compresses a mini-symphony of sleigh bells, trumpet, and banjo into less than four minutes of Van Dyke Parks–like bliss. Woodwinds generated by a tiny toy keyboard waft through "When You Wake Up Feeling Old," a fake bassoon turns "She's a Jar" into a melancholy beauty, and birds chirp and voices sigh alongside a bright George Harrison–like guitar in "Summer Teeth." Bennett and Tweedy reference the Cure's "Just Like Heaven" synthesizers in "I'm Always in Love," Elvis Costello's *Armed Forces* power pop on "Candyfloss," and the Beatles' "A Day in the Life" alarm clock in "Nothing'severgonnastandinmyway(again)." With nothing but time and cigarettes on their hands, they were delighted to find that if they slowed down the latter song, it provided a musical bed that synched perfectly with the chords of "My Darling." And so they pulled off a bit of studio sleight of hand that Brian Eno might have appreciated.

The album title started with a bad joke. "I got summer teeth: some are teeth, and some aren't." "A horrible joke—that seemed appropriate," Tweedy says. "I mean, I didn't want to call the album *Small Sorrow*, even though that's what it started out as. I got in my head that 'summerteeth' meant something elusive or fake, but had a beautiful name."

To execute this beautiful deception, Bennett became something of a one-man orchestra. He conjured otherworldly sounds on a bulky keyboard instrument known as a Mellotron—the same instrument that gave the Beatles' "Strawberry Fields Forever" its woozy, disorienting texture—and piled on a baby grand piano, an out-of-tune upright piano, bells, tambourine, synthesizers, lap steel, EBow guitar, baritone guitar, banjo, and backing harmonies. When the Nashville-based Coomer and the New Orleans–based Stirratt weren't readily available, he threw on drums and bass as well. And then he added hand claps.

The studio was a new toy waiting to be explored. Wilco had

never used Pro Tools before this album, and now they would exhaust its possibilities: throwing eighty tracks of vocals on a song, picking sixteen, and then editing them into a finely tuned choir. "In Uncle Tupelo, we didn't have the expertise or the equipment to do something like that," Tweedy says. "So we made a record within our limitations. When we got to *Summerteeth* and saw the possibilities available to us, we thought we'd be foolish not to try it. It's like when multitrack recording became available in the '60s. If the Beatles were around today, I'm sure they would've at least experimented with Pro Tools to see what they could do."

Yet the technology binge didn't leave much room for the other band members. "It almost required that fewer people be involved, because if everyone had been there, there would have been a lot of sitting around and grousing while we were playing around with the possibilities," Tweedy says.

"It was a circling of the wagons, and John and I felt left out," Ken Coomer says. "It was Jeff and Jay feeding off each other not just musically, but other vices. There was a bonding going on, and it didn't involve just music. Jeff didn't go to rehab, but he should've, in my opinion. Jay was taking painkillers, antidepressants, and wasn't in much better shape. The band was different. There really wasn't a band, just two guys losing their minds in the studio."

Jay Bennett didn't see it that way. He was on a roll, at the peak of his creative powers. To him, the long hours in the studio were a form of therapy. He could lose himself in his music, his gadgets, and his relationship with the band's principal songwriter. "Jeff and I were pretty much of one mind," he says. "We would get together and record and write without those guys. We would write songs, talk about plans or emotions, or share things. We had similar emotional issues, psychological issues, the anxiety attacks. We helped each other and learned from each other."

Bennett's skills complemented Tweedy's. "I know what I want to hear, and I know how to play it generally on the guitar," Tweedy says. "But I don't know sometimes how to get there efficiently. I know what the effect is, in nonmusical terms. Jay can often do that. On the other side of it, Jay can have great musical ideas that might be beautiful and elaborate and ornate, that connect on an intellectual level but not necessarily on an emotional one. It sounds like he went to music school. So his ability to filter that stuff through the way I see things made *Summerteeth* what it was."

"Geography was key," Bennett says of the duo's *Summerteeth* bonding. "We were in Chicago, and the other guys weren't. I was pretty ignorant to other people's feelings, because the work we were doing was so satisfying. I know Ken and John were wondering if they had a place on that record. The band was never good at fully addressing issues, at getting to the core of things and fully resolving them. Think big extended Woody Allen family, from *Interiors*—that's what communication was like in Wilco. When John and Ken would come in to do something, it would just be very fuckin' frustrating. Ken wasted a lot of time trying to redo my drum parts. So, out of loyalty, we'd waste two days at six hundred dollars apiece to let Ken try to replace my drums. Loyalty in Wilco, back then, was worth at least twelve hundred dollars."

The rhythm section's confidence could not be brought back that easily. "There was definitely something fruitful about the actual work, but the dynamic around it was diminishing returns," Tweedy says. "It was inevitable that not everybody was going to be happy."

"I would show up in the studio, and 'She's a Jar' would be in its final form, which was an unprecedented way of working in the band," Stirratt says. "I'd think, 'I should be really mad, but it's so beautiful.' Some of the technology was used in really musically constructive ways, like with 'Via Chicago.' And other times it just struck me as overkill. Like some weird form of damage control. I thought what we had in Austin was really beautiful. The story of *Summerteeth* is Jay bought a Mellotron and he was going to use it, no matter what. It was lovely, but it was overdone. Once they got going on the overdubs, they didn't stop. And nobody in the band stepped up to stop the madness."

Stirratt saw a twisted spiritual quest playing itself out. "It reminds me of [Joseph Conrad's] *Heart of Darkness*," he says, "where you knowingly extend the creative process for the purpose of exploration or redemption, or whatever it is you're looking for. Jeff is a great songwriter in the sense that he doesn't separate a lot of things personally from the music, and I think that's what people love about it. But the studio became an end in itself, a place to go to get away from something. The beautification process became a plague. Like there's something wrong, but nobody is saying exactly what it is, and because of that it felt wrong to me in some way. Was it the great record that got away? I don't want to overstate that. I couldn't listen to it after it came out. It felt too dense, claustrophobic. With a little distance, I can appreciate the beauty of what it is. But I still think we achieved more of the essence of the songs on the original demos."

Years later, Tweedy would agree with his bassist. "I wish now that I left those lyrics naked, that we hadn't spent so much time trying to cover them up," the singer says. "I wasn't as brave as I could have been. It didn't work, because there was no way to conceal some of the openness of the lyrics. Every song on that record was about the same situation but from a different point of view: this is the way the drunk would handle the situation, or this is the way the total lovesick guy would handle it, or the better-adjusted or more farsighted guy. I tried to work closer and closer to some version of healthiness."

Though *Summerteeth* did irreparable harm to some of the relationships within Wilco, the richness of the music on it is undeniable. Despite more limited roles, Stirratt and Coomer made stellar contributions to the album: amid the shifting textures of "A Shot in the Arm," Stirratt's bass drives the melody with beacon-like clarity while Coomer's timpani brings a Hal Blaine–like drama. The overall arch of the music is stunning. Tweedy's damaged protagonist—his version of Randy Newman's "untrustworthy narrator"—slowly works his way toward some measure of hope. It's telling, however, that the album's most redemptive moment—the orchestral finale of "Pieholden Suite"—contains no lyrics. Instead, Tweedy wiped out the third verse to let the music wash over him, and the listener, as if it could somehow heal them both.

In the end, his narrator is looking beyond his despair to "a future age" when he will float "High above / The sea of cars / And barking dogs / In fenced-in yards." It may be a drug reference—Tweedy claims it isn't—or it may be about transcending the emotional holocaust he has just described in the album's previous songs. The music floats and twinkles like one of the filmmaker Wim

Wenders's angels, a surreal reminder of the world beyond life's dirty windshield: "Let's turn our prayers / Into outrageous dares / And mark our page / In a future age."

At a time when his world outside the studio was tilting toward darkness, Tweedy made some of his most beautiful music. "I was really conscious of that," he says. "A lot of times I write things as wishful thinking, or as reminders, because I can invent a person that can believe that to sing it. And in doing that, I feel I'm taking some proactive step to being that person. Not an ideal necessarily, but an extension of myself that becomes highlighted, to where I can define myself more by someone who takes the world a bit more openly, in hope that one day I could actually become that person."

The one truly upbeat song, "Candyfloss," ended up buried, tucked away as a hidden track at the end of the CD. At one point it was intended as the album's centerpiece, but as the songs got more dire, "Candyfloss" stuck out like a sugarcoated impostor. "The record just went past it," Tweedy says. "See ya later, 'Candyfloss.' Go hang out with your bubblegum buddies."

Like its narrator, *Summerteeth* is an imperfect album. The music went too far, was too sumptuous for lyrics as raw as an open wound. But its ambition is stunning and its execution frequently breathtaking, and it threw another curve at those who thought they had Tweedy and Wilco figured out, including their record label.

The band that made *Summerteeth* barely resembled the rough-hewn outfit Joe McEwen had signed only four years earlier, and with this new batch of intricate pop songs it risked alienating the fan base it had nurtured through even the sharpest turns of *Being There*. McEwen loved the album despite its drastic reinvention of Wilco's sound and saw it as another step forward. But his ability to protect his protégés from record-label politics was eroding as corporate interests began to supersede artistic concerns. The approval of an experienced talent scout no longer carried as much weight in Warner's corporate corridors. "In the past you'd always be proud to have great artists that were kind of midlevel sellers," McEwen says. "But that day was coming to an end because it became all or nothing, not just at Warners but throughout the music industry."

By the time *Summerteeth* was released in March 1999, a disillusioned McEwen had already left the label, costing Wilco one of its staunchest allies.

It was the end of a decade in which Warner Brothers slowly scuttled its reputation as the most artist-friendly of all the major record labels. It had forged its reputation by installing music-savvy connoisseurs in key positions and since the 1960s nurturing the careers of artists such as Neil Young, Joni Mitchell, Van Morrison, Ry Cooder, Van Dyke Parks, Bonnie Raitt, and Randy Newman. The philosophy had been to develop career artists rather than quick-hitting wonders and to stick with them through even poor-selling albums in the belief that over the long haul the artist and the label would both benefit.

But that philosophy began to crumble when Time Inc. and Warner Brothers Inc. consolidated their empires in 1989, among the first in a wave of corporate mergers that would transform the entertainment business as the millennium approached. The first sign of rupture occurred in 1992, when, rather than support Ice-T in the outcry over the protest song "Cop Killer," recorded by the rapper's death-metal band, Body Count, Time Warner caved in to public pressure and pulled the song off Body Count's self-titled debut album. Ice-T was Wall Street's idea of a nightmare: an articulate and outspoken black man from the inner city exercising his free-speech rights at a corporation that also housed middle-American institutions such as *Time* magazine. Later Ice-T would be cut loose from his contract, and the rapper's recording career never recovered.

The man who signed Body Count, Howie Klein, was president of Wilco's label, Reprise, when *Summerteeth* was released. "We were supposed to be there for the artists, not for fucking Wall Street," Klein says. "But there was pressure from the corporation to get rid of the problem. After Ice-T was let go, Warner Brothers was never the same."

Money had always been the driving force in the music industry, but now the stakes were much higher; the merger had left Time Warner Inc. with a debt load of $16 billion, and it was hemorrhaging millions of dollars a day in interest payments. The pressure was on to have hits now, and anything that wasn't an instant success became expendable. It was a sign of the times: shareholders' profits and daily stock quotes meant more than artistic integrity.

The forced departure of the label's two most respected executives—Mo Ostin and Lenny Waronker—followed the Ice-T debacle. For more than two decades they had insulated the label's music-obsessed foot soldiers from corporate meddling. The company soon became a revolving door of disenchanted executives. Four chairmen drifted through Warner Bros. Records in less than two years.

Gary Briggs, a Reprise product manager at the time, describes an atmosphere of paranoia in the company's Burbank, California, offices: "There were twenty-year executives who were starting to panic. 'Oh, my God, I'm gonna lose my gated-community house, my BMW, my expense account, my stock options.' Everyone in the upper echelon of the company no longer felt safe, which caused more pressure to show results and to deliver hits. Without hits, none of us had job security."

"Every day the corporation became more and more powerful inside of the company, and suddenly our focus no longer became the artists, the consumers, or even the employees," Howie Klein says. "It became the fucking Wall Street analysts."

Like Joe McEwen and many other old-school Warner executives, Klein was a music man above all. A 1960s radical who had booked the Who, Jimi Hendrix, and Pink Floyd in their infancy while attending the State University of New York at Stony Brook, he went on to deejay at a progressive-rock radio station in San Francisco. There, he formed the 415 Records label and had success with several noteworthy underground acts, including Romeo Void, Pearl Harbor, and Wire Train. He kept the label afloat by paying himself a one-hundred-dollar-a-week salary.

At Reprise, Klein considered Wilco one of his cornerstone acts, a modern equivalent of the label's revered franchise players: Lou Reed, Neil Young, Joni Mitchell. They may not have had a lot of hits, but they were the type of artists who would give the label credibility in an era of now-you-see-them, now-you-don't MTV bands. Klein didn't blink when McEwen broached the idea of releasing *Being There* as a double CD, and he was content to let Wilco produce its own albums without the label's input. "The philosophy of Mo and Lenny had always been 'Do what's right for the artist and you'll end up doing what's right for yourself,' " he says. "My faith in Wilco was rewarded many times. Nobody could like *Summerteeth* more than I did. I have it in my iTunes player to this day. The songs are incredible."

Despite Klein's enthusiasm, the album got a lukewarm reception at Reprise's radio-promotion department. Though Wilco had never particularly geared its music toward pop or rock radio, in the post–Mo Ostin Warner era, executives looked everywhere for hits to fatten quarterly profit statements and please stockholders. There was less time to wait for bands to break big. And so the radio department would try to edit Wilco's singles to please programmers, lopping the fiddle off the "Casino Queen" radio single to make it less twangy or excising the horns from the radio version of "Monday" because brass sections hadn't been heard on the charts since the heyday of Blood, Sweat & Tears. Wilco played along. "Tweedy didn't agree with the changes, but, God bless him, he allowed us to circumcise his art," says Gary Briggs. Besides, as long as Warner let him make the albums he wanted to make, he had no problem with its marketing schemes for radio, a world he neither knew nor cared much about.

None of the edits made Wilco much of a presence on commercial radio, which in the Ry Cooder and Randy Newman era of Reprise wouldn't have been a major problem. The Time Warner era was a different story, however. "That's when 'artist development' as a phrase was disappearing from the record industry because the corporate takeovers were happening, the cutbacks were starting to happen, and it was all about quarterly numbers," Briggs says. "Upper management was under a lot more pressure not to be so precious about artist development. Success was no longer viewed as a long-term thing, but on a record-by-record basis."

The pressure mounted to break a hit off *Summerteeth*, to find a song that would take the album to platinum-level sales. A song in heavy rotation on commercial rock stations was still the quickest way to sell an album. Wilco would've undoubtedly benefited from a marketing strategy that played to its strengths: a strong-selling touring base, a loyal core of fans, an ability to make conceptually unified albums that held up over time. But in this more profit-conscious era at Warner, patience was in short supply, and Warner saw nothing but risk with *Summerteeth*. "There was a feeling that they'd blown it in a way," says Briggs. "It was a great record, but it was Jeff as pop genius rather than as alt-country guy. That alt-country audience accounted for 70 percent of Wilco's sales base, and it still does. But that record shut the door on the No Depression era of Wilco."

What's more, the powers that be didn't hear the proverbial "single," despite the lusher pop production.

Briggs found himself in a *Twilight Zone* episode, where he was being asked over and over again for something he couldn't possibly deliver. "The head of radio promotion came up when I first brought him the *Summerteeth* demos and said, 'Can you go back to Chicago and tell Jeff that we really need him to deliver a "One Headlight." We think Wilco could be another Wallflowers,'" Briggs recalls. "And I just said, 'What the fuck? You really want me to go back and say that to Jeff Tweedy?' I went back to Jeff, and I think he knew right then and there that no one was getting him."

But Reprise's A&R department, headed by David Kahne, was undaunted. It wanted another song. "That's a pivotal moment in the band's history," Bennett says. "The band said, 'Yes, we will do that, once and once only.' That's the only time someone made us aware of the 'overnight-success knob.' The 'instant-fame knob.' The 'Goo Goo Dolls knob.' You give us this, and we'll work the knob, they said to us. They were extremely apprehensive asking us to do this. Our response was, 'You're going to pay us to go into the studio and write, record, and play a song?' Of course, that's what we love to do! They expected us to say, 'Fuck you.' But we wanted to show that this was a cooperative venture. A lot of bands who sold as many records as we did at the time didn't even get a chance to make another record, so we figured we owed them one. But only one. Up until then, we'd pretty much been left alone. It was the first time we were forced to acknowledge that we were part of the big corporate rock world."

Tony Margherita saw it as a make-or-break moment for the band, one they couldn't let pass them by. "I felt like the record was going to fall victim to this political shit if we didn't go along," he says. "It was the lesser of two evils. I didn't think the record would be marketed in anywhere near the way we wanted it to if we didn't go along. Jeff was emotionally spent from working on this record for as long as he did. To get up and do it again was not pleasant. But the label agreed to pay a whole bunch of recoupable expenses. Basically they paid us to record one more song that they could bring to radio. We weren't going to spend our money on something we viewed as being artistically unnecessary. To us, it was a test for Reprise as much as it was for us."

It was the band's first encounter with David Kahne. The head of Reprise's A&R department had enjoyed Howie Klein's trust since the 415 Records days, when Kahne served as the label's in-house producer. Kahne had a reputation as a no-nonsense professional with a Midas touch in the studio. He had worked on hits by the Bangles, Sugar Ray, and Sublime, among others, and he was intrigued by the song Wilco had come up with: "Can't Stand It." With a little studio tweaking, it might have a shot at radio.

Gary Briggs held his breath. "Jeff got on a plane, came to L.A., went into A&M Studios to David's room, and they sat down and dissected the song and basically reconstructed a few parts," Briggs says. "The intro was different, and they cut out a big portion of the bridge and added some elements, like the bells. Between the two of them they reconstructed the song within a day, and the end result is what you hear on the album. I was a nervous wreck putting the two of them in the studio together because David's this nerdy, well-schooled producer guy; he looks like he could be a fuckin' librarian, you know, and putting Jeff Tweedy in the same room as the librarian always really scared me. But they started talking music, and a mutual respect developed."

David Kahne was pleased, in a reserved sort of way. "Jeff told me he liked what we came up with," he says. "It was good, it was pleasant working with him."

Jeff Tweedy tried to be a good sport about a process he openly loathed, but was willing to try—once. "Impressive skills were being displayed," he says, "but with scientific detachment. Working with David Kahne was like going to the dentist."

"It was a really tight, professional, meticulous mix," says Jay Bennett. "[Kahne] created the hook with the response vocal. It

took what Jeff and I did, and improved it. It is better than the original in all ways: melody, fidelity, arrangement. Jeff felt the same
way, otherwise it never would've gotten on the record."

By all accounts within the Reprise hierarchy, Wilco sucked up
its pride and delivered the goods with "Can't Stand It." With its
bright guitar riff and jaunty rhythm, embellished by tubular bells,
it was just enough of a departure from Wilco's previous music—a
burnished blue-eyed soul track that put a contemporary spin on
Alex Chilton's Box Tops—that it couldn't easily be dismissed by
programmers as just more of the same. With Kahne's gleaming
mix, Reprise felt confident it had a solid shot at radio play.

"David Kahne was right to ask for another song," says another
Reprise exec and Wilco ally, Bill Bentley. "I've played 'Can't Stand
It' for people who hate Wilco and they go, 'What's that?' I still
believe you could put that song out today and have a hit single."

Gary Briggs had his fingers crossed. "We thought this could be
the mass-appeal multi-format song that we never had had before,"
he says. "In other words, we thought that we would start it at
Triple-A radio, move it into rock stations, and then go mainstream.
We thought that lyrically, melodically, and groove-wise it was all
there, that the timing of the sound was right. We all thought this
was the one."

It wasn't.

"Can't Stand It" made the usual rounds at Triple-A radio in
1999, a world that Wilco had already dented with the modestly
successful "Outtasite (Outta Mind)" off *Being There*. Triple-A, or
Adult Album Alternative, is a specialized format catering to discerning listeners older than the key rock demographic, primarily
listeners between the ages of fourteen and twenty-four. It's not a
format known for breaking bands into a million-selling sales level.
For that, Reprise needed to establish "Can't Stand It" at modern-
rock stations such as KROQ in Los Angeles, WKQX in Chicago,
and WXRK in New York.

Briggs was crushed when "Can't Stand It," like all the rest of
Wilco's Reprise singles, fell short. "It went Top 5 on the Triple-A
format," he says. "It was Top 10 on the rock chart. But we just
couldn't cross it over to alternative. And the bait on the hook to
get Tony and Jeff to agree to do the remix was that we'd work it

at alternative. But it was never fully serviced to the format. There were other radio priorities at Warners at the time, bands like Green Day that already had a built-in younger alternative audience. I don't think our own radio department was convinced that Wilco was an alternative-rock band. They were still perceived as alt-country, even though this record didn't sound alt-country at all. That's when Jeff lost all respect for the A&R division of the company."

Bill Bentley couldn't blame him. "We were competing against ourselves at radio," he says, "because you have one, maybe two slots to go after, and you have to pick one band to spend the majority of the dough on—and it wasn't Wilco. I was ashamed of us, and I was ashamed of our label."

Though Reprise ended up spending about $350,000 to promote *Summerteeth*—including payments to independent radio consultants who greased the wheels at major commercial stations—it was not an extravagant marketing push by major-label standards. The five multinational corporations that dominate the music business spend easily three times as much to push acts onto the radio. For pop performers such as Jennifer Lopez or Janet Jackson, multimillion-dollar promotional campaigns are considered the norm. Bands with less built-in mass appeal have to scrape for the crumbs, and if Wilco wasn't exactly groveling, it never got to the banquet table with the label's priority acts.

Summerteeth was allowed to fade away quietly as Warner Brothers' radio and marketing departments turned their focus to other, easier-to-market bands. The album ended up selling less well than *Being There*, and it took four years to finally top 200,000 copies.

As it became clear that *Summerteeth* was becoming yesterday's news, Margherita and Klein lamented its demise. "You can't tell me that making a great record doesn't matter in the music business," Margherita said at the time, "or else I'm going to quit." Klein, who was as baffled by the failure of *Summerteeth* as Margherita was, looked glum. His response brought no argument from Wilco's manager: "I won't say it doesn't matter, but I will tell you that it doesn't matter nearly as much as it should."

The increasingly troubled relationship with Reprise Records aside, Wilco had never been more successful as a band. In many ways, the music industry—Time Warner Inc., radio programmers, marketing executives—existed in a parallel universe to the one occupied by Wilco. By 1999 the band had moved into its own recording-and-rehearsal space, a forty-four-thousand-square-foot third-floor loft on the Northwest Side of Chicago outfitted with mixing boards, guitars, keyboards, computers, phones, faxes, drums, desks, living-room furniture, a shower, and a handful of engineers and gofers. The band was earning more than $1 million on the road, and band members were pulling down salaries, plus tour bonuses, that ranged between fifty thousand and eighty thousand dollars a year. Tweedy was making substantially more from songwriting royalties, but he also diverted a percentage of that income to the other band members, whether they contributed to the songwriting or not.

With success came grumbling and jealousy. *Summerteeth* had exposed fractures in the band, with Bennett and Tweedy dominating the songwriting and recording while Coomer and Stirratt were left to wonder if they still had a role. Bob Egan's departure and

Wilco's increasingly elaborate studio creations required the addition of a multi-instrumentalist, Leroy Bach, who was brought on board for the 1998 tour following *Mermaid Avenue*. Bennett and Bach had become friends while attending the University of Illinois at Champaign during the 1980s, and Bach had gone on to play in the Chicago instrumental bands 5ive Style and Uptighty, as well as record and tour with Liz Phair. Born in Chicago in 1964, Bach was skilled at blending; with his self-effacing personality and his talent on a number of instruments, he was the ideal addition for a band that didn't need any more volatility.

Joining Wilco and feeling truly a part of it would prove entirely different matters, however. At the Guinness Fleadh in New York during the summer of 1998, the estranged *Mermaid Avenue* bedfellows—Wilco and Billy Bragg—played separate sets promoting the same album. Egan, who was touring with Bragg, ran into his successor backstage.

"Congratulations on your new position, Leroy."

"Well, nobody's really welcomed me into the band yet."

"I know exactly what you mean. So here it is," Egan said, extending a sympathetic hand. "Your official welcoming."

Just as Uncle Tupelo had been shattered by a debilitating lack of communication, Wilco was weakening under the weight of too many things left unsaid. When Stirratt called Margherita's office in early 1999 looking for information on the band's next tour, he got into a snippy conversation with the manager's new secretary. He felt like little more than a hired hand. Soon after, the bassist left New Orleans and moved to Chicago.

It was Stirratt's way of reintroducing himself to Wilco's inner circle. Though a gifted songwriter, he had landed only a single song on Wilco's albums: "It's Just That Simple," on *A.M.* In the years after, geography and unspoken frustration kept Stirratt at arm's length from Wilco's primary decision makers: Tweedy and Margherita, and, later, Bennett. In the winter of 1996, the bassist had invited Coomer, Bennett, and Max Johnston to New Orleans to write and record in a side project they dubbed Courtesy Move.

"We were realizing that (a) our names weren't on Wilco's deal with the record company and (b) the money was questionable, so fuck it, let's go record," Coomer says. "The fact that John and Jay had songs that weren't getting on Wilco records was the main impetus for it."

Courtesy Move recorded an album's worth of songs, but only one seven-inch single was ever released (several songs later surfaced on non-Wilco recordings by Bennett and Stirratt). Tony Margherita was not pleased. He told Stirratt and the others that they were undermining the "team" and that they should shelve the project until *Being There* was up and running. It was a difficult demand for them to swallow, particularly because Jeff Tweedy had been moonlighting all along in Golden Smog.

"Looking back, it wasn't politically smart on my part to do that," Stirratt says. "I invited Jeff too, but he was home with his new baby. It really alienated us from Jeff and Tony."

Stirratt never found a comfortable way to collaborate as a songwriter with Tweedy. Whereas Bennett supplied Tweedy with tapes filled with chord changes and musical beds that required a vocal melody to complete, Stirratt preferred to demo fully arranged songs suited for his voice that left little room for Tweedy's input. After *A.M.*, it took several years before Stirratt could find an outlet for his songs that wouldn't raise Tony Margherita's ire. Working in his home studio between Wilco tours and albums, Stirratt wrote, sang, recorded, and produced two lush albums of baroque pop songs under the name the Autumn Defense; he also began collaborating on folk-pop duets with his twin, Laurie Stirratt, who moved to Chicago after her marriage to Cary Hudson and their band, Blue Mountain, disintegrated. Once John Stirratt moved to Chicago, he and Tweedy rebuilt their relationship.

"I haven't struggled too much coming up with songs, but I have struggled with loving and embracing them and wanting to see them through to the end," Tweedy says. "And John's been great about pushing for stuff. If John is game for it, it's probably something that's gonna happen. If it's something that John is not that into, he'll keep his mouth shut, and it becomes apparent over time that it's not working."

For Tweedy, who has always craved the feedback of trusted listeners—the late-night phone calls to Heather Crist, the long drives with David Dethrow, the acknowledgment of Brian Henneman, the unabashed cheerleading of the Golden Smog boys—Stirratt was a vital foil. Since he wasn't involved in the songwriting process, he could be more objective about the songs. And his increasingly proficient bass playing and high harmony vocals, plus his smiling buoyancy onstage, made him a low-key constant in a band rife with more fragile or volatile temperaments.

"I certainly had plenty of songs to sustain a band," Tweedy says. "There weren't enough of John's songs, or there wasn't enough of a dialogue, to establish an equal, Uncle Tupelo–type songwriting partnership, and I don't think anyone had any illusions that that was going to be how the band would work. I wasn't willing to go back to writing half an album a year. But I definitely wanted ideas from everybody and input on my songs. Mostly what I've stressed is, do you have anything you're working on that I could be involved in shaping, or something that I could write the melody for? I'm not the greatest singer in the world, and I have to write the melody to be able to sing it."

"I never felt stymied in this band," Stirratt insists. "I was always made to feel as if my opinion counted, and that I could give it any time, and that it would make a difference in how the music was presented. Jeff may have been the primary songwriter, but he never went out of his way to separate himself from the rest of us. I think he always saw us as a unit, and encouraged us to think like one."

Still, a perception persists on fan message boards devoted to Wilco's music that Stirratt is essentially Tweedy's yes-man. Jeff Tweedy laughs. "I find it to be the opposite," he says. "The way I characterize it is I look to him for approval."

The relationship between Coomer and Tweedy was more volatile. Just as Jay Farrar had once forced Coomer to get through an Uncle Tupelo show while the drummer was suffering from food poisoning, Tweedy sadistically kept calling for encores during a Wilco show in Indianapolis while the ailing Coomer was vomiting into a bucket next to his trap kit. "Come on, I think we can get him to do one more," Tweedy announced as the audience roared and Coomer staggered to his drum stool like a sad circus act. Years later, Tweedy and Coomer got into a tiff onstage that erupted into a near fistfight. After an exchange of verbal buckshot in time-honored gangsta tradition ("Fuck you!" "No, fuck yooooooou!"), the singer dived through the trap kit, and the two combatants rolled on the stage behind the toppled drums, fists poised. No punches were thrown, and to this day Coomer doesn't know exactly what set Tweedy off: "Being on the road does strange things to people."

Yet Coomer's personality as a drummer couldn't be denied. He had a loose, laid-back feel for a groove that was derived as much from southern soul as from rock, yet he could hammer with John Bonham–like force when necessary. Not for nothing did the band frequently encore during its 1996–97 tour with Jonathan Parker wailing Led Zeppelin's "Immigrant Song" while Coomer waged war on his kick drum. The Nashville native was a natural talent, and strong-willed enough to know it. He did not want to put up with too much fussiness in the studio. If he played a part well, he saw no reason to keep plugging away at it ad nauseam, in contrast to the mad scientist Jay Bennett, who could spend the better part of a day tinkering with a rhythm track. It was an attitude perfect for *Mermaid Avenue*–style spontaneity, but it ran counter to the more studio-intensive direction of albums such as *Summerteeth*.

Coomer also filled a role as the band's goodwill ambassador, the affable bear of a man who could always be counted on to keep a backstage party rolling or to act as entertainment director on the bus or in the hotel room with his large stash of bootleg movies and comedy tapes.

Even though Bennett had emerged as Tweedy's closest collaborator in the band, he also was made to feel like he was on the outside looking in. The multi-instrumentalist's desire to produce artists outside Wilco was regarded harshly by Margherita. The manager accused Bennett of "whoring around the Wilco sound" after he produced a number of albums by singer-songwriters such as Tim Easton that used most of the band as a rhythm section. The most noxious side effect of Wilco's success was a perception within the band at its lowest moments that not all the spoils or credit were being shared equally. "There was an illusion that this was a band," Coomer says. "People would be shocked when we'd tell them that. We were hired guns, glorified sidemen."

"Mo' money, mo' problems," says Jonathan Parker, who often found himself put in the position of sounding board for the grousing band members. "The more successful the band got, the more the others felt like they were being undervalued. They'd never say anything to Jeff or Tony. I think to a large extent they realized everyone was expendable. I'd say stuff like, 'Cheer up, you're in Wilco for God's sake! It's not that bad.' "

Tweedy recognized that things were askew around the time of *Summerteeth*. "That was a period that ran smack in the face of having a band," he says. "And right or wrong, whether I was wanting to hide from the scrutiny of rabid Uncle Tupelo fans or just wasn't emotionally mature enough to want to take on the responsibility of being a band leader, but from *A.M.* on, I really depended on wanting everybody to feel like it was a band, the idea of a band, and did more and more things over time to institutionalize that feeling, like saying every song is written by Wilco, sharing publishing, doing things just to reassure everyone it's equal. Which is also unrealistic. There isn't much chance of people outside the band treating us like that. It's more about treating each other with respect, and as long as we understand that at the end of the day I'm going to bear most of the responsibility for what this is, good and bad. Democracy is a very unrealistic and difficult thing in the context of a band. It's best to hope for benign dictatorship."

Tweedy's ability to lead was impaired by his personal turmoil. On the 1999 tour of Europe, he started bottoming out. He fell off the wagon in Scotland, sharing a bottle of red wine with Jonathan Parker as he moped through a Father's Day several thousand miles from his son. Before opening for R.E.M. at a soccer stadium in Bologna, Italy, Tweedy suffered one of his worst anxiety attacks yet. "He's pale, they call the medic, they're giving him oxygen, he's shaking," Coomer says. "He's having a severe anxiety attack, bawling his eyes out. And somehow he gets it together just in time, five minutes before he has to go on."

By the time the band was back in its rehearsal loft in Chicago to record more Woody Guthrie songs for *Mermaid Avenue Volume 2*, Tweedy was guiding a band riddled with morale, health, and self-esteem problems. These sessions produced some of Wilco's finest music, but they also were in many ways a sad indication of just how dysfunctional the band had become, especially the relationship between Jeff Tweedy and Jay Bennett.

"The *Mermaid Avenue 2* loft session was the most harmful to the band," Tweedy says. "I was kind of out of it, not just because of drugs but from being morbidly depressed and sad, and, if anything, drugs were a symptom of it, wanting to find some way to be functional, not necessarily to get high. I've been a classic self-medicator my whole life. I have an enormous amount of drive to do stuff, and it's been very difficult for me to handle these dips and valleys of energy that I'm prone to, so at different points in my life I've tried different things to push me through that valley. And I feel very lucky that for some reason I've had a real self-preservation instinct, to get pretty disgusted with myself pretty quick, that once things like drugs aren't working, that it's coloring my enthusiasm for things, or coloring my ability to see things clearly and understand what's going on, I get scared, and I hate it, and I do whatever it takes to eliminate it from my life."

Tweedy struggled to pull out of his dive. As fuzzy and warm as the pills made him feel, as much relief as they were providing from the onslaught of migraines, he slowly came to grips with larger fears about dependency and the deteriorating quality of his life. In 2003 he tried a more organic approach: surgery on his septum combined with a diet free from dairy, wheat, and sugar. Though his migraines continued, the fallout was less severe.

But in late 1999, Tweedy felt as lost as he had ever been. "It created an environment where I was happy that someone was going to rally the troops or be more on top of things," he says. "I pictured that being the case in any good working band, that when someone is not quite up to par, not full of inspiration, there are people around to pick him up. I think that also can be very dangerous, because it happens in tons of relationships, where one person is happier when another person is sad, feels more useful, and doesn't see it for what it is, but allows it to inflate their sense of importance and bolsters their self-image. It's not necessarily malicious. It's the belief that people want to have that they're taking care of someone, or this recording needs to get done, and I'm gonna do it. But having someone around who believes that nothing will get done without them is pretty unhealthy. Aside from that, Jay wasn't in much better shape than I was. Long story short, Jay was happiest in the band when I was the least coherent."

Remarkably, Wilco's music making on *Mermaid Avenue Volume 2* was exceptional. Bragg had plenty of tracks left from the Dublin sessions, but Wilco insisted on returning to the Guthrie archive for fresh inspiration. "Remember the Mountain Bed," a nine-verse tone poem, comes off like an annotated, chorus-free version of "California Stars." It's a six-minute meditation on mortality, and Wilco's treatment of it is masterly. The sparse music gently drapes the narrative, with Bennett and Stirratt nearly whispering their harmonies. Tweedy's voice confides in the listener, embracing a lyric that sounds as though Guthrie were peering inside the singer's life at that moment and wishing him Godspeed:

My greeds, desires, my cravings, hopes, my dreams inside me fight
My loneliness healed, my emptiness filled, I walk above all pain
Back to the breast of my woman and child to scatter my seeds again.

"Secret of the Sea" is a Bennett pop extravaganza, a parade of guitars that shift from the Far East to George Harrison's *All Things Must Pass* to a Nashville honky-tonk in the space of two and a half minutes. The sparse reverie "Someday Some Morning Sometime" turns into a surreal dreamscape, golden particles drifting through space. The illusion is created by filtering a vibraphone through a space echo, which Tweedy and Bennett dubbed a "delayaphone." They recorded Tweedy singing over his acoustic guitar, then in the mixing phase removed the guitar from the track until the very end. The effect is ghostlike and enchanted, the remaining instruments finishing chords that are no longer audible.

In general, the two *Mermaid Avenue* albums heartened those listeners who felt Wilco was pulling away from the rootsier sound of *A.M.* and Uncle Tupelo. "We thought it was the record that sounded the most like what we imagined people think we sound like," Tweedy says with a laugh.

He knew the next Wilco album would be vastly different. "Someday Some Morning Sometime" held the key, Jeff Tweedy says: "To me that recording was a piece of the puzzle that led to *Yankee Hotel Foxtrot.*"

CHAPTER 15

O n May 14, 2000, Jeff Tweedy stepped onstage for the first time with the two people who would most influence his music for the next four years. Neither of them happened to be in Wilco.

Tweedy had spent the previous winter driving around with Jim O'Rourke, long before he got to know him personally. Sharing a house with two children and a wife whose office hours were diametrically opposed to his nocturnal lifestyle, Tweedy did most of his listening in his car, cruising the winter streets with cigarette smoke leaking through a crack in the driver's side window, an unfastened seat belt, and a nonstop parade of newly discovered music oozing from the tinny speakers. Just as he had once whiled away his nights back in Belleville immersed in the new worlds created by P.I.L.'s *Flowers of Romance* or Black Flag's *Damaged*, Tweedy could drive in circles for hours if properly transported by the CD spinning in his dashboard. When O'Rourke's 1997 solo album, *Bad Timing*, found its way into his drive-around collection, it never left.

"It ended up blowing my mind more than just about any record I'd heard in the last five years," Tweedy says.

Bad Timing consisted of four epic instrumentals blending O'Rourke's guitar fingerpicking with orchestrations for horns and strings. It sounded worlds away from the type of music Tweedy had been presenting to the public since the first Uncle Tupelo album. But Jim O'Rourke was the type of artist Tweedy always admired, the type of artist he longed to be: not easily categorized, free to discombobulate, delight, and surprise as he moved with stealthy purpose between seemingly disconnected musical worlds.

By the time Tweedy got to know him, O'Rourke had participated in the making of two hundred albums, encompassing everything from a limited-edition self-released CD of "solo electronics" to collaborations with the legendary New York City noise-rock avatars Sonic Youth, a band he eventually joined full-time. Born in 1969 in Chicago, O'Rourke played jazz in high school and studied composition at DePaul University. When a teenager, he was already collaborating with the British avant-guitar maestro Derek Bailey and has since worked with a Who's Who of the world's most renowned underground musical innovators and improvisers: Japan's K. K. Null, Sweden's Mats Gustafsson, the Red Krayola's Mayo Thompson. His own recordings, both as a solo artist and with bands such as Gastr del Sol and Brise-Glace, are notable for the way they merge a bewildering and seemingly incompatible array of influences: the orchestrations of Jack Nitzsche, Van Dyke Parks, and Charles Ives; the fingerpicking of John Fahey; the atmospheric drones of Tony Conrad; the wickedly dark comedic lyricism of Sparks.

If there's a unifying thread, it's that O'Rourke is less interested in reinforcing established strengths than in taking himself—and the artists he works with—out of their comfort zones. He's aborted a number of his own finished albums because he deemed them too similar to his previous releases. His preferred mode of artistic expression is confrontation; he once showed up at a punk concert in Chicago in the guise of a surly, chain-smoking clown. "I'm shy, but I'm not afraid to look stupid," he says. "I'm more interested in making people confused. That's a better forum for thinking about things, because if you don't confuse people, they just go on to the next thing."

It was an attitude to which the audience-baiting Jeff Tweedy of Shepherd's Bush Empire 1997 could relate. Tweedy also had a background in experimental music, though it was better concealed, emerging only sporadically in the more obtuse passages of songs such as "Sunken Treasure" and "If That's Alright." While skipping classes at Southern Illinois University Edwardsville, he'd park himself in the library and check out John Cage and Karlheinz Stockhausen records. During his pre-Tupelo days in Belleville, he hung out with a couple of would-be industrial noise rockers in love with feedback and oscillators, a midwestern response to the British extremists Throbbing Gristle. Their band, Un-Film, shared a 1988 compilation of experimental music with one of O'Rourke's early bands, Illusion of Safety, among others.

O'Rourke had spent considerable time slumming in the singer-songwriter world between laptop-guitar concerts and computer manipulations. Collaborating with Edith Frost, Chris Connelly, the Aluminum Group, and other artists, he demonstrated an ability to illuminate and dramatize the elegance of their songs as a musician and producer.

When Tweedy was invited to play at the Noise Pop festival in Chicago with a collaborator of his choosing in May 2000, he had no idea if O'Rourke had even heard any of his music, but he knew he wanted to collaborate with him. The festival promoter had suggested a more obvious pairing, with the Mekons' Jon Langford or Sally Timms, artists who were steeped in the same punk-folk singer-songwriter tradition. "I know those people and like them, but it seemed to me that it would be pretty understandable," Tweedy says. Instead, he had the promoter contact O'Rourke.

"I was shocked he wanted to play with me," O'Rourke says. "I had liked *Summerteeth* quite a bit. I appreciated *A.M.* and *Being There* for what they were, but they were less to my taste: there were too many 'tasty licks.' People filling up the space with constant musical commentary instead of letting the songs breathe. But with *Summerteeth* I saw the instruments being used more as a part of a larger arrangement, and there was an interesting mishmash of styles going on in the songwriting."

O'Rourke had done his homework before he met Tweedy. "I knew Jeff had been in a noise band way back when," he says. "I knew he came from a similar background, but I didn't realize he'd retained those interests. When we met, he didn't realize that I'd been paying attention to singer-songwriter music. We surprised each other."

When they met at O'Rourke's apartment a few days before Noise Pop, they didn't play at first. Instead, they listened to vinyl records on a turntable: the British folk rockers Roy Harper and the Trees, the minimalist composers Arnold Dreyblatt and Phil Niblock, the glam rocker T. Rex. That got the juices flowing, and they began improvising chord changes for new songs. It felt good, and they agreed to meet again the next night at the Wilco loft. O'Rourke asked if he could invite a friend, a drummer named Glenn Kotche.

Kotche, born in 1970 in Chicago, had been playing in bands since junior high school and had studied percussion at the University of Kentucky in Lexington. There he hooked up with the masterful singer-songwriter Paul K. and recorded an album, *Love Is a Gas*, with K.'s band, the Weathermen. It was produced by the Velvet Underground's Maureen Tucker, whose thundering tribal sound jolted rock drumming in the 1960s. Though Kotche had played in high-school orchestras and drum ensembles, Tucker showed him how to develop and orchestrate different drum parts across the entire width of a rock tune. Kotche continued with that approach when he returned in 1997 to Chicago, where he quickly developed a reputation as a drummer who set aside his ego to serve the song and the person singing it.

"All my training had pointed me to think about the whole song rather than my individual contribution," Kotche says. "Trying to assimilate what each situation needed, and coming up with parts that would serve the overall goal rather than trying to put my stamp as a drummer on there."

Backing the singer-songwriter Edith Frost one night at Lounge Ax, Kotche found himself sharing a stage with O'Rourke, who was sitting in—a common occurrence at the Lincoln Avenue club, which had become a rec room of sorts for Chicago's underground music community. "He had this tiny set—a floor tom, a hi-hat, and a snare—and he was just able to do so much musical stuff with it, paying so much attention to the space and color in the song," O'Rourke says. "It was blowing my mind." Kotche would frequently augment his kit with welded homemade sculptures; like jazz drummers, he used his kit not just to play with rhythm but to embellish melody and deepen harmony. O'Rourke was soon calling Kotche to join him for every recording session requiring a drummer.

Darin Gray, Tweedy's old friend from Edwardsville, Illinois, met O'Rourke in the early 1990s at Lounge Ax when Gray's band, the Dazzling Killmen, shared a bill one night with O'Rourke. They bonded over their mutual appreciation of obscure avant-garde musicians and immediately vowed to play together. They formed the improvisational noise combo Brise-Glace and have continued to collaborate ever since. While working on O'Rourke's *Eureka* album in 1997, Gray got a firsthand look at his friend's favorite drummer.

"The thing that first struck me about Glenn was that he was the most prepared musician and person that I'd ever met," Gray says. "He'd have a clipboard with piles of notes he'd made from a tape of music Jim had given him. He would have extensive notes on a minute of O'Rourke's music, all these ideas for how he could approach it. I'd never seen a drummer do that before or since. At the same time, he had no ego about it. He was this incredibly schooled musician who could be content to play his bass drum or a shaker through an entire song, if that's what was needed to make the song work."

When the prospect of working with Tweedy emerged, O'Rourke immediately knew that Kotche should be involved. It would prove to be a galvanizing meeting for all three.

"I had my head down and felt isolated for a long time," Tweedy says. "During Uncle Tupelo, we were really vigilant guards at the gate of what was acceptable. Right or wrong, I accepted that and tried to make it work. And Wilco hasn't been so much about that, but I got it into my head that the best way to work was to not pay attention to what other people were doing. Working with Jim and Glenn really opened my eyes to something I had intuited for a long time but not honored. And that is that musicians inspire and help each other. The best thing you can do is open yourself to their inspiration and creativity and absorb and learn."

The session at the Wilco loft was so informal, the three musicians lounging on couches as they played, that any inhibitions quickly dissolved. "It was like turning on tap water," O'Rourke says. "The ideas just flowed."

Kotche, who had been used to working with O'Rourke's meticulous bar-by-bar instructions, was left free to improvise. That night the trio developed the songs that would later surface on their debut album, *Loose Fur*, released in 2003.

"On 'Laminated Cat,' a song Jeff brought in, Glenn put two drumbeats on top of each other and basically made that song," O'Rourke says. "He had a sense of arrangement, a big-picture guy, none of that—what do journalists call it?—'post-rock' playing, which really isn't about the song at all."

Tweedy jump-started lyrics by doing word exercises: writing down all the verbs that describe what a fireman does, picking out random nouns from a stray copy of *TV Guide*, and then finding new meaning in the debris of the collisions and juxtapositions. Lines such as "classical music blasting masks" and "you boil hearts and discuss birds" jumped from his lips, the disarming directness of "Screen Door" a distant speck in his rearview mirror.

"We didn't really have a group identity with the lyrics, but it was weird how they intersected," O'Rourke says. "My songs are about the sexual misadventures of decrepit people—it's an absurd way of looking at some very hurtful material. And Jeff takes the angst route. But we usually ended up with the same reading on the 'pain' meter."

Tweedy also began asserting himself as a guitarist, albeit an unconventional one. He was no Jay Bennett–style gunslinger on the instrument, and he knew it. A more than competent acoustic guitarist, Tweedy felt free to explore a more personal vocabulary on the electric guitar during the sessions with O'Rourke and Kotche. On O'Rourke's "So Long," he smeared and splattered notes as though he'd been woodshedding with the free-jazz recordings of James Blood Ulmer rather than emulating a more obvious hero like Neil Young. The solo has a weird logic all its own, as if the song's melody were being sucked backward through the arrangement before resolving. "It's like watching the end of *Zabriskie Point* in reverse," says the art-film buff O'Rourke, referring to the 1970 Michelangelo Antonioni movie, which climaxes with a surreal orgy in Death Valley. "All Jeff's previous music had led me to believe he didn't have that in him. It was stunning to hear something that developed and personal coming out of him on the guitar."

Just as Antonioni's movie polarized cinema buffs, Tweedy's Noise Pop performance rejiggered expectations about his music. Wilco fans who showed up at the Double Door on May 14 to watch Tweedy perform, perhaps hoping that he'd dust off old favorites such as "Screen Door" or "Gun," were in for a surprise. The set opened with an eleven-minute version of "Laminated Cat," which, like O'Rourke's *Bad Timing* mini-epics, sounded like it was in no hurry to go anywhere in particular. It was a radical transformation of a song, "Not for the Season," that Wilco had been working on in the studio but was never able to interpret in a way that Tweedy felt captured its original spirit. In the Wilco incarnation, "Not for the Season" sounded like an arena-rock Anthem, circa *Born in the U.S.A.* With O'Rourke and Kotche, the song began to feel like Tweedy imagined it when he wrote it, even though the trio barely had any time to rehearse. It emerged spontaneously, the three converging rather than pouncing, as if enjoying the process, the struggle, the tangents and the mistakes, every bit as much as the final destination.

It was a lesson learned from *Bad Timing*, and when Tweedy speaks of O'Rourke's solo record, at times he sounds like he's fixing his aspirations for his own music. "When I first heard *Bad Timing*, I sort of dismissed it," he says. "I thought, 'I can do this; I do this on my couch every night.' But I kept going back to it, and I started to drive around with it, and I spent a lot of time alone with it. It's not passive listening. It's pretty, and it works as background music, but to really understand it, you have to give it the attention Jim did when he was making it. And that's a lot to ask of many people. The patience of the arrangements really appealed to me, the idea that it's not about how fast you get from point A to point B, but savoring every second of the journey."

"So Long" came next in the set, with Tweedy's guitar splattering notes and Kotche dropping out as a timekeeper to add new scenery every step of the way on a menagerie of percussion. There were noisy rave-ups on Cyril Tawney's English folk ballad "Sally Free and Easy" and T. Rex's "A Beard of Stars." Even the most straightforward performance—a cover of Utah Phillips's murder ballad "Rock Salt and Nails"—proved too extreme, at least for Natalie Merchant. The singer was in town after touring with Wilco and offered to join the boys onstage. But she bailed out when she was offered a song about a husband's violent solution to his wife's infidelity. Tweedy sang it instead.

The performance was far short of brilliant, the impromptu band meandering as much as it cohered. But through the uncertainty Tweedy could feel a door opening. New insights into the process of making music flashed, and the singer came off the stage buzzing with certitude. He'd been reinspired working with O'Rourke and Kotche, and he didn't want to lose the feeling. The three would clear their schedules to record an album, fleshing out the song skeletons they rattled at the Noise Pop festival and adding a few more originals. The trio didn't even have a name yet—they eventually settled on "Loose Fur"—and the six-song album they recorded through the summer of 2000 would not officially surface for another two and a half years, but it laid the groundwork for the next phase of Wilco. The studio recording finds the drummer concerned less with traditional notions of timekeeping than with providing an orchestral backdrop for the singers; guitars that flit between atonality and fingerpicked fragility; and shape-shifting arrangements that bridge pop and noise, rock and trance. The music encompasses folkish gentility ("Chinese Apple"), free-form guitar ("So Long"), and rustic meditations that mutate into feedback-saturated chaos ("Liquidation Totale"). That same year, Tweedy also enlisted Kotche to help record the drifting instrumentals for the soundtrack to the movie *Chelsea Walls*.

Sue Miller noticed a profound change in her husband, especially after he met Kotche. Jeff was feeling healthier than he had in years, and he had discovered a new collaborator, a kindred spirit. "He was getting openly excited about things, which he never does," Miller says. "It started with Glenn, the dynamic between him and Glenn. Everything was Glenn, Glenn, Glenn. He was in love with him. And he was in love with the music they were making."

Kotche's personality was closely aligned with Tweedy's: he was easy company, soft-spoken, smart, and keen to shake himself loose from clichés. His attitude was the polar opposite of "I do what I do," Max Johnston's lament in the difficult days before he parted ways with Wilco. Kotche was willing to try just about anything musically and had the chops and smarts to pull it off.

"When Jim and I got together, I felt like we could do no wrong with Glenn," Tweedy says. "He was bringing unbelievable sensitivity and musicality to what we were doing. He was listening to everything we were doing, responding to it, and lifting it beyond. He was steering the ship in many ways. It was exciting because it didn't feel like there was any ownership of ideas. No one could tell where the ideas were coming from. I felt I had been in tune with improvised performing for a long time, because that's how I write. I make songs up. I would turn off my mind and play with the tape recorder rolling. But to play improvised music with other people, I never felt good enough. So it was cool to be playing that kind of music with a world-class guitar player who was actually encouraging me to play guitar, and this incredible drummer. I immediately wanted Wilco to feel like that experience."

In the band's loft studio, Wilco was struggling through the early stages of the album that would become *Yankee Hotel Foxtrot*. The quintet capped off the year with a string of midwestern shows, culminating at the sold-out twenty-two-hundred-seat Riviera in Chicago on November 22, 2000. It was in many ways a typical tour ender: loud, brash, a bit sloppy. Competent but perfunctory— a letdown from past Thanksgiving-weekend blowouts that was imperceptible to the fans, perhaps, but apparent within the band. The show exposed a group that had become too comfortable with its sound, pleasing the fans while spinning its wheels.

"There was almost like a revue quality to the shows: a big band, bombastic," Stirratt says. "I can understand something needing a change after that."

"We got used to painting with broader strokes," Tweedy says. "Not just because we were playing bigger places, but our work ethic wasn't geared toward practice. All the time and energy was going into making records, because practice wasn't much fun. There wasn't much room for flexibility, because we were becoming a loud rock band and we had given up on subtlety."

By December, Wilco had accumulated more than enough songs to turn in an album. But Tweedy wasn't satisfied. The new music felt nothing like what he'd been making with Loose Fur; the songs were there, but their emotional center remained out of reach. Tweedy couldn't put his finger on why, though he had a few notions.

On December 17, he was to play a solo concert at the Abbey Pub, only a few blocks from his house in Chicago. Kotche showed up about forty-five minutes before the concert with his wife, Miiri Shin, and his sister-in-law to watch his friend play, only to be summoned backstage.

Kotche returned to inform his companions that he wouldn't be able to sit with them.

"Where are you going to be?" his wife asked.

"Onstage."

"I got in Jeff's car, drove back to the Wilco loft, and grabbed a couple of drum pieces," Kotche says. "I played blind on a lot of the stuff, feeling my way through songs I'd only heard, but never played."

"This is Glenn," Tweedy announced to a capacity audience surprised to find another musician onstage. "He wanted to be on the guest list, and he had to pay for it."

The experience wasn't much different from the one Kotche and Tweedy had when they first met seven months earlier and immediately started improvising songs. They turned on the faucet again, and the music flowed. With his light strokes and brushes, Kotche swathed Tweedy's songs in subtlety and shade. The singer spent most of the night smiling and bantering good-naturedly with the audience between songs, a twenty-three-song set that ranged back to his Uncle Tupelo–era cover of the mountain-soul traditional "Satan, Your Kingdom Must Come Down" through songs so fresh they hadn't been released yet. Among them was "Heavy Metal Drummer."

"She fell in love with the drummer, she fell in love with the drummer, she fell in love," he sang.

Jeff Tweedy could relate.

CHAPTER 16

"IT WAS A TRAUMATIC YEAR"

Ken Coomer, a gifted drummer with a big heart and little patience for replaying his parts in the studio, was not particularly cut out for the new Wilco. As *Summerteeth* gave way to *Yankee Hotel Foxtrot*, the quintet tended to construct and then deconstruct tracks, looking for new angles of attack. The bash-'em-out days of *A.M.* were long gone. With its own studio space, the band could create and tinker with tracks at its leisure, and the band's most studio-savvy member—Jay Bennett—began outfitting the space with keyboards and recording equipment. The quintet experimented with multiple takes and varied approaches to each song; it was not unusual to hear as many as ten distinct versions of a track, each of them with at least some merit. Bennett, with his microscopic attention to sonic detail and technical expertise, thrived in this world. And Jeff Tweedy, who wasn't interested in retracing his steps, welcomed the possibilities it opened up for his songs.

By December 2000, Wilco had worked out more than enough songs for a new studio album, and had it been released at that point, it's difficult to imagine anyone—Wilco's fans and quite possibly even their record company and rock radio stations—com-

plaining, if only because the music so readily lived up to expectations. "Magazine Called Sunset" was a sighing, up-tempo piece of
orchestral pop that compressed the lush *Summerteeth* sound into
two and a half minutes. "Kamera" came on like a Phil Spector
anthem, with Coomer's thunderous "Be My Baby" accents. "Not
for the Season" surged into bombastic Springsteen territory;
"Alone" shimmied with the sly charm of Doug Sahm, complete
with touches of rinky-dink organ, à la the Sir Douglas Quintet's
Augie Meyers; and "Nothing up My Sleeve," with its offhand
whistling and gruff harmonies, found Tweedy and Bennett playing
John Lennon and Paul McCartney in folk-rock mode, circa the
Beatles' "Two of Us."

But Tweedy felt underwhelmed. He knew he'd already covered this ground. The new album felt less like a step forward than
a hybrid of *Being There*, with its sprawling, name-the-influence
rock moves, and *Summerteeth*, with its more elaborately produced
pop songs. Several songs that he considered crucial to the new
album—"I Am Trying to Break Your Heart," "Reservations,"
"Ashes of American Flags"—still weren't in shape, despite numerous attempts to find suitable arrangements.

Outside the Wilco loft, Tweedy had found a musical and personal confidant in Glenn Kotche. As the year wound down and the
Foxtrot sessions dragged on, a decision dawned that would be drastic in its scope, dramatic in its timing, and downright inexcusable
in its execution.

Tweedy initially entertained the idea of bringing Kotche into
the Wilco fold as a temporary sideman to add percussion but soon
thought better of it. "Playing solo shows, playing with Glenn, playing in Loose Fur made me realize how important it was to have
Wilco feel like those experiences," Tweedy says. "I played this
whole show in December with a drummer who theoretically
didn't know any of the material, and it felt more fluid and exciting
than 90 percent of the shows I'd done in the last three or four
years. That was too much information to ignore. I became more
certain that this is how music is supposed to feel, and I got braver
about doing something about it."

But Tweedy's bravery stopped when it came to picking up the
phone.

A few days before recording was to resume in January 2001, Tony Margherita called Coomer at his Nashville home and told him not to bother boarding a plane to Chicago. He was out of the band, to be replaced by Glenn Kotche.

Margherita didn't have much to say: "We need to make a change. Jeff doesn't feel like it's working out."

"So why doesn't Jeff call me?"

"He's going to."

Coomer unraveled, overcome by tears of betrayal. "Looking back, I was in slight shock," he says. "Eight years ended in one fifteen-minute phone call. It was like being evicted from your family. I thought it was very bush-league and chickenshit for Jeff not to call. If you want to make a change, that's his prerogative, but be man enough to tell me why to my face. I can face myself in the mirror every day and know I didn't sell anyone out in that group."

The drummer is still dumbfounded that his eight years playing alongside Tweedy had been swept aside without so much as a warning shot. "No one expressed any dissatisfaction to me until Tony's phone call," he says. "There was some issue made that I wasn't living in Chicago. But I pulled Tony aside numerous times, saying, do I need to relocate? I told him I'd rather not, but for the good of the band I would. And he says, 'Your Southwest Airlines ticket is sixty bucks from Nashville. Don't worry about it.' So I took him at face value. And John moved to Chicago to become more a part of it, but he was not any more involved in the song-writing than he had been."

Coomer had his tiffs with Tweedy over the years, and he'd butted heads with Margherita many times about what he felt was a lack of respect and financial compensation for the non-Tweedy majority in the band. But, more crucial, it was becoming increasingly apparent that Coomer and Tweedy were outgrowing each other, Jonathan Parker says. "Coomer's specialty was not playing the same part twice," says Parker, who had become the band's stage manager. "Often they'd do the same song twice in a row in the loft, and Coomer would do something completely different each time. And Jeff couldn't ask him to do the same thing twice without getting a lot of attitude. Jeff would say, 'That's not the same kick-drum pattern that you had on the last take,' and all you'd hear is sticks flying across the drum booth and Ken saying, 'I'm a fuckin' drummer! Do you want to come in here and try to do any better?' I think Coomer is stupid if he didn't see it coming."

"I was prepared for him to hate me and to hate the band," Tweedy says. "But at a certain point he stopped listening to the songs, and Glenn is completely tuned in to the nuances of the songs. It would be lying to Ken to pretend it's right anymore. I made a decision to honor inspiration as opposed to honoring loyalty to a friend. It was about loyalty to the music and to the band, and making the band better. It's not that Ken wasn't a good drummer. But he wasn't the right drummer anymore."

Tweedy has one regret: "I should have called him. But at the time, I felt it was a band decision, and that Tony should call him first, and all of us would follow up with calls. By the time I did make the call, I don't think he wanted to talk to me."

It was a harbinger of things to come. Over the next year, Tweedy would be faced with several major decisions about his band and music that would require decisive action. As he came to each crossroad, he became more sure of himself. "He is not the most assertive person in the world," Sue Miller says. "He can't even order a damn pizza. I have to. He's one of *those* guys. But when it comes to his music, he got more assertive about everything. He handled the Ken situation really badly. Jeff feels terrible about it, and I feel terrible about it. But it's a decision where I think he finally accepted that he was the leader of the band, and that he needed to do something for the good of the music that was really hard for him to do on a personal level."

For Jonathan Parker, the Coomer firing was a wake-up call. "Jeff's a little boy at heart," he says. "There's an innocence there that enables him to write these beautiful songs. But there were a few things like the Coomer firing that made me think, 'You have no compassion.' Between him and Tony, they could be very decisive in letting people go without any notice. Tony's attitude was like, 'You're lucky to be working for us. Tweedy's your meal ticket.' Tony would say stuff to me like, 'Pretty soon it's just gonna be you and Jeff up here.' A few of the guys in the band would joke that the management motto was 'We'll burn that bridge when we get to it.' It's going to come back and bite them in the ass someday."

John Stirratt called Coomer the day after the drummer was fired. "That was definitely a big moment: Do you go with loyalty, or do you go with making a better record?" Stirratt says. "Jeff told me he just didn't think he could get his ideas across to him any-more, that there wasn't any sort of higher unspoken communica-tion with Ken anymore, that everything had become a struggle. I understood that coming from a songwriter, but being complicit in that, I still have major regrets about how it went down." Leroy Bach wrote Coomer a letter, which the drummer still cherishes. Tweedy left a voicemail message a couple weeks later that Coomer never bothered to return.

"I played with people who were my friends practically all my life," Jeff Tweedy says. "It's a really hard thing to do, keeping that together. We all grew up on this myth of the Beatles—a utopian vision of a rock band. But even those guys beat the shit out of each other over what they played. They had George Martin to steer the ship. I'm sure Ringo Starr and George Harrison didn't feel all that connected at times. There was dissatisfaction, and the competition between Paul and John. It was all in service of music."

Bennett agreed. He'd grumbled about the rhythm section since *Summerteeth*, when he usurped some of Coomer's parts, as well as Stirratt's. Of all the band members, the bassist was the most trou-bled about the drummer's dismissal. He'd played with Coomer since the Uncle Tupelo days, and he felt he could be next on the chopping block. "Jay was the first guy to introduce politics into the whole situation," Stirratt says. "He was a big part of getting rid of Ken. He wanted me out of the band, right toward the end of *Sum-merteeth*. I think Jay started seeing the band as just him and Jeff, and everybody else as pretty much disposable."

"Some of the songs we were having trouble nailing with Ken," Bennett says. "The songs were ones that I had a hand in writing: 'Kamera,' 'Poor Places,' 'Ashes of American Flags,' 'Radio Cure.' We're talking about the heart of the record, the emotional center of the record. Ken was headstrong. He was also enthusiastic, and at the end of just about every Wilco track ever made, you could hear him saying, 'Oh, man, that's the one.' But we weren't like that anymore as a band. We were like, 'It might be the one. Let's try it a different way.' He lost his patience for that. A lot of those songs could have gone many different ways, but Ken over time decided he could only take them one way. That played into my motivation of going along with Jeff. I didn't want to see a bunch of the songs I'd written with Jeff go down the tubes because someone is not getting with the program. I participated in the decision selfishly. I sold out Ken Coomer to get certain songs on the album. With hindsight, I shouldn't have done that. I was being selfish."

Bennett was going through his own battles with depression, but his way of dealing with it was outwardly different from his bandmate's. Whereas Jeff Tweedy couldn't help but wear his feelings, Bennett tucked his personal turmoil inside a workaholic exterior. "Jay was running around doing everything in the studio while we were making *Yankee Hotel Foxtrot*, to the point where we were like, 'Dude, you have to pick one or two things at a time, and do those,' " Coomer says. "There was a lot of manic energy. We were all wondering, 'What's he on?' We were watching a guy burn out before our eyes."

Only months before Coomer was let go, Bennett had sought out the drummer in his hotel room on the road for a soul-baring conversation. "Out of the blue Jay pulled me aside and said he wanted to talk," Coomer says. "It was the most emotional and heartfelt conversation, I think, I ever had with anyone in the band. He was going through some stuff, and he basically told me how important I was to him. It reminded me of this bird I had for eleven years, a cockatiel, and one day he lands on my head, then jumps on my shoulder, talking to me. It was like he was seeking me out. The next day, he crawls in his cage and dies."

The issue of whether Coomer was the best drummer for Wilco came up constantly in the era of *Summerteeth* and beyond. "Jeff's sense of loyalty overwhelmed his sense of the music having to be perfect and to his liking for a long time," Bennett says. "But when he met Glenn, that changed."

Kotche found himself dropped into a beehive of anxiety. Not only did he have to deal with a roomful of new bandmates who had just been rocked by the departure of a friend; he and the band also had to put on their game faces for a camera crew beginning work on a Wilco documentary.

"I walked into the loft and Jeff pulls me aside and says, 'Ken's out of the band,' " the filmmaker Sam Jones recalls. "I look around and you could feel this air of depression hanging over the place. And I'm thinking, 'What did I get myself into?' "

Jones, a Los Angeles magazine photographer, approached Wilco about documenting the creation of an album in the mold of François Girard's *Thirty-two Short Films About Glenn Gould* or Jean-Luc Godard's *Sympathy for the Devil*. Jones also is a music buff and Wilco fanatic, and a songwriter and musician in his own right. He flew to Chicago in the fall of 2000, and he and Tweedy broke the ice by talking music until closing time at an Italian restaurant. Jones was in, almost over his head. By the time he completed his documentary, *I Am Trying to Break Your Heart*, released in the summer of 2002, he had captured one of the most compelling insider views of music making on film since the Beatles' star-crossed *Let It Be*.

Jones could not have dreamed he'd be documenting a story with this many plot twists. Tony Margherita offers a Cliff's Notes summary: "Two major departures in the band, problematic making of the record, problematic reception from the label, and then no record deal. It was a traumatic year."

It started with Kotche taking Ken Coomer's place while Jones's cameras rolled. "It was dreadful putting Glenn in that situation," Stirratt says. "But he was so prepared it was really easy for us to play with him from the first day. He was a little tighter drummer than Ken, and it took the pressure off pretty quickly. Like, hey, this isn't going to be so bad."

For Tweedy, the most troublesome song had been "I Am Trying to Break Your Heart." It contained only three chords and went through five verses before reaching anything resembling a chorus. But the singer considered the words crucial to mapping out the themes he had envisioned for the album. The musical backdrops devised during the Coomer era struck him as repetitive and static. Before he officially invited Kotche into the band, Tweedy had huddled with the drummer at the Wilco loft, where they listened to one of the singer's favorite albums, P.I.L.'s *Flowers of Romance*. It's essentially an extended dialogue between John Lydon's hectoring voice and Martin Atkins's dry, devastating drumming, a stunning example of a rock percussionist not just pounding out a groove but actually shadowing, enhancing, and sometimes stalking the vocal and shaping the song.

An inspired Kotche jumped off the couch and behind the drum kit. "I just started laying down patterns that I thought would work for the song," he says, "and Jeff was listening. 'Try that. That's it.'" Kotche turned the song into a percussion tour de force, devising two separate but complementary rhythm lines on a trap kit and a set of hubcaps, and then embellishing them by running handheld electric fans across piano strings, tapping away on floor tiles, and pounding crotales (tuned metal discs with a distinctive bell-like sound). It offered myriad options for the final mix of the song, a tapestry of percussion that could be woven in and out of the arrangement.

Kotche injected the rest of the album with fresh ideas as well. He transformed "Kamera" with a small, tight groove that could've been lifted off an early-1980s Prince album, locking in behind Tweedy's conversational vocal in a way that a half-dozen earlier incarnations of the song couldn't. For "Radio Cure," Kotche created a steady pulse on a Turkish hand drum and then a faster tempo on a brush-stroked snare, which were then run through a gauntlet of effects until they morphed into what sounds like a keyboard or a treated guitar. The drumming became a sonic illustration of a lyric about disintegration.

Within a month of Kotche's arrival, *Yankee Hotel Foxtrot* was no longer treading water, and the band could see the end in sight. "Glenn made the songs happen," Bennett says. "He could do what was asked of him and brought good ideas to the table. He's an extramusical drummer—not more or less talented than Ken, but certainly different in the kinds of things he was able to bring to the songs. After that, no one could curse Jeff for sponsoring this great musician into the band. It was the right decision."

Tweedy was beaming in Wilco's loft as he played with the album's final sequence. *Yankee Hotel Foxtrot* had shifted from a big rock-pop extravaganza into something more esoteric, atmospheric, and emotional. Its foundation consisted of three songs, placed at the beginning, middle, and end: "I Am Trying to Break Your Heart," "Ashes of American Flags," and "Reservations."

It was as personal an album as Tweedy had ever written, but its imagery was more poetic and evocative than that on his previous albums, blending the me-you directness that had informed his lyrics through *Summerteeth* with surreal wordplay. It was a record influenced by sound as much as text; Tweedy had been driving around with the shortwave-radio transmissions collected on the *Conet Project* box set for years, subjecting friends trapped in his car to the sound of anonymous, static-encrusted voices repeating strings of numbers or phonetic letters. Tweedy heard something strangely moving in these vaguely forlorn voices, one of which gave the album its title as it intoned the words "Yankee . . . hotel . . . foxtrot."

The recordings got Tweedy thinking about geography, distance, the desire for human connection in a time glutted with media, apathy, and convenience stores. "I started writing from the viewpoint of America as this imagined space, the America that exists in everyone," Tweedy says. "There is nothing more abstract to me than the idea of a country. These solitudes exist so apart from each other in this sea of white noise and information. And the beautiful thing is they keep transmitting to each other in the hope that somebody is going to find them. And the beauty is that people still do, still find some meaning in another person, in a relationship, find some way to communicate, even though more often than not it's in a way that's not what they intended. Because some communication is better than giving up or not communicating at all."

The language of *Yankee Hotel Foxtrot* is more impressionistic than explicit, the narrator adrift in a land of false prosperity. It's the subject of the Band's second, self-titled album, the rustic Americana evoked by "Up on Cripple Creek" and "The Night They Drove Old Dixie Down," transposed to a twenty-first-century landscape of disposable Dixie cups, cash machines, and diet soft drinks. And like *The Band*, *Yankee Hotel Foxtrot* becomes a universe unto itself, immersing the listener from its opening fragmented swirl to its lingering fade nearly fifty-two minutes later.

The songs are deceptively simple, the arrangements are not. "Ashes of American Flags" began as a primitive John Lennon–like chord progression, cycling back and forth between a B and a G, but gained luster, thanks to a chance encounter with an Igor

Stravinsky recording that struck Tweedy as a perfect fit for the song's coda. Though Stravinsky's estate denied permission to sample the composition, Wilco was undeterred: Tweedy, Bennett, and company took the composer's serial music and cut it up, tromped on it, and then ran it backward through a synthesizer to create a lost-in-space fade. It's the album's most disorienting moment, and when it drops into the lap of "Heavy Metal Drummer," it's a blessed relief. The transition—backward Stravinsky, a handful of drunken piano chords, a low-fi drum machine—is a key moment in the album's story line. "Heavy Metal Drummer" arrives as a necessary reminder of what the narrator has lost, a nostalgic look back at the cover bands on St. Louis's Laclede's Landing that Tweedy once despised, now seen as a reminder of youth, bliss, innocence.

The ten-second transition from "Ashes of American Flags" into "Heavy Metal Drummer" would become a central scene in Sam Jones's documentary. Bennett had overseen the recording and engineering of the album, and now he was taking a crack at mixing it. For this crucial phase—mixing was where the final draws would be made on how the individual instruments and voices blend on the finished tracks—the band moved from the Wilco loft to a thousand-dollar-a-day studio on Chicago's Near North Side, Chicago Recording Company, the same studio where they had recorded the bulk of *Being There*. There, they had to sort through countless reels of tape and versions of each song to find a definitive take. After a year in the studio, this final push up the mountain nearly undid the band.

Jonathan Parker summoned Tweedy to the studio when Bennett and the rest of the band began butting heads over the intro to "Heavy Metal Drummer," a work stoppage that was costing the band serious money. Tensions between Bennett and the rest of the band had nowhere to go; decisions had to be made, and fast, but no one was in a giving mood. As Bennett took on more of the engineering responsibilities, in addition to co-writing some songs with Tweedy and playing a variety of guitars and keyboards throughout, there was a growing sense of separation between him and the rest of the band.

"He increasingly saw himself as the guy who came in to work

the session and call the shots, and nobody likes that, especially in a band that had been together six years at that time," Stirratt says. "He was very talented and willing to dive in, in a way that the rest of us weren't. There were racks of stuff lying around everywhere, lots of clutter, and he thrived on that personal organizational chaos. He was like a mad scientist in there, wearing the same clothes for days at a time, staying till all hours of the night working on God knows what."

Bennett does not dispute the idea that he took on too much. "I bit off more than I could chew; I wore too many hats," he says. "But I thought *Summerteeth* was missing something, so I took control of *Yankee Hotel Foxtrot* to avoid that happening again. The price I paid was in my personal relationships with the band."

The songs for *Foxtrot* had been recorded on four different tape mediums, opening up a maze of possibilities that only Bennett could readily untangle. He frequently was the first Wilco member at the studio and often the last to leave, keeping a pair of assistant engineers toiling over sonic minutiae till 4 or 5 a.m. each day. It was an exhausting schedule that left Bennett invested in the album to a degree that made the other band members shake their heads. "Jay owned all the gear, so he was the only one who could operate some of the stuff," Parker says. "He loved the fact that he was the only one who knew what version of what went where. Confusion was a Jay Bennett tactic to maintain control."

Tweedy showed up at the studio with a throbbing migraine when "Heavy Metal Drummer" was being mixed. He didn't care how the problem was solved, as long as the sound he envisioned was realized. To him, the transition into "Heavy Metal Drummer" was nearly as vital as the song itself. He didn't want to hear a mix of the song without it.

After Bennett and Tweedy bickered for a few minutes—"I don't have to understand you all the time"; "Why couldn't you just say, 'I understand what you're saying'?"—Jones's camera followed Tweedy into the bathroom at the recording studio and peered over a toilet stall as the singer vomited. He washed his face, grabbed a diet Coke to wash away the acrid taste, and returned to the studio. He tried to make peace with Bennett by slinging an arm around his bandmate's shoulder, but Bennett remained intent on getting in the last word. The sequence is discomfiting to watch, to the point where it feels choreographed. Bennett insists that Tweedy didn't throw up during the quarrel; Tweedy says he did. "I had a very bad migraine, and I probably would have wanted to throw up whether we were arguing or not," Tweedy says. "But it's not out of sequence, I guarantee you." What's indisputable is that the two erstwhile soul mates and collaborators were going in opposite directions, that their differences had become magnified in the final mixdown pressure cooker.

Tweedy has the mind of an old-school record collector, the type of listener who hears albums as a whole. "Jeff is a vinyl-record fan living in a CD age," Bennett says. "He saw records in terms of how songs were sequenced and how they fit together, whereas that didn't matter nearly as much to me."

What mattered most to Bennett were songs, particularly the songs he had a hand in writing. He felt that a number of worthy tracks got left on the cutting-room floor as Tweedy strove to build and sequence the best album rather than a collection of the most accessible songs. "It was dumbfounding to me that 'Candyfloss' almost didn't get on *Summerteeth*, and when it finally did, it was an unlisted track," Bennett says. "I was disappointed that 'Magazine Called Sunset' and 'Cars Can't Escape' weren't on *Yankee Hotel Foxtrot*. As far as I'm concerned, melody is king, and those songs are hugely melodic, hugely catchy. So you replace two songs like that with two noisy ones; it's totally understandable to me why a record label would have a problem with the final track sequence, no matter what kind of statement Jeff is trying to make. We are from two different worlds when it comes to things like that."

Tweedy was more excited about doing something fresh. He sensed that the type of album he hoped to make was within reach but that it needed a new set of ears to allow it to break free from the morass of inter-band politics that was beginning to envelop the project. Since discovering an instant camaraderie with Jim O'Rourke the previous May, Tweedy had always figured that he would call on his new friend to mix at least one track from *Yankee Hotel Foxtrot*. He saw that Bennett was burning out on the project,

and so was he. The arrangements were dense, dizzying, and daunting, like nothing Wilco had attempted before, but Tweedy realized
that the songs were getting lost in the production.

He asked O'Rourke to take a crack at "I Am Trying to Break
Your Heart," and it took O'Rourke three days to wade through
the noise to find the backbone of a song, to crack its code, but the
results blew away everyone in the band. Even Bennett was
impressed. "It was a freaky, fucked-up song, and he made sense out
of it," he says. "He did a good job."

Nonetheless, tension arose between Bennett and O'Rourke.
While O'Rourke was mixing at Soma studios in Wicker Park,
Bennett continued to create disc upon disc of musical beds that he
wanted O'Rourke to consider for the final mixes. "It was less
about being helpful and more about being paranoid—he wanted to
make sure that he would be represented on every track, regardless
of whether it was needed musically or not," O'Rourke says. "I
could understand why people close to him were getting fed up."

"You get in trouble lobbying for your parts," Kotche says,
"because you're not thinking about the song anymore."

Contrary to popular perception, O'Rourke didn't bring out
the noisier elements in *Foxtrot*; instead, he stripped away much of
the abrasiveness to bring out the melodies underneath and
heighten the drama. With "I Am Trying to Break Your Heart," he
added a few Serge Gainsbourg–like keyboard parts that gave the
song a musical spine. He then wove Kotche's five separate drum
and percussion lines through the arrangement, fading them in and
out to give the song a sense of motion that the three-chord,
chorus-free narrative couldn't have sustained on its own. Once he
got done, the song had morphed from an unfocused sound-effects
display into a coherent musical journey.

It opens with a kaleidoscope of distorted keyboards and off-
kilter percussion that suggests an early Pink Floyd track, circa *The
Piper at the Gates of Dawn*. Tweedy's voice is relaxed, almost sleepy,
as if he's continuing a conversation he began in a dream. Slowly
reality intrudes: "What was I thinking when I let go of you?" After
more than four minutes, the disparate threads of sound that shoot
through the mix are suddenly pulled together by a handful of

gospel piano chords, and the song lurking within is fully revealed, a majestic anthem pulled from chaos.

Unlike *Summerteeth*, where the production was developed to counterbalance the dire lyrics, *Yankee Hotel Foxtrot* uses the music to enhance, complement, and even comment upon the lyrics. "As a general practice, I'm always conscious what the lyrics are," O'Rourke says. "For a song to work, you have to pay attention to the plot, and everything in the mix needs to serve the song. I don't want to put things in there just because it sounds cool."

O'Rourke got the go-ahead to mix the rest of the album. He was honored to do it, but he sensed that Wilco was putting its career at risk. "I took away 80 percent of the noise on the record, which is the reverse of what people expect of me," O'Rourke says. "People are of the opinion that I make intentionally obscure records, that I ruin them. So the second Jeff asked me to mix the record, I said to him, 'I will get you dropped from your record label.'"

O'Rourke did more than just turn knobs and push fade switches on the mixing board. He added keyboards, guitar parts, and even pedal steel guitar to various tracks, with Tweedy's blessing. He also suggested a radical restructuring of "Poor Places," flipping the original verse and chorus and having Tweedy redo his vocal. Midway through the song, Wilco morphs into Loose Fur, with only Tweedy, Kotche, and O'Rourke playing on the track. Tweedy initially was upset about rewiring one of his songs but soon saw the merits of the new version. Stirratt wasn't tickled about the revamp, but he understood the motivation. The song had been the sole master Jeff Tweedy had served faithfully through his entire career, and that wasn't going to change now.

"I thought it was a great decision to bring Jim in," the bassist says. "When I go back and listen to the record before Jim got a hold of it, I realized it was *Summerteeth 2*. There were elements of it that were buried. We had a chance to make a complete departure from that, and Jim helped us do it. It was liberating to give it to someone else. It's less dense, more open, even with all the textures and sound collages."

"We were being merciless about tracks," Tweedy says. "Taking tons and tons of stuff that had been there for months, some of the things even established as a hook, and saying the song doesn't need it."

To dismiss the album, as some critics have subsequently done, as folk songs distressed by an overlay of indiscriminate noise is wrongheaded. Rarely has "noise" been so judiciously and carefully sculpted in the service of melody and narrative. That is never more apparent than on the concluding track, "Reservations," where sound actually takes over for lyrics to act as a kind of summary statement for the album. For all the sonic machinations, *Yankee Hotel Foxtrot* is about finding one's way through a world glutted with impersonal distractions, and finding one thing that matters. In "Reservations," the narrator discovers what it is: "I've got reservations about so many things, but not about you."

A celestial orchestra swathes the lyrics, then lets them drift away. The half-speed coda evolves over four luminous moments, the instrumental fade so slow and gradual that the music imperceptibly melts into the stillness. The song, the room, and the listener dissolve into silence. "The song wasn't a contender for a single or anything, I knew that," Tweedy says. "But I'd never felt so certain about anything. To me, that last section exposes what the rest of the record has been about. Whenever we'd listen to it in the loft, people would sit there listening long after the song was over. It was mood altering."

The world of *Yankee Hotel Foxtrot* was as complete as Jeff Tweedy could make it, and he didn't want anyone—least of all a record label—messing with it. All the turmoil, the messy personnel changes, the studio arguments, had led to this moment. The man who once had trouble placing a pizza order had never felt more sure about anything he'd had a hand in creating. His certainty would nearly prove to be Wilco's undoing.

CHAPTER 17

F rom a business standpoint, Wilco's timing couldn't have been worse. They finished *Yankee Hotel Foxtrot* in June 2001 and sent a copy of the CD into the black hole known as Reprise Records, at this point a virtually leaderless record company.

Reprise's parent company, Time Warner, had just entered into a $156 billion merger with America Online. Warner Brothers Records and its subsidiaries, including Reprise, were being pressured to cut costs, a mantra of the corporate consolidation era. Warner Music Group had ended 2000 with a 15.6 percent market share, down from 20 percent in the mid-1990s, and six hundred jobs were on the chopping block in 2001.

Among the employees shoved out the door at the company's Burbank, California, headquarters was CEO Russ Thyret, a thirty-year company veteran and a music fan who had fought hard and spent tens of millions of dollars to keep bands such as R.E.M. on the label. Howie Klein, the longtime president of Reprise, was offered a buyout, and he decided to jump ship rather than watch it sink. While Warner Brothers Records waited for Tom Whalley to extricate himself from a deal at Interscope to succeed Thyret, a recent acquaintance of Wilco's—David Kahne, the head of the A&R

department—reentered their lives. With Klein gone, and Whalley still months away from arriving, the fate of *Yankee Hotel Foxtrot* was in Kahne's hands. Wilco could not have picked a less advantageous time to make their boldest musical statement yet. Warner Brothers was no longer in the boldness market. Instant hits—successful formulas that could easily be deciphered and exploited by radio programmers—were the priority. Everything else was expendable.

"When downsizing a company, bodies and bands had to go," says Gary Briggs, looking back on his final months as a Reprise executive. "Everyone at Reprise was trying to create something at radio to save their asses. Everyone wanted to be a winner before the new regime walked in. For the first time in my twenty-three years at the company, I felt it was being run by fear. It had nothing to do with the quality of the music. It was about how the fuck am I going to keep my job when every day I see fifteen more people carrying their boxes out to their car?"

Tony Margherita had been sending work-in-progress CDs to the band's new A&R representative, Mio Vukovic, who'd been assigned by Kahne to handle Wilco after Joe McEwen left the label. Vukovic was not particularly a fan of Wilco's; his background had been in dance music. His primary qualification for overseeing Wilco, several Reprise staffers say, was that he wasn't busy with too many other bands so he could handle a new assignment. Unlike his relationship with McEwen, who trusted the band implicitly, Margherita knew he needed to keep Vukovic in the loop as the band recorded its new album if it was to get a fair shake at the label. Vukovic reported to Kahne, and Margherita didn't want a repeat of the *Summerteeth* we-don't-hear-the-single scenario. But the more Vukovic heard of *Yankee Hotel Foxtrot*, the less he liked. What's more, he sensed the band didn't much care for him. "Mio was having conversations with David Kahne, saying, 'These guys aren't listening to me. They aren't being receptive. They don't respect me. Everything I suggest they throw back in my face,'" Briggs says.

"Word would get back from Mio, and he'd say something like, 'You guys are just getting further and further away,'" Margherita says. "Mio had heard the original stuff cut with Ken Coomer, and then the new stuff cut with Glenn. The more we sent, the less he seemed to get it. It would take some time to get a response from him each time. At best we were getting lukewarm responses. It was getting frustrating. I would rather have them tell me they hated it, rather than this shrugging-the-shoulders bullshit. It was clear before anything went down we were gonna have problems."

The band had spent less than $200,000 recording and mixing *Yankee Hotel Foxtrot*, a pittance by major-label standards. Rather than waiting for label executives to make up their minds about the album, Tweedy and O'Rourke flew to London to oversee the mastering of the final sequence. It was the point of no return. Handing in a mastered recording to a major record label was the music-biz equivalent of throwing down the gauntlet: take it or leave it.

Wilco didn't hear back from Reprise for two weeks, an ominous sign. In the last week of June, as Reprise staffers threw a farewell bash for Howie Klein, Vukovic finally got back to Wilco and said the album needed more work before the label could even consider releasing it. But the band's hard-line tack made it instantly apparent that "more work" wasn't going to happen. As far as Wilco was concerned, the album was mastered and ready to go. Within a few days, Vukovic was calling Margherita back to discuss an exit strategy. "Maybe you should just put this record out yourself," the A&R man suggested.

Margherita's face brightened for the first time in weeks. He could finally see a way out of this mess. "I took that as a great development, not a terrible we're-getting-dropped development," he says.

Much like Jay Farrar's decision to quit Uncle Tupelo, Reprise's rejection of *Yankee Hotel Foxtrot* initially stung Jeff Tweedy. Then he began to envision the next step. When it came to music, Tweedy had a bulldog determination that was not always evident in other aspects of his life. "My feelings were hurt for a few days," the singer says, "and then I got over it."

Vukovic was essentially a messenger rather than a decision maker, shuttling between Kahne and Margherita. "He was being made the fall guy for a decision that wasn't very popular among the rank and file," one Reprise staffer said. It was Kahne, in his capacity as the vice president of A&R, who essentially washed his hands of the album, and the band. He had seen enough radio potential in *Summerteeth* to offer his services for a couple of remixes. On *Yankee Hotel Foxtrot*, he heard a dud. "I heard nothing I wanted to work on in terms of making it more accessible for radio," says Kahne.

"I listened to the whole record, and I didn't think it took a step forward or a step backward," Kahne says. "I thought the production was more abstract. It had a raw quality to it, a humor and playfulness that I found interesting. It wasn't slick, and it was very cohesive. I think it would have been offensive to Jeff if I had tried to bend a song toward radio."

Kahne took a dim view of Wilco's prospects if they put out *Yankee Hotel Foxtrot* at Reprise. "Most of the big record companies are pretty heavy radio-oriented companies now," he says. "You can make any kind of a record you want, but at the end the word 'radio' always comes up. And if you don't have a song for radio, you're in trouble."

Kahne's attitude reflected a fundamental shift in the way Warner Brothers did business. "The idea used to be to cultivate artists, even if they didn't have hits," says Bob Merlis, one of the longtime Warner executives sent packing in the consolidation era. "There was an aura at the label which brought us bands like R.E.M., who signed with us because this was the label that had Van Dyke Parks," a cult artist who had recorded with Brian Wilson. "Now the corporate environment is completely different. The attitude once was, let an artist make a great record, and we'll find a way to sell it. Now it's all about cost-per-unit-sold analysis."

The attitude at the major labels was shifting toward blockbuster hits at the expense of almost everything else. Their hand was being forced not just by corporate shareholders looking for a quick return on their investment but by a radio industry that was losing its taste for adventure. Corporate consolidation had narrowed the pipeline to radio to the point where any hint of individuality had all but been expunged from the airwaves. After the Telecommunications Act of 1996 deregulated the radio industry, Clear Channel Communications of San Antonio, Texas, went on a massive buying spree, locking up more than twelve hundred stations in major markets nationwide. The cost of doing business with radio stations had always been steep, but now it was prohibitive. Only the biggest artists could afford to play.

Record companies were funneling as much as $300 million annually to radio stations through independent promoters to gain access to programming decisions. Most labels say it takes at least $100,000 just to get a song on radio, with no assurance that it will be added to a station's regular rotation, much less become a hit. These promotional campaigns can add up quickly: it can cost a label more than $1 million in promotion costs for a major hit single, which is why the marketing expenses—including radio-promotion money—for recent multiplatinum albums by artists such as Alicia Keys and Jennifer Lopez range from $14 million to $20 million, according to industry insiders.

For a band that had never sold more than 300,000 albums domestically, such spending would have been absurd. Wilco had never been a radio-oriented rock band anyway. Now it was being told it had no other choice: give us singles, or take a hike. For Howie Klein, the way his old protégé Kahne nudged Wilco off Reprise was symptomatic of everything that was wrong with the music industry. "Mo Ostin and Lenny Waronker ran the company for decades and set the tone by hiring people who love music, because they wanted a bigger view than 'Is this a hit?' " Klein says. "We would determine that a band could go all the way, and we would support them financially and emotionally until they did. But sometimes it would take four or five albums for a band like that to make it, and we'd get constant pressure from above to drop them—'They're losing money, put your resources somewhere else.' But in those days it was easy for the talent people to force the corporate guys to back down. It's a lot less easy to do that now in the record industry. The corporate hand is so much stronger now, there is no comparison."

To Kahne, the notion that Wilco was a "heritage" band in the Warner Brothers tradition of artists such as Neil Young, R.E.M., Joni Mitchell, Van Morrison, and Randy Newman wasn't even a factor. The long-term future of the label was no longer an issue. If an album that he green-lighted failed to break at radio and sell millions, Kahne implied, he wouldn't be around long enough to profit from his allegiance to artistic integrity. "I just don't think about heritage bands," Kahne says. "I'm a producer, and I think of music song by song and band by band. Heritage band or not, it's got to be in the music. I'm just listening to see if I can add something to it, or even like it. The flavor of the record company, a lot has to do with heritage, but at the same time it's a changing company."

On his way out, Klein pleaded with Kahne to hang on to Wilco. "Artists like Jeff Tweedy are leaders, not followers," he says. "It takes years for radio and the public to catch up with them. I have a lot of faith and trust in David Kahne. He came and told me he didn't get it. He explained to me that Wilco wasn't coming up with singles and that the company was becoming so radio driven that we wouldn't be successful with them. When he told me what he wanted to do, I told him he was making a big mistake. Not just for Wilco, but for the company's sake. I thought it was a tragic loss for the company, because I remain convinced that Wilco will eventually sell lots of records, and that when they do, they'll be doing it for someone else, not us."

Klein's anachronistic views were a big reason why he shuffled off to an early retirement in his Griffith Park home in Los Angeles. He understood the fundamental contradiction that the record business had embraced, to everyone's detriment.

"The record business started out as a frontier industry, with people who loved music and saw an opportunity to make some money in a nontraditional business," says Michael Ackerman, a Los Angeles entertainment lawyer who has worked on numerous record deals for bands. "Now it's become a traditional established business, a multibillion-dollar business, so the focus is on standard business methodology: bean counting along the lines of reducing expenses, reducing staff, reducing risk. But I didn't think that's completely applicable to the music business. There are things inherent in music that don't translate to a standard business. One of them is the notion of creating art, and taking risks to create that art. You cannot sum that up in a quarterly business report."

It took a month for the paperwork to be wrapped up for Wilco's departure. Meanwhile, Warner Brothers personnel tried to salvage the rift, to no avail.

"I never said this record would end their careers, as some people claim," Kahne says. "I like Jeff and I like the band. I think the album could have come out exactly as it is on Warners or Reprise if they insisted. But it all started with a conversation with Tony about whether it was good for the band to put a record out if it wasn't going to get any support at radio."

Margherita appreciated Kahne's frankness. Without any allies in the key decision-making jobs, he sensed that Reprise would have let *Yankee Hotel Foxtrot* fade quietly and would irreparably have harmed the band's ability to make another album. Death by neglect was a scenario he could not tolerate. "I tried to tell people who were trying to persuade us to change our minds—and I got a lot of those phone calls from Warners people as the paperwork dragged on—that staying on Reprise could kill the band, that it could be the worst thing to happen to us," he says. "I told them if you really care about Wilco, then let us get the hell out of here."

Phil Quartararo, president of Warners at the time, kept checking in with Margherita to see if the company could make amends in any way. But he had little power to reverse the decision. His hands were tied until Tom Whalley moved in as CEO, still months away. Margherita asked only that Quartararo make the band's exit as quick and painless as possible. "They realized that this would be written about in a way that would not make them look good, that this was symbolic of what was wrong with the record industry, that this would be Exhibit A: 'Reprise Fucks Wilco,' " Margherita says. Wilco's lawyer, Josh Grier, had negotiated a relatively inexpensive buyout with Reprise: for fifty thousand dollars, Wilco could walk and take *Yankee Hotel Foxtrot* with it. It was an amazingly generous offer, but then Reprise went one better. "After they accepted the fifty-thousand-dollar deal, we were happy," Margherita says. "Right in the final stages of that, they called us up and said, 'How about if we give it to you for free?' The whole thing was like this insane dream."

"My sense of it was that it was such a debacle for them that it became a matter of 'What's another fifty thousand dollars?' " Grier says. "It was about let's get these guys out of here before it gets any worse. In talking to Phil Quartararo, they were trying to stop the bleeding as quickly as possible. I think they all agreed they were going to get the money sooner or later because the band's back catalog was going to continue to sell."

The oddest aspect of Reprise's purge was that Wilco hardly made a dent in the company's budget. The band was a self-sustaining success story on tour, selling out most of its shows at one-thousand-to-twenty-five-hundred-capacity theaters nationwide and pulling in annual seven-figure revenue. Its albums sold steadily if not spectacularly. In the two years after Wilco's departure, Reprise sold an additional 187,000 copies of the band's first three albums without spending a penny promoting them. "The problem with Wilco at Warners wasn't that they weren't making money; it's that they weren't making enough money," Grier says. "The problem with the industry in its current state is that a band that is profitable on a certain modest level is still not worth bothering with."

"Wilco didn't do anything wrong except be themselves. I once got sued by another label for similar reasons," Neil Young says with a laugh, referring to a lawsuit brought by David Geffen against him in the 1980s for making "unrepresentative" albums. Young won his court battle with Geffen and eventually moved back to Reprise, the label that originally signed him in the 1960s. "They're scared to get rid of me now," he says. "They know it would be a huge disaster for them if they did."

Elliot Roberts, Young's longtime manager, says Wilco "got caught in a game where thinking about the bottom line is at an all-time high and things like class or artistry really don't matter much. The people running record companies are not looking to sign a Ry Cooder or a Tom Waits or a Joni Mitchell, artists with a genuinely personal vision of how to make records. Those kinds of artists don't get record deals today. You try acting like Neil Young and they say, 'Next.' "

Despite its efforts to make amends with Wilco, Reprise got exactly what it feared: a public-relations black eye. If Kahne didn't appreciate the long-term worth of Wilco, others inside and outside the label certainly did. Journalists across the country began picking up the story after the details first surfaced in the *Chicago Tribune* on August 15, 2001.

"Ten bands have signed since Wilco dropped," Kahne insisted soon after Wilco's departure. But after Tom Whalley took over as Warner CEO, Kahne and Vukovic were cut loose. Their efforts to serve the short-term interests of Warner Brothers had backfired.

The Wilco exit gutted morale at the label. "It never should have happened," Gary Briggs says. "One of the most embarrassing moments in my career at Warner Brothers was the day they let Wilco go. It broke my heart, and it told me I no longer have a home there." Briggs left the label to work in artist management.

Warners hustled to assure their artist roster that this was not a sign of things to come. Cult bands with middling radio success such as the Flaming Lips were the beneficiaries. Much like Wilco, the Lips were a self-contained operation that Warners briefly indulged. The Lips once released a box set of four CDs, *Zaireeka*, designed to be played simultaneously on four stereo systems, and in 2003–2004 were filming a sci-fi holiday movie, *Christmas on Mars*, with Warners money at the singer Wayne Coyne's house in Oklahoma City.

"We are benefiting from the label's regret over Wilco," says Coyne, sounding very much like a kid let loose unsupervised in the corporate candy store. "We are living in the golden age of that being such a public mistake. The people on Warners said, 'We'll never have a band like Wilco feel like we don't believe in them again.' They'd tell me that it would never happen to us. And what a great day for me! Making money at the end of the day is how people at labels keep their jobs. But they realized with Wilco that keeping your job is more than that. Being part of that decision [to let Wilco go] seemed like the wrong thing to be doing, regardless of the money."

Wilco came out of the ordeal with exactly what it wanted—its album and its freedom—and when Jeff Tweedy made the rounds at music-industry executive suites in New York City in August 2001, he was being courted by thirty record labels, most of whom wanted to sign the band for hundreds of thousands of dollars in advance money and immediately release *Yankee Hotel Foxtrot* without altering a note.

David Kahne tried to put a positive spin on the development. "People are painting Warner Brothers as the evil empire in all this," he says, "but it worked out great for the band. It seems antithetical to the idea that's being circulated of the big, bad corporation screwing over the little band."

If anyone got screwed, it was Reprise. When Nonesuch

Records—another, smaller member of the same Warner Brothers empire to which Reprise belongs—finally signed Wilco in November 2001, the irony was not lost on Jeff Tweedy. He had gotten one of the biggest corporations in the world to pay for his new album twice. "It's a bit of a rock 'n' roll swindle," Tweedy says, referring to the notorious 1980 movie about another disenchanted Warner Brothers act, the Sex Pistols.

"I felt like we were robbing the bank from inside," says Tony Margherita, still amazed by the turn of events two years later, "and I was waiting for someone to kick the door down and arrest us all."

CHAPTER 18

"A CIRCLE CAN ONLY HAVE ONE CENTER"

In one of Jeff Tweedy's notebooks, the private journals where he keeps the scraps of lyrics, poems, and drawings that provide the foundation for his music, several pages are devoted to a sequence of tiny numbers, written in descending order from 1,000 to 1. The neat ballpoint figures must have taken half an hour to complete, a lasting reminder of an anxiety attack that Tweedy quelled by giving himself a homework assignment that demanded all this concentration.

Panic attacks bring on feelings of inexplicable fear of death. They sap the victim of power and courage; the heart races, the breath quickens, the head spins, the skin crawls. On a solo tour in 2001, in the weeks immediately before *Yankee Hotel Foxtrot* was mixed, Tweedy was a trembling mess backstage most nights. But he had learned how to fight back, or at least how to manage his fear in the minutes before a show. Though his anxiety could be debilitating, the attacks also heightened and sharpened his senses, made him somehow more attuned to the world outside his four walls of isolation, made him feel more connected to the people waiting to see him. On certain nights, he felt like he was in the audience, waiting for the doors to open, the anticipation rising in his chest. Onstage he could hear himself singing the words, as if the song were being shaped by someone else. The intimacy he found in that space—a space where it seemed impossible to separate singer, song, and listener—satisfied him in ways that few other experiences ever could.

When he would strum "War on War," it was as if he were talking to himself: "You have to learn how to die / If you wanna wanna be alive." The song had become a public form of meditation, a way for Tweedy to get outside himself, his self-awareness melting away. It was a feeling that he wanted to experience again and again.

"When I first heard 'War on War,' I felt that writing that song was one of the steps he took to getting through tons of turmoil," says Tweedy's longtime friend David Dethrow. "That's how you build character and endurance, by taking risks and going through a ton of garbage. In the end you come out defeated or a lot stronger. Jeff can come off as kind of quiet and passive, but he's actually a very driven person."

"It's like Jeff has a split personality, and one side takes over when he gets onstage," says Tweedy's wife, Sue Miller. "The anxiety attacks happen a lot at his solo shows, and it freaks me out sometimes. But within minutes of going onstage, it's like something takes over his body, and I can see the change."

Tweedy had been self-medicating his entire adult life. But after wearing out booze, pot, and then painkillers, he was sick of it all. He struggled to wean himself off his dependencies. His health was returning, his confidence was quietly escalating, and the possibilities in his music opened up again.

"What made Jeff get better? Feeling like shit just got to be unbearable," Miller says. "He didn't just snap his fingers, but he never went to any program. It was just willpower."

At the nadir of Tweedy's depression in 1999, Lounge Ax was on its last legs, eventually shuttering for good in January 2000. The club Miller had co-owned for more than a decade with her partner and friend, Julia Adams, found itself squeezed out of existence by a gentrifying neighborhood and a new landlord. That same year, Miller's mother died; Tweedy was called home from the road to attend the funeral, then rejoined the band the next day so as not to cancel any more dates. A few months later, Sam Tweedy was born. Sue Miller had her hands full trying to keep her home and business running. She wasn't in a position to realize that her husband's health was bottoming out. There was never a crisis moment, just a slow decline in the grip of migraines, pharmaceuticals, and depression.

The last two weeks of Lounge Ax's existence, Wilco joined a stellar lineup of independent bands in saying good-bye. The performance was a sloppy, punch-drunk funeral for a rock club, with numerous guests sitting in—the Mekons' Jon Langford, country-soul chanteuse Kelly Hogan, R.E.M.'s Scott McCaughey, even a Billy Bragg impersonator. A couple of fans elbowed their way in front of the stage and began dancing woozily to the sea-chantey rhythms of "Walt Whitman's Niece."

"We wanted to play here one last time," Tweedy told the audience, "only we didn't want to practice."

"He got pretty low down around the time Lounge Ax was closing, and I'm like an oblivious idiot because I'm going through my own problems with the club and before that with my mom," Miller says. "Now, as I look back, I see it all loud and clear, but I didn't see how bad it had become at the time. After Lounge Ax closed, Jeff really committed to getting healthy. He's been down a few times since then because of the migraines, but never as bad as it was back then. I think he realized it was just more important to be a healthy person and be a good father, a good husband, and a good band person than to be this fucked-up miserable guy."

So when Reprise flicked *Yankee Hotel Foxtrot* off its release schedule in the summer of 2001, Jeff Tweedy wasn't about to let the opinion of a record company he barely recognized anymore get the best of him. In early July, Wilco played a handful of midwestern dates to road test the new material and break in the new lineup with Glenn Kotche behind the trap kit. The Reprise rebuff was only a few days old when the band gathered for a free show before tens of thousands of fans on a sun-soaked July 4 afternoon in Chicago's Grant Park. Backstage, Tweedy casually talked about Reprise's rejection notice as though he were discussing a piece of irritating junk mail he'd just received. He was much more enthused discussing his latest obsession: the 1970s German art-rock band Neu! It was an odd way for a major-label artist to behave; but then, Jeff Tweedy never really looked at himself as a major-label artist. He viewed himself as a guy who made up songs, and it just so happened that a multinational conglomerate had thought enough of them to put them out. He felt uncertain about many things in life, but music was not one of them.

"I wasn't really worried about paying the bills, because I knew that Jeff was still writing great songs and had a great record that somebody would put out," Sue Miller says. "We had friends in Chicago on labels like Drag City and Touch and Go who would've put that album out in a second."

The band opened its Grant Park concert radiating an understated confidence, energized by the prospect of playing new songs in front of a large hometown crowd. At the morning sound check, Glenn Kotche was a bit self-conscious about a trap kit that was easily twice the size of Ken Coomer's, resembling a small aircraft carrier. "I feel like Carl Palmer up here," he said, blushing as a visitor greeted him. But Kotche's kit had nothing to do with progressive-rock bombast and everything to do with meticulous preparation. The kit was so big because every piece of equipment—from the chimes and plastic tubing to the crotales and homemade sculpture—had a job to do, a color to add that would make a specific moment in each song more vivid.

"Once we got on the road with Glenn, my appreciation for him grew," Jay Bennett says. "Whereas Ken was a great stylist, a great drummer who made music, Glenn was a great musician who happened to be a drummer."

Even though the setting was more suited for beach balls and barbecue than challenging art-rock songs, Wilco opened with a full dose of *Yankee Hotel Foxtrot*. The epic "I Am Trying to Break Your Heart" was Kotche's baptism by fire, and the drummer instantly made his impact felt, deftly shifting the sonic scenery behind every verse with an array of percussion. When Leroy Bach's gospel piano chords finally kicked in, the song surged, and the crowd began to sway. "War on War" followed, with Stirratt chopping away on a twelve-string acoustic guitar while Bach moved to bass and Bennett played keyboards. On "Airline to Heaven," one of the band's Woody Guthrie collaborations, Wilco turned into a traveling jubilee, with tambourine banging and a slide guitar whining. More new songs arrived later: the sprightly bounce of "Kamera" gave way to "Ashes of American Flags," which was sucked into the noisy undertow of Bach and Bennett's four-fisted keyboard attack. Stirratt, always the best gauge of how the music's flowing onstage, beamed his approval. A small horn section joined for "I'm the Man Who Loves You," and Tweedy handed off the guitar solo to Bennett, who hunched over his instrument and bent the strings as if to savor every note.

It was a priceless Bennett moment, one of those let-it-all-hang-out solos that had endeared him to the fans. That recklessness informed his life; he had survived no fewer than eleven car crashes virtually unscathed, yet still refused to wear a seat belt, as if to push fate as far as he could. In the studio, his energy left bandmates and engineers inhaling his fumes. At Grant Park, he was at it again, driving through a solo while ignoring the safety precautions. The fans loved it, applauding long and hard when he had finished. A few minutes later, Bennett walked offstage with a wan smile as a Wilco band member for the last time.

J eff Tweedy drove to the Wilco loft on a steamy August evening a few weeks after the Grant Park show. When Tweedy met him in the parking lot and invited him back inside, Bennett already had an inkling of what was coming.

"A circle can only have one center," Tweedy told Bennett. Even in firing one of his bandmates, Tweedy spoke in the metaphors of a songwriter. He was reclaiming his band, a band that he felt was being compromised by the man who had once been his closest collaborator.

Looking back on that conversation, Bennett now can muster at least a hint of humor. "Ah, but an ellipse has two focal points—in hindsight, that should have been my comeback," he says. "It was not an uncomfortable conversation. But it was pretty nuts-and-boltsy coming from a guy with whom I'd just written the last song on *Yankee Hotel Foxtrot* ['Jesus, etc.'] only a few weeks before. For me the big question that has never been adequately answered was, 'When did I become the guy you couldn't make music with?'

Because my last music-making experiences with the band seemed to produce some improvement. I also knew we were gonna sign a new record contract and I wasn't gonna be on it. I felt I deserved to be on that contract, but I knew Jeff would never go for that. I think Jeff knew that he couldn't sign another record contract with me in the band based on the fact that Wilco had become pretty fucking collaborative."

Yet the collaboration was irrevocably strained. "I don't think we are right to be making music together anymore," Tweedy said, and even if Bennett didn't like what he heard, he knew that the singer was coming from the heart. The dynamic in the band had shifted with Coomer's departure and Kotche's arrival. The bond that had developed between the drummer and Tweedy was undeniable; meanwhile, Bennett had distanced himself by taking on more responsibilities as an engineer during *Yankee Hotel Foxtrot*. In the studio, he acted like he saw himself no longer as an equal of the others but as Tweedy's peer. The aborted mixing session at the thousand-dollar-a-day Chicago Recording Company was the breaking point. Bennett was bickering with everyone and giving orders. It got so bad that Stirratt, Bach, and Kotche had to flee one afternoon to a nearby bar to share a drink and grouse about their increasingly aloof bandmate. In early August, everyone in the band except Bennett gathered on Tweedy's back porch and reached a unanimous decision on his ouster.

After his conversation with Tweedy, Bennett drove to his home in the Chicago suburb Arlington Heights and placed a tearful dawn phone call to his old college friend Edward Burch. He'd been writing songs with Burch sporadically for a decade, and now he needed reassurance. A few weeks later, the two songwriters were hunkering down in Bennett's basement studio, working on much of the same equipment that the former Wilco multi-instrumentalist had used to record *Summerteeth*. They would release their elaborately orchestrated folk-pop debut album, *The Palace at 4 A.M. (Part 1)*, on Undertow Music, a Chicago record label run by Bob Andrews, Uncle Tupelo's old tour manager. It shared its release date—April 23, 2002—with Wilco's *Yankee Hotel Foxtrot*. Bennett insists it was a coincidence.

In the immediate aftermath of his firing, Bennett enumerated for interviewers exactly what instruments he played on what Wilco songs and how big of a role he played in the songwriting. His role, he said, was every bit as crucial as Tweedy's in developing the band's music. In the Wilco documentary Bennett tells the director, Sam Jones, "Jeff was threatened by me, it's clear, by the attention I was starting to get."

Bennett's dismissal set off a passion-stoked debate on Wilco fan-club sites that has continued for years. Some saw it as a mistake or as a symptom of an out-of-control Tweedy ego. "I thought [Jay] was the one who brought Tweedy's visions to life," one fan declared. Wrote another, "Seems like the Tweed-meister can't work with one person for too long . . . The dictatorship reigns supreme."

As he had with Ken Coomer, Jonathan Parker saw it coming. He could side with naysayers, who saw it as the end of Wilco's golden era, but he feels Bennett left Tweedy and the band with no choice. "Personality-wise, it was the right move. Musically, I think it was a big mistake," Parker says. "The fan in me thinks, 'You're not going to find a better lead-guitar player.' If he could have only kept his ego and personality in check and realized his place was a rung below Jeff Tweedy, I think they'd still be going. But there was a saying going around for a while within the band: Jeff gave Jay just enough rope to hang himself with."

Bill Bentley, one of the band's biggest boosters at Reprise, was stunned. "I'd seen Jay and Jeff do a duo tour right around the time of *Being There*, and it was like them against the world," he says. "There was a bond there that you could feel in the music. When Jay left, people were like, 'Whoa, what's Tweedy going to do in the studio?' But in a way, Tweedy needed a guy like that as security blanket, because he'd always had Jay Farrar. And I think for a while, Jay Bennett spurred him on, and Jay Bennett is a great artist in his own right. But their relationship wasn't necessary or healthy for Jeff's long-term growth. I think once again Jeff kind of outgrew it."

Within the band, there was not much debate about what needed to be done.

"We had a band meeting without Jay, and there was a real unified commitment to letting him go," Tweedy says. "The mixing session before Jim O'Rourke got involved was the watershed moment. It was insanity. When Jim got involved, it had a bolstering effect: a wonderful vibe with everyone discussing the music openly and frankly, nobody clinging to ownership of parts or songs that were deemed expendable by everyone else. It made it really hard to go back to the idea of working in an environment that we all knew was so wrong."

Stirratt still chafes at what he sees as Bennett's "martyrdom." "It will be so easy for people to say that this is the only guy who had a voice in the band outside Jeff and he was removed," the bassist says. "And that's just a sham. He had a voice in the band, and would have continued to have one, and been a big part of the band. But the situation just got unbearable. He just wasn't a lot of fun to be around."

Several conversations with Bennett find him still wrestling with his feelings. He was rebuffed several times trying to call Tweedy, and he was hurt. But he had also continued to insist that Wilco owed him merchandising and songwriting royalties, and between songs at his post-Wilco concerts he sniped at Tweedy.

Two years later, closure still eludes him, even as he insists he didn't feel betrayed by Tweedy's bombshell. "The sense of betrayal, if there is one, is that Jeff broke up with me before I had a chance to break up with him," Bennett says. "I wish I had the balls to say it first. I would confide in Leroy [Bach], telling him that I didn't think I was long for this band, that I felt it was time to move on. But I never said anything to Jeff like that. So when Jeff brought it up first, it took me a couple days to get over that punch to my ego. Now it's a case of 'Who cares who said it first?' It was the right thing to do."

In 2003, Bennett opened his own recording studio on the Northwest Side of Chicago, not far from the Wilco loft. There, I encountered him after twenty-three straight sixteen-hour days. He was wearing a wool hat over shoulder-length hair that had twisted into dreadlocks. A butane lighter hung by a string from a water pipe over his desk as he worked his way through a pack of cigarettes. His dirty clothes were soaking in an industrial washbasin around the corner. He looked exhausted, but he chose his words carefully. He tried to focus on what made his seven years in Wilco the most satisfying musical experience of his life. Time had soothed, if not fully healed, the wound left by his sudden ouster.

"Psychologically, Jeff got healthy and realized he wanted his band back," Bennett says. In the first flush of anger over his firing, Bennett had told me that Tweedy had "thrown the baby out with the bathwater." When I remind Bennett of those comments, a small grin passes, as if he were reminding himself of the personal devastation he felt in the immediate aftermath of his firing. Now he barely has time to think about Wilco or what might have been. He is preoccupied with new music and a new business and with finding a healthier, more balanced lifestyle. "Looking back," he says finally, "I'm pretty glad we didn't salvage it." The tears in his eyes convey a different answer.

CHAPTER 19

"JUDAS!"

Scott McCaughey, the frizzy-haired R.E.M. sideman, spent the penultimate week of the summer of 2001 at the Chicago home of his old friends Jeff Tweedy and Sue Miller. McCaughey was in Chicago to record an album for his side project, the Minus 5, and he was psyched: Wilco was going to be his backing band during a weeklong recording session. The songs he'd written were some of the best of a career that stretched back to the early 1980s with his Seattle power-pop band Young Fresh Fellows. The Fellows had been regulars at every club Sue Miller had ever booked, and shared bills with Uncle Tupelo in the late 1980s. Now the idea of being in the studio with a few old pals sounded like an inviting way to spend the waning days of a beautiful Chicago summer. But on the morning of September 11, 2001, a teary-eyed Jeff Tweedy woke up McCaughey to an unimaginable new world.

"It was a horrible day, obviously," McCaughey recalls. "A lot of tears and just a general feeling of helplessness. We were supposed to record that day, but nobody could think about that for a while. We ended up at the studio later that night, almost out of desperation. We were all looking for something to do besides watch the news. It became a refuge. The attitude was, 'Let's just try to create something good in the world right now. It's not like it's going to change anything, but at least we can feel like we're putting out something positive.' "

The engineer that night at Soma studios was Mikael Jorgensen, the twenty-nine-year-old son of a Danish immigrant who ran a recording studio in Manhattan. "Just being able to play was an escape," he says. "I didn't know the guys that well, but I was amazed that they were literally arranging songs in the studio lounge, and then going in and recording them right after, very much live. I remember thinking that Jeff was a great listener, in that he was able to make quick decisions on what made a song work and envision how it fit into the bigger picture. I had worked on a lot of records for people like Stereolab and Bobby Conn but never worked with a bunch of guys who worked as quickly, and outwardly were so enthusiastic about what they were doing. It was like they were throwing themselves into this work at a breakneck pace."

For Tweedy, the Minus 5 recording session was a welcome opportunity to play a supporting role for a musician he admired. Over the years, McCaughey, Buck, and Tweedy had become friends, separated by geography and increasingly complex careers but bound by their ongoing enthusiasm for music. When McCaughey was in need of a backing band for the latest batch of Minus 5 songs he'd written between R.E.M. tours and recording dates, Tweedy and Wilco were a natural choice. But McCaughey wasn't exactly sure what band would show up until he arrived in Chicago on the evening of September 9.

"I didn't meet Glenn until the morning of the first recording session," McCaughey says. "When we started talking about this project, Ken Coomer was still in the band, a great guy who I really loved. Then it seemed every few weeks something new and cata-strophic would happen to Wilco: 'Ken's not in the band anymore.' Then it would be, 'Jay Bennett's gone,' and, last but not least, 'Oh yeah, we got dropped by our record label.' It's a good thing I trusted Jeff because otherwise I might have sensed something was wrong."

McCaughey's sense of humor was a marvelous tonic in Wilco world. Though the mood was upbeat in the weeks after Reprise dropped *Yankee Hotel Foxtrot*, rehearsals had been by far the most intense in the band's history. They'd gone from a band that didn't practice much to one that worked eight hours every day at the loft. Tweedy, Stirratt, Bach, and Kotche knew they had something to prove with Jay Bennett out of the band, and the stress was apparent. "I'd be lying if I said we didn't feel a little bit of pressure to prove ourselves," Stirratt says. Tweedy would grumble after practice to Jonathan Parker about muffed notes. He wanted the band to sound better than ever.

"It has crossed my mind a lot, how we would be perceived without Jay," Tweedy said a few days before McCaughey arrived in Chicago. "When I say that I don't think the band has ever sounded better, people will take that as a slam at Jay. And if I were to say we're sorely missing him, it wouldn't be true. But there is an energy and a freshness in the band that wasn't there before."

Wilco's travails soon became trivial in the face of world events. With the World Trade Center suicide bombings as a backdrop, it's little wonder that McCaughey's Minus 5 album *Down with Wilco* sounds so forlorn. "I try to catch a piece of the sky, but I fly too low," McCaughey sings on the album's opening song, "The Days of Wine and Booze." The album's a small gem of orchestrated pop; as co-producer, Tweedy nudged McCaughey to play more piano. Overall, the tone of the album is far removed from the wise-guy power pop that had been McCaughey's standard mode of operation since Young Fresh Fellows. The first night in Chicago, Tweedy played McCaughey an album that he hoped would serve as a loose template for the recording session: *Time of the Last Persecution* by Bill Fay, an obscure English folk singer. In the early 1970s, Fay recorded two albums in which he sang gently over orchestrated arrangements. His finest moment is "Be Not So Fearful," a song that worked its way into Tweedy's solo sets for the next two years, its lyrics forever linked in the singer's mind to that horrendous week in September:

Be not so nervous
Be not so frail
Someone watches you
You won't fail

"Through all the divorces the band was going through—Ken and Jay, and Reprise—it was a horrible time," McCaughey says. "I think Jeff took some heart from that song, and then what happened on September 11 only made it more meaningful."

When the week was finished, the new, four-piece Wilco made its live debut as McCaughey's backing band at the Abbey Pub. The band wrestled with the notion of playing a concert so soon after a national tragedy. But the more they thought about it, the more apparent their decision became. "It was four days later, and it was the first chance everyone had to exhale," McCaughey says. "The attitude was, 'We've had enough of being shut indoors. Let's go out and drink and hear some music.' It was necessary for everybody."

Two days after the show, Tweedy was cruising the neighborhood, a box-set collection of 1970s pop hits rotating through his dashboard stereo. Right now, perhaps for the first and only time in his life, he needed to hear Melanie's "Brand New Key" and Rose Royce's "Car Wash," if only "to take my mind off stuff."

"Jeff is an emotional person anyway," Sue Miller says. "And he was overwhelmed by this. Scott and Jeff were sitting around the TV set all week in a stupor. They played music to make themselves feel better. So the decision to go on tour right after that was a hard one for him to make. I think he needed it, the band needed it. But at the same time, he never likes to leave the kids, and this was especially hard. There were a few more tears than normal this time when he left."

"Be not so weak, be not so frail"—Bill Fay's consoling lyrics kept cycling through Tweedy's daily routine. Every action seemed elevated, every small gesture seemed to speak volumes. His head was clear about what mattered to him, about what he had to do. The band had been playing *Yankee Hotel Foxtrot* songs in the practice space for months, and the words had taken on a haunting new layer of meaning in the last week: "Tall buildings shake, voices escape singing sad sad songs"; "I would like to salute the ashes of American flags"; "Moving forward through flaming doors, you have to lose, you have to learn how to die, if you wanna wanna be alive."

"Our record was originally scheduled to come out on September 11," Tweedy says, a trail of cigarette smoke marking his direction on the first gray Monday afternoon after that infamous day. He grips the wheel tighter to steady a left hand that is trembling slightly. "We made a record about America, and now it feels like these personal moments are politicized in a way I couldn't have imagined. What happened last week is a reminder that this is the world we're faced with every day. We face death every day, whether we choose to acknowledge that or not. Last Tuesday, you couldn't help but acknowledge that. And so the last week, there was a lot of debate within our band about whether we play or not, do we go on tour or not. How do we respond to this? And we came down on the side of any act of creation, any positive direction. Because it's all directly in the face of death and destruction and hate."

Tweedy apologizes. "It's important for me to talk about this, but I'm not sure the emotions aren't getting the better of me." He pauses, then begins again. "I've never not wanted to leave my family more than I don't want to leave right now, but music is an important part of our lives. This isn't a war on America or an attack on buildings; it's an attack on people, and it's an attack on their spirit. And the only thing you can do to combat that is to create something, to just keep on doing. In my case, that means making music. It's a thousand times more important for people to do now what they philosophically said they did before Tuesday."

Jeff Tweedy once stood aghast as his former bandmate Jay Farrar did a bizarre Bono imitation, mocking the pompousness of the U2 singer. In Uncle Tupelo's world, stadium-rock blowhards were the enemy. And Tweedy has shied away from writing songs with political messages or making speeches from the stage about his political beliefs. He wasn't going to change now. For him, simplifying the music into words that could fit on a bumper sticker would've cheapened it.

"We're not U2," Tweedy says. "We're not the biggest rock band in the world. But we are part of the fabric of certain people's lives who have tickets and are waiting to see us. And there is no doubt in my mind that for some people out there, we are one of the threads they are hanging on to. And I think what we have to do as a band is to make those people aware of how we need them as much as they need us. To me, music is love, and I need it in my life just as much as they need it in theirs."

Jeff Tweedy had devoted two albums to the question of how much music really mattered in his life. Now he had his answer.

Sue Miller knew and nurtured countless musicians she had met at her old club. She went into her marriage with one of those musicians, Jeff Tweedy, with eyes wide open. As her younger son, Sam, weaved a toy car through an obstacle course of table legs in Miller's kitchen, she addressed the subject with her usual frankness: "I wouldn't ever want to put the question to him 'If you had to choose between your wife and music, which would you choose?' I just don't want to go there. But I'm not really jealous of it. I was a little irritated when he wanted to bring a guitar on the one vacation we took to Hawaii, though."

Jeff Tweedy hadn't figured it all out, not by a long shot. But he had a better idea than the guy who wrote *Being There* and *Summerteeth*. "I look back now, and I wonder how I could be so myopic," he says. "The person I was when I wrote those lyrics on *Being There* and *Summerteeth* is a person who was resisting change. I didn't know if I loved my life as a husband and father, because I didn't know if that would mean I couldn't love music as much anymore. If music could ever mean as much to me ever again. If I let go of this, will I even care about it anymore? And doing those albums, I came to some healthy conclusions. Where I am now is that music is still the most important thing in the world to me. It has sustained me my whole life. It still helps me every day.

"But I don't have to deny loving something else. I have no problem taking care of my family and my kids, and being there for them, and they have no problem that their dad is a freak for music. My fear was based on a ridiculous notion: that there's only so much love. But love is exponential; it grows the more things you learn to love. I had to learn that. I am still learning it. But I think I turned the corner where it's not tearing me apart anymore."

The next day, September 18, Wilco confirmed that they would not wait to release *Yankee Hotel Foxtrot* through official corporate channels. Instead, they began streaming the entire album on their wilcoworld.net Web site to coincide with a tour in the fall of 2001.

The move came at a time when the record industry was immersed in a contentious debate over the merits of free music on the Internet. File-sharing services such as Napster had opened up new avenues of distribution that cut out the record companies, and the labels complained that the rogue operations would decimate CD sales and artists' incomes.

Artists were torn over the merits of file sharing. On one hand, digital distribution offered instant access to their fans. On the other, it provided no mechanism for paying royalties. Yet the vast majority of musicians didn't receive royalties from their record labels anyway. Most were so deeply in debt to their record companies because of recoupable expenses such as studio time, video and marketing costs, and tour support that they had no hope of ever making a penny from their record sales. Jeff Tweedy's old friends in the Jayhawks had become poster children for the skewed economics of the music business when in 1995 it was revealed that they were more than $1 million in debt to their record label and managers. The band likely would never sell enough albums in its lifetime to recoup that debt. Tweedy himself had to go to court to extract royalties that were a decade overdue from his first label, and was still not making money from his Reprise Records sales, thanks in part to the reduced royalty rate he agreed to take so that *Being There* could be released as a double CD.

When Wilco launched the *Yankee Hotel Foxtrot* Net-stream on September 18, it essentially decided to let fans preview its new album without charge. On the first day, the band's Web site logged fifteen thousand visits, more than eight times the normal traffic. In subsequent months, visits to the site quadrupled. The band was gambling with its livelihood, but music fans starved for substance were tuning in to the band in record numbers.

On the road that autumn, the *Foxtrot* Internet campaign had its intended effect: though the band was breaking in new material, the fans were not only familiar with it but also singing along with many of the new songs. The record-company executives came courting. When Wilco played two sold-out shows at the fifteen-hundred-capacity Town Hall theater in midtown Manhattan, a handful of A&R executives clustered backstage, waiting patiently to touch the hem of Jeff Tweedy's rumpled shirttail and to offer awkward compliments (most using a variation on the mantra that Wilco had become "America's answer to Radiohead").

"That was a weird, *Spinal Tap* moment," says David Bither of Nonesuch Records, one of the executives in line to shake Tweedy's hand. "There were people from a few labels down there in this basement backstage, all waiting for our number to be called, like we were in some doctor's office. At that moment, it became really apparent that Wilco was a sought-after band."

Tweedy was in an astonishing position. The record business was finally coming to his door, asking for his music. All along, he felt that he'd been getting away with something, using the big labels to put out his music, even though he assumed they were only hoping that one day he might produce the elusive radio hit. Now, whether they got his music or not, they were bidding for it. Danny Goldberg, the president of Artemis Records, showed up at his house in Chicago for a pizza dinner, although Sue Miller had to come up with the cash for the delivery boy. Another executive called up a journalist in Chicago, pleading, "What's it gonna take to sign Wilco?"

Such questions made Tweedy's eyes roll. He scanned the artist rosters of several labels that made strong bids and knew right away where he didn't want to be. He was most intrigued by a handful of larger independent labels, but he knew that with all the attention on the band, *Yankee Hotel Foxtrot* would be too much for these smaller operations to market.

"I felt we needed a certain amount of resources, and I wanted a record company that was capable of selling hundreds of thousands of records," Tony Margherita says. "I wasn't ready to put a ceiling on this album. Some of the other scenarios, like doing our own label or working with some of the indies, weren't going to be capable of selling more than 100,000 records. That level wasn't that interesting to me. I just think there's a big audience out there for this band, even at their weirdest, and I wasn't ready to be put into a world that couldn't tap into that."

Tweedy settled on Nonesuch, a relatively small, artist-intensive major-label subsidiary of Warner Brothers staffed by about a dozen people. The label specialized in quirky artists, many outside the rock spectrum: the classical composers Steve Reich and John

Adams, the avant-garde performance artist Laurie Anderson, the quirky folk-pop chanteuse Sam Phillips, the jazz guitarist Bill Frisell. Tweedy found an easy rapport with Bither, Nonesuch's senior vice president of A&R; much like Joe McEwen, Bither was a man of discerning musical taste whose record collection Jeff Tweedy would've been proud to call his own.

"I was very surprised when Reprise let Wilco go, but in a way they're in a different business than we are," Bither says. "The demands on big labels to have radio hits are enormous. We've never been a radio-driven label, and I think that appealed to Jeff."

The label had a reputation for putting out beautifully packaged, pristinely recorded albums that found an audience the old-fashioned way: through word of mouth, with an occasional assist from National Public Radio and the more adventurous Triple-A commercial stations. In 1997, Nonesuch had released an album of Cuban folk songs recorded in Havana by the guitarist Ry Cooder and a group of mostly forgotten seventy- and eighty-year-old native singers and musicians. That album, *Buena Vista Social Club*, ended up selling millions of copies, cracking the *Billboard* Top 200, and inspiring an Oscar-nominated documentary by the German filmmaker Wim Wenders.

The parallels were not lost on Bither. Sam Jones's Wilco documentary was in the pipeline, scheduled for theatrical release in the summer of 2002, and the Nonesuch executive was impressed by the loyalty of Wilco's fans. To him, Wilco was a band that connected for all the best reasons: its charisma was in the music, and it had an unspoken integrity that translated from album to album. "I was up-front with Tony Margherita because I admitted there were two things that we as a label knew little or nothing about, and that was the commercial pop spectrum of radio, and MTV," Bither says. "We just don't go there, and we can't go there. There are too many people who are really good at that, and it's not something that we should get involved with. Tony didn't have any problem with that. He said, 'Well, we don't go there either, by and large.'"

When *Yankee Hotel Foxtrot* was finally released on April 19, 2002, it became the biggest hit of Wilco's career. Even though the songs on the album had been widely circulated on the Internet, Wilco fans bought the album in unprecedented numbers. In its first week, the album sold 55,573 copies and debuted at number 13 on the *Billboard* pop-album chart—both peaks for the band. Two years later, it had topped 400,000 sales domestically and was creeping toward gold-album status, without radio or MTV support.

The goodwill and commercial success bought the band time to work out the growing pains of its new, four-piece identity onstage. Without Bennett, there was more space in the music. Tweedy became the band's principal guitarist by default, exploring a more fractured style that on one night could be riveting and the next could seem aimless. He also fiddled with a laptop computer at his feet, a development that did not please the purists in the band's audience. Bach found himself developing parts for two hands that had once been played by four. Kotche began putting his imprint on the songs with a style diametrically opposed to his predecessor's. And John Stirratt stepped into the void left by Bennett to play bass lines that were more ornate and melodic in their construction while continuing to add counterpoint harmonies that made the songs soar. Even though the raw material was much the same, the music was vastly different from the loud, romping, tidal-wave guitar approach that had defined the band in concert from 1997 through 2000. It now took on a more spacious, atmospheric quality, and the contrasts in tempo and volume became more pronounced. Whereas once Tweedy confronted his audience by screaming at them, now he'd bring the music down to an almost-unbearable hush. It was a development that was greeted negatively by some of the diehards, who saw the band as irredeemably weakened by Bennett's departure. The nonstop rock had yielded to a more textured brand of folk music, a kind of junkyard Americana that had more in common with Tom Waits, Sparklehorse, and Califone than with Ryan Adams of Whiskeytown or Rhett Miller of the Old 97's, the new golden boys of alternative country. For the finishing kick at its shows, Wilco was still strapping on the electric guitars and blasting out "Casino Queen" and "Monday," but they weren't the main course anymore.

"It's a challenge to reconcile these things in our minds," Tweedy says. "We're trying to present a pretty wide range of music and make it cohesive. We go to play festivals overseas, and we see the bands that are totally geared up to play in these big outdoor settings. They have big songs, and they paint with broad strokes, and I'm thinking, 'Should we just throw together all of the most rocking, hit-you-over-the-head straightforward songs and put them in a set and have a good time?' Sometimes we probably should have done that. But we're all getting comfortable with the idea that what we do is not always completely appropriate. It's not completely appropriate to stand in front of people baking in the sun and play acoustic guitar for ten minutes, with slight electronic manipulation going on behind it, and then kick into 'Casino Queen.' It's confusing. But it's more honest about who we are, and how we listen to music, and what we care about. I don't care more about art than I do about people; I think what we do is more how people really are."

The idea of making his audience and himself uncomfortable had been one of Tweedy's guiding principles; it energized him, brought him to a place where he felt more alive than if he were just doing what was expected. Every time he had begun to feel hemmed in or dictated to, whether it was following Johnny Cash in New York City or playing with Jay Bennett in a loud electric rock band, Tweedy had opted for confrontation rather than compliance, radical change rather than the status quo.

In a show at the Pageant in St. Louis in 2001, Darin Gray saw a profound difference in the band's approach. "There was all this space in the music that Jay Bennett wasn't filling up anymore," he says, "and the audience response was, 'What's going on?' It was Jeff's way of keeping himself interested in the music. He knows his music history; he knows the artists who kept at it the longest were the ones who kept changing. Like Bob Dylan or Neil Young, he's doing all the wrong things in all the right ways. It's the same music he'd be doing in front of five people in his living room. So what if there were three thousand people there? They were gonna have to meet him halfway."

That attitude was one of the main reasons Tweedy and Wilco continually found themselves second-guessed by Reprise Records and the music industry in general. "His inclination is always to make decisions for the benefit of the song and not for anything else," says Wilco documentary director Sam Jones, who watched Tweedy construct and then deconstruct countless songs while making *Yankee Hotel Foxtrot*. In the movie *I Am Trying to Break Your Heart*, Tweedy tells Jones, "There's no reason at all not to destroy [the album] . . . We made it; it's ours to destroy . . . but in a creative and liberating way."

"That was the big question I had throughout the process," Jones says. "I kept seeing them leave a lot more radio-friendly stuff by the wayside. I was incredulous at first. 'You guys really do not care if the radio does not play your stuff or if you sell a lot of records?' I finally realized that Jeff doesn't care. He just doesn't have it in him. All he really wants to be allowed to do is make records. I asked him about the money, and he said, 'Sure, I want to be able to feed my family and provide security for them and have a nice house.' But his idea of a nice house is really modest. He doesn't have aspirations to have the nice things that money can buy. He doesn't use those things. He has such a rich interior life that he doesn't appear to have much use for the exterior world."

Jay Bennett could never get his head completely around Tweedy's instinct to push the music past the breaking point. "I'm willing to challenge my notion that melody is the most important thing, and Jeff has written songs with a lot of melodic space," Bennett says. "He didn't stop writing those songs, but he stopped wanting to present them that way or put them on albums. There's an open-mouth-insert-foot kind of thing going on. There's a little bit of David and Goliath that he always wants to be involved in. Like he doesn't feel fully present if there's not a little bit of that going on: him taking on 'The Man,' or taking on what's expected of him. It was frustrating to me after a while."

From album to album, Wilco's inability to define its "sound" frustrated even the band's allies at Reprise. "The way Jeff Tweedy thinks is not the way a major record company would want any of their artists to think," the former Reprise executive Gary Briggs says. "I've heard song demos of his and said, 'God, that is built for radio, Jeff!' And I'd go back two weeks later and he'd completely sabotaged it. As soon as you get to that chorus with the big hook and the big payoff, he would throw a wrench into the spokes, because he hated formulas more than anything. I loved him for that, and I hated him for that. Because I felt he'd deconstructed something that a lot of people might've liked. But Jeff wasn't interested in formula songs, especially once he got around to making *Summerteeth* and *Yankee Hotel Foxtrot*."

One longtime record-industry executive, Peter Koepke, who had run several labels before being forced to the sidelines in the consolidation-crazed late 1990s, admires Tweedy as an artist but thinks he's a liability to any major label. "Jeff Tweedy is a twat," Koepke says. "He is the quintessential 'difficult' artist. A double CD from an artist who never even had a gold record? Please. I'd say he's taken far more advantage of Reprise than they have of him. He may be on a big corporate label, but he acts like he's on an indie, making records for a small group of devoted fans."

Jeff Tweedy chuckles when the comment is relayed back to him. "To people who say I'm acting like an indie artist on a major label I say, 'I don't know any other way.' I've been trained historically to not expect things I make to go through the roof, that if I make the record I believe in, it will grow incrementally, and that the record I made three years ago will be more appreciated now than the record I'm currently making. I tried to think around those things with *A.M.* and *Being There*—those were records that were as 'commercial' and directly stated as I could make. When somebody makes a piece of music, and they aim for a target and hit it, that purity is lost on a lot of people, because what it may communicate to future generations is the love for money or the desire for fame. But the ability to do that is human, and it's insanely powerful and profound to connect with a fan like that. Some people in the record industry may not think so, but I would welcome that sort of connection. But that's not something I could even think about, let alone control. The only kind of 'direct marketing' we've ever been good at is going out and playing for people. And the only thing I can be confident about is that I do everything I can to stay focused on the act of making music, not how it will be perceived or how much it will sell. Because as soon as I do that, the music is fucked."

In the post–Jay Bennett era, Tweedy saw the possibilities for Wilco's music open up again. Mikael Jorgensen, a skilled recording engineer and keyboardist who had spent several years working with Tortoise's John McEntire as an engineer at Soma, knew a thing or three about electronic music. But he was impressed when

Tweedy played a "solo" on a laptop computer and distorted it with a foot pedal, creating an eerie slide-guitar effect on the Minus 5 song "Dear Employer." "It was exciting to see someone use the computer in a creative musical way rather than in the typical way that most techno-music people use it, which is very dry and sequenced," Jorgensen says.

Bennett found such experimentation problematic. "Jeff had this computer program where you can squiggle lines on the screen that would make different noises," he says. "That was a toy to me, and I made it apparent to Jeff that I felt that way. I mean, literally four minutes later [Tweedy's older son] Spencer was playing on it. The germ of creativity can come from toys, but it comes more often from a good melody. We saw things like that more and more differently."

Tweedy didn't see computers as usurping melody or even standing in for a band; he wanted them to enhance the songs, to push the songs into areas he hadn't yet explored as a songwriter and musician. It's why he approached Jorgensen about manipulating the sound in Wilco's live show, essentially doing a live mix of the band's performance. Though some rock devotees saw this as heretical, the idea of processing and manipulating live sound has a long tradition in underground music, from the Jamaican dub reggae of King Tubby and Lee "Scratch" Perry to the angular indie rock of the Boston quartet Mission of Burma. During its early-1980s life span, Mission of Burma considered its sound mixer an integral part of the band, though he never appeared onstage. Martin Swope would lurk behind the sound board during shows and record the band's performance, then play the reel-to-reel tapes backward or alter their speed to add an extra layer of chaos to that already being created by the more visible portion of the band.

Jorgensen began to play a similar role in Wilco, starting out behind the mixing board and eventually moving onstage, where his Macintosh PowerBook was augmented by keyboards. He would season Tweedy's acoustic guitar, Kotche's drums, and Bach's keyboards with electronic effects and throw in samples of previously recorded sounds: Kotche's cymbal scrapings, a droning D chord from a classical symphony recording to augment the ending of "A Shot in the Arm," and bits of radio static from the *Conet Project* box set that had been so integral to the sound and vision of *Yankee Hotel Foxtrot.*

The bespectacled keyboardist was derided as "laptop boy" on some of the band's Internet message boards, his presence another reminder to the diehards that Wilco wasn't in *Being There* mode anymore. When the self-titled Loose Fur album was finally officially released in early 2003, two and a half years after it had been recorded, it was greeted with a mixture of respectful tolerance and outright derision on many Wilco sites. Here was the precursor of the sonic experimentation on *Yankee Hotel Foxtrot*, the moment when Jim O'Rourke and Glenn Kotche found their way into Jeff Tweedy's world. It was an uneven mix of skewed pop songs, adventurous and sometimes indulgent but never pat or predictable. To some observers, it was another head-scratcher destined to confuse record labels, confound radio programmers, and seriously cheese off even some of the loyalists who were wondering whatever happened to the guy who wrote "Screen Door" and "Black Eye."

"Save your money on the Loose Fur," a disgruntled fan posted on one Internet site devoted to Wilco's music soon after *Loose Fur* was released. "I've suffered through it now several times hoping that it would reveal its qualities after multiple listenings; the only thing it's revealed is that somebody's got to get Tweedy away from O'Rourke before it's too late."

It was a sentiment shared to an extent by Darin Gray. "Glenn and I would joke that these two guys probably should have never met," he says. "Because they have a lot in common, not all of it good. They have preshow anxiety that is just debilitating. I think at some point they question whether or not they're going to even do the show. Running away—it seems like an option at some point."

Only a few weeks before *Loose Fur* was released, Tweedy and Kotche joined O'Rourke and Gray for two sold-out performances at St. Ann's Warehouse in Brooklyn, New York, focusing on the more experimental non-Wilco material in their combined repertoire. The performances were preceded by minimal rehearsal as Tweedy and O'Rourke sneaked through a gap in their busy touring schedules with Wilco and Sonic Youth, respectively. But the performances were not nearly as skittish as Loose Fur's debut show at the Chicago Noise Pop festival in 2000. Gray was added to play bass, leaving Tweedy and O'Rourke free to raise a twin-guitar ruckus, the songs spiraling to noisier, dizzier heights.

At the second show some of the growing resentment among the Wilco faithful about Tweedy's detour into more abstract musical terrain spilled over. "You suck, Tweedy!" a fan shouted as a ten-minute "So Long" wound down. "Judas!" another yelled, as if to equate Tweedy with Dylan, who had endured similar epithets when the erstwhile folk messiah dared to crank up the electric guitars with the Hawks on his 1966 tour of England.

The hostility was enough to cure Tweedy of a hellish migraine. "It had been a long time since I'd played in front of something other than a cultish environment, where people don't feel as free to voice dissent," he says. "It was fun having people yell at me. It keeps me on my toes. Jim got more upset than me. He's very protective. He kind of dotes on me, which is sweet, like I'm some old blues guy, this naive artist, under his wing. But what he didn't realize is that I found it refreshing. I took more abuse in that one night than I have in a long time. It makes me feel like I'm on the right track."

CHAPTER 20

"BE NOT SO FEARFUL"

It was fitting that the release of *Loose Fur*, a modest side project that essentially documented the studio improvisation of three friends, coincided with the anointment of *Yankee Hotel Foxtrot* as the 2002 album of the year. Without *Loose Fur*, there might have been no *Foxtrot*, at least in the form it was released. Though the record industry conveniently ignored *Foxtrot* when it came time to make Grammy Award nominations—imagine how embarrassed Reprise executives would've been had the album won—it topped *The Village Voice*'s annual poll of the nation's critics in a landslide over Beck's *Sea Change*, the Flaming Lips' *Yoshimi Battles the Pink Robots*, the Streets' *Original Pirate Material*, and Sleater-Kinney's *One Beat*.

Wilco was now enough of a cause célèbre that even *People* magazine cited the album as one of the year's best, alongside the works of multimillion sellers such as Bruce Springsteen, Norah Jones, the Dixie Chicks, and Justin Timberlake, in its 2002 roundup. Yet the band still had enough of a hip, anticorporate cachet that the album found its way into many Internet and fanzine Top 10 lists, as well as winning considerable airplay on college radio stations. Janet Weiss, of the punk band Sleater-Kinney, cited

Yankee Hotel Foxtrot as a band favorite, an album the trio listened to constantly while touring in their van.

Could a backlash be far behind?

Robert Christgau, pooh-bah of the *Voice* music section, led the charge in the same issue in which several hundred critics voted *Yankee Hotel Foxtrot* No. 1. Christgau proclaimed the results "the worst one-two finish" in the poll's three-decade history and cited Wilco's winning album and Beck's runner-up as "two of the dullest works of well-turned semipopularity ever to contemplate their own impotence."

It was a sign of Wilco critiques to come; Sam Jones's *I Am Trying to Break Your Heart* documentary inspired countless underground responses, most of them sarcastic. The best of them was a sharply humorous parody by a masked band of punk rabble-rousers known as the Goblins. Their self-released DVD, *I Am Trying to Take Your Cash*, found one of the Goblins nearly forgetting to unzip his mask before blowing lunch into a toilet after quarreling with a bandmate. A widely circulated MP3 file of unknown origin distilled Jones's movie to a seven-minute audio play with actors playing the roles of Jeff Tweedy, Jay Bennett, and Jim O'Rourke. In the satire, a self-important Tweedy requests that O'Rourke provide him with "a poster boy for indie-rock-martyrdom-in-the-face-of-corporate-America type of sound."

Wilco was enjoying the freedom that "semipopularity" had brought them. Between tour dates, the quintet recorded hours of new music, enough to fill several albums. Six songs appeared on their Web site on the first anniversary of *Yankee Hotel Foxtrot*'s release, available free to fans who owned the CD, and the band streamed or Webcast numerous concerts on its 2002–3 tours. With as many as ten thousand fans visiting wilcoworld.net daily, the band had built a grassroots following that was expanding annually. The quintet capped off two years of touring behind *Yankee Hotel Foxtrot* in September 2003 with two sold-out shows at Chicago's Auditorium Theatre, selling out eighty-four hundred tickets weeks in advance. The $200,000 weekend by itself could have covered the recording budget for *Yankee Hotel Foxtrot*.

There was no telling at that point what the next Wilco album would sound like. The only certainty was that it likely wouldn't sound much like anything Wilco had recorded before, that the reference points for the band's "sound" would once again be scrambled and realigned. It was the only way Jeff Tweedy wanted to work. His discomfort, his own sense of surprise, would tell him when he was on a promising path.

A Reprise executive who knew the band well once said that if Tweedy thought he'd written a pop hit, he'd find a way to sabotage it. In the course of countless hours of interviews, anger rarely figured in Tweedy's responses. But this time the indignation rose in his voice. It was the first time I sensed just how adamant, even intimidating, Jeff Tweedy could be when anyone aimed to mess with his music.

"Sabotage in the minds of some people we've worked with at record companies is us going the full hundred yards to make something that is exciting to us," he says. "To me, that's the fulfillment of the promise of a song. Sabotage to me would be to make a song something other than what I believe in, for the sake of commercial success. That's sabotage. That's contrary. What we've done has never been contrary. I've never been a contrarian; I've never made stuff to fuck with people. I've made stuff because I want to fuck with myself."

Jonathan Parker, who left Wilco in 2002 after years of service on the road and in the management office, had seen enough shows to vouch for Tweedy's response, even if it meant waving good-bye to a sound he loved. For him, there has never been a better version of Wilco than the one that rampaged across North America in a swirl of booze, pills, braying guitars, and flying deli trays in the months after *Being There* was released. "They changed after *Summerteeth*, and they changed even more when Jay Bennett left," Parker says. "They lost a step in my eyes when they got rid of Jay. But it did make it a different, or more interesting, band in Jeff Tweedy's eyes. The guy is not afraid to evolve. He's turned his back on a lot of cash cows such as the No Depression scene, the two-guitar thing with Jay Bennett, the idea that he could have been this Ryan Adams–like rock star if he wanted to play along. He could have been more successful and more of a household name by now had he played any of those cards. Now he's ditching the pure-pop thing. Maybe that's his destiny. Jeff just wants to be known as the guy that you can't put your finger on. What is Jeff Tweedy going to do next? You can't put him under your thumb and say, 'Jeff Tweedy is this: he's all flannel and acoustic guitars.' He's not. That's Jeff in a nutshell: a guy who doesn't want to be labeled."

In January 2003, Tweedy played three solo acoustic shows at the Vic Theatre in Chicago. The performances were sold out and attended by his wife, children, and parents, along with forty-two hundred fans. Alone onstage, Tweedy looked thin and pale; he had lost fifteen pounds during the previous tour in the grip of daily migraines. In a few weeks, he would check himself into a local hospital to have surgery on his septum in the hope that it might bring some relief. But now the music would have to do the job. It ranged from the caustic "Millionaire" ("Wish I could fuck you like he thinks he does / Before he falls asleep / But I've never been that tired") to a joyous "Heavy Metal Drummer" (in which he playfully mentioned each of the bands that had been nominated for a best alternative-album Grammy ahead of Wilco).

He embroidered the simple chords with fingerpicking that evoked the untutored intricacy of Bob Dylan on his back-to-back acoustic albums of 1992 and 1993, *Good As I Been to You* and *World Gone Wrong*, or the tumbleweed Segovia-isms of Willie Nelson. As he bent notes, the barriers between his playing and his personality melted away; even as he concentrated on his fingers moving across the fret board, his face radiated delight, a becalmed satisfaction. There was nothing on earth he would rather have been doing. On the middle night, he closed with Bill Fay's "Be Not So Fearful," and he didn't so much sing it as whisper it in the audience's ears, his lips pressed to the microphone: "Be not so fearful . . . Be not so sorry for what you've done." The words came gently, unhurried, a meditation more than a song.

Henry Miller once found the proper words for such a moment. They were words that Jeff Tweedy had likely stumbled across in the hours he had devoted to the great author's canon, from the story *The Smile at the Foot of the Ladder*. In it, Miller describes the "gift of surrender," the art practiced by those "emancipated beings . . . [who] live in the moment, fully, and the radiance which emanates from them is a perpetual song of joy."

For a few hours onstage, the pain of a migraine recedes, and the moment is subsumed in measures and beats and the sound of fingers squeaking on guitar strings.

For his thirty-fourth birthday in 2001, Sue Miller's gift to her husband was a guitar lesson from Richard Lloyd of New York new-wavers Television. In the midst of the 1970s' CBGB scene, the dueling guitars of Lloyd and Tom Verlaine evoked '60s psychedelic and progressive bands more than many of their punk-era peers. Tweedy adored the band, and the way Lloyd's skewed harmonics opened up the fretboard in particular. In three hours, he filled up a notebook with new possibilities after Lloyd showed up with a guitar at the Wilco loft.

On the road, Tweedy would practice electric guitar by himself in his hotel room for hours, or play along with squalling freak-outs by free-jazz saxophonist Albert Ayler or avant-garde guitarist Derek Bailey. His sound was rude, spasmodic, visceral, but Tweedy's love of noise wasn't well-received by Jay Bennett, whose technical knowledge dwarfed the singer's. When Tweedy would try a guitar solo in the studio, Bennett would shrug dismissively or laugh out loud. It was yet another example of how the two collaborators were splitting apart. But after Bennett was ushered out of the band, Tweedy threw his inhibitions aside on the 2002–03 tour after *Yankee Hotel Foxtrot*.

"It took me two years to learn how to be confident in something I've been doing for a lot longer," he says. "I practiced scales and theory at home, and then just started going for it in the shows. I became confident enough that even if I hit a 'wrong' note, I'd be quick enough on my feet to integrate that note into the solo. I got myself into the mind-set of always being on the edge of a cliff, and nothing bad can happen."

In November 2003, Wilco arrived in midtown Manhattan to record what would become their fifth album, *A Ghost Is Born*, with Jim O'Rourke as producer. It was O'Rourke who initially encouraged Tweedy to keep pushing with his guitar playing in Loose Fur, and the singer's growing confidence on the instrument would become central to the recording sessions. Whereas *Yankee Hotel*

Foxtrot and *Summerteeth* had taken live band recordings and then filtered them through an elaborate and sometimes arduous studio-as-instrument deconstruction, the process was reversed for *A Ghost Is Born*. Songs were performed and then edited on Pro Tools computer software in Chicago. Once satisfied with the arrangements, the band then learned how to play them live, with minimal over-dubbing.

"All those things you can do with Pro Tools and all the emotional buttons you can push with just purely sonic things I think can be done with just plain old music," Tweedy says. "I love all the possibilities that modern recording techniques allow, but I couldn't picture the idea of really wowing anyone with some crazy evolution of the *Yankee Hotel Foxtrot* sound."

It was typical of Wilco's career so far. With every new album, they produced not just a timid progression, but a left turn down a dark alley. The latest twist presented Tweedy in a new, unlikely guise: lead guitarist. Much of *A Ghost Is Born* was cut with the band playing together, and Tweedy's guitar solos flowed out of the energy in the room. But this wasn't simply noodling for noodling's sake, in the jam-band tradition of the Grateful Dead and Phish. This was a more controlled brand of guitar chaos. Lloyd is a master of composing solos rather than simply free-associating them into shape, and Tweedy and the band worked out a ferocious coda to the tender "At Least That's What You Said" that plays like a tribute to his mentor. The guitarist flirts and jousts with Kotche's increasingly agitated drums, until both fall back exhausted in a feedback haze.

For "Spiders (Kidsmoke)," a song that had been turned every which way by the band on the road without ever arriving at a satisfying arrangement, Wilco finally found the sweet spot by laying down a trance-like rhythm that wouldn't have sounded out of place on one of Neu's German art-rock albums in the '70s. Tweedy's guitar darts in and out, squeezing between vocal lines to provide disruptive commentary, patiently building the tension, then shifts into a galvanizing power-chord section. The two impulses—fractured lead lines and monolithic chords—volley back and forth over nearly eleven minutes, building a relentless momentum that steamrolls any hint of self-indulgence.

The haunted atmospherics of *Yankee Hotel Foxtrot* are dialed back a touch, but linger long enough to frame some sturdy melodies in a lovely ambiguity. Keyboards hover like an opium fog over "Wishful Thinking," and O'Rourke shrouds "Muzzle of Bees" in a delicate lattice work of acoustic finger-picking. On "Company in My Back," Tweedy sings of "hissing radiator tunes," as if to foreshadow the album's penultimate song, "Less Than You Think." What had once been the briefest moment in the Wilco songbook becomes its longest recorded work, a fifteen-minute epic, thanks to an extended coda that consists entirely of various electronic contraptions and synthesizers oscillating through a series of effects boxes—Wilco's answer to Lou Reed's experiment in drone, "Metal Machine Music." Each band member created his own sound installation in the studio, then let it run unattended. In the mixing afterward, the noise was sculpted into a slow-moving arch that peaks, then fades, the poltergeist of the album title shrieking to life and then drifting out of the room. The piece is followed by a straightforward, two-minute pop song, "The Late Greats," that serves as something of a commentary on what has just happened. "The greatest lost track of all-time . . . you can't hear it on the radio, you can't find it anywhere you go."

"Less Than You Think" is "the track that everyone will hate," Tweedy says with a laugh, arriving like an uninvited guest near the end of what is the most straightforward, tradition-bound Wilco record since *Being There*. "I know ninety-nine percent of our fans won't like that song, that they'll say it's a ridiculous indulgence. Even I don't want to listen to it every time I play through the album. But the times I do calm myself down and pay attention to it, I think it's valuable and moving and cathartic. I wouldn't have put it on the record if I didn't think it was great. We've been doing sound installations like that for the last couple of years in the loft to amuse ourselves, and there's something beautiful about making music that doesn't have any author. Nobody 'plays' anything, and it goes hand in hand with the notion that 'there is so much less to this than you think.' I wanted to make an album about identity, and within that is the idea of a higher power, the idea of randomness, and that anything can happen, and that we can't control it."

For Tweedy, the opposite of that random beauty is the world described in another new track, "Hell Is Chrome." In it, the narrator is beckoned by the devil, who offers a world "where everything was clean, so precise and towering." It's a world that Tweedy has done his damnedest to reject, even to the point of turning over his band every few years. Just as the 2002–03 touring lineup had gelled into a formidable live ensemble and recorded a new album based on that premise, it splintered. Leroy Bach told his bandmates weeks after the completion of *A Ghost Is Born* that he was quitting. Unlike earlier Wilco departures, where members were literally pushed out, Bach left while he was still missed. It was the type of risky, unexpected gesture that Tweedy could appreciate, even as it saddened him.

"I was hurt because I'll miss him," Tweedy says. "But at the same time, I admire him for doing it. Wilco is a pretty good deal for a lot of people. You can pay the rent. It's a good place to be. But what I've discovered is that when people lose interest in the music, they may not even admit it to themselves, because the environment is pretty cushy, so they aren't going to leave until they're told to. That happened with some other guys in the band. I think Leroy just didn't want to do it anymore and wasn't going to put himself through it for the sake of a steady paycheck. It's the same reason Leroy was so valuable when he was in the band, because he didn't think like that."

Within a few weeks, Wilco had retooled again, hiring multi-instrumentalist Pat Sansone, Stirratt's songwriting partner in *Autumn Defense*, and Nels Cline, a masterful West Coast jazz-punk guitarist who shares with Tweedy a distinctly nontraditional approach to the instrument. The new six-piece lineup began touring even before *A Ghost Is Born* was to be released in June 2004, prompting another reconfiguration of Wilco's world, another test for fans already dizzy from watching the band's revolving-door lineup and sound come and go.

Consider the formidable band that is in Wilco's past: Coomer on drums, Bennett on guitar, Bach on bass and keyboards, Bob Egan on pedal steel, Max Johnston on fiddle and other stringed instruments. Tweedy shrugs and smiles. In his present and future,

there are bands just as powerful, new musical avenues just as exciting. Otherwise, he says, why bother? "I stay inspired by not even
remembering what I liked a year ago."

Two months after Bach's departure, Tweedy abruptly checked
himself into a Chicago rehab clinic. It was his latest attempt to con-
tain the vicious cycle of migraines, anxiety attacks, and prescription painkillers that had once again overtaken him. The decision
forced cancellation of a European press junket, put Wilco's tour
plans in doubt, and prompted his record label to delay the new
album's midyear release by at least two weeks.

There was only one certainty: As difficult as it was to live with
migraines, it was even more difficult for Tweedy to live without
music. Somehow, he'd be back.

In the pale light of his family room at 2 a.m., Jeff Tweedy is listening to the latest addition to his stack of homemade cassettes.
A tape recorder clicks on, and the sound of Tweedy's voice and
guitar makes the room feel smaller than it already is. "It's called
music—I invented it!" Tweedy says as he listens to a playback of
Wilco's rehearsal that night. He flashes a tolerant smile as he hears
the singer fumbling his way toward an uncertain destination. But
the song gathers strength, and the singer audibly grows more confident as he and the band lock in. Tweedy clicks off the recorder
and apologizes. "We still got some work to do," he says. But he is
quietly pleased with the performance, even if no one besides him
and his bandmates will ever hear it.

"That's the beauty of music," he says. "Because when it feels
right, it does feel like you invented it—because you did. You
invented it for yourself."

ACKNOWLEDGMENTS

Without the cooperation of Wilco, this book would not have been possible, and I am grateful to them. From the outset, Jeff Tweedy and his bandmates, past and present—Leroy Bach, Jay Bennett, Ken Coomer, Bob Egan, Max Johnston, Mikael Jorgensen, Glenn Kotche, and John Stirratt— were unfailingly generous with their time and forthcoming with their answers despite my sometimes intrusive questions. Not once did they seek to read, steer, or impede my efforts, even though I explored a number of delicate subjects that they had rarely, if ever, publicly discussed before.

Dozens of people inside and outside the worlds of Wilco and Uncle Tupelo went above and beyond in aiding my research. I am especially grateful to Bob and Jo Ann Tweedy, and to Sue Miller, for opening their homes and their archives to me. Tony Margherita also shared hours of conversation, provided leads, and paved the way for interviews crucial to rounding out the band's story. To everyone I interviewed for this book (including several whose quotations do not appear anywhere within the text but provided invaluable background information or confirmed certain details) my sincerest thanks: Michael Ackerman, Bob Andrews, Bill Bentley, David Bither, Peter Blackstock, Billy Bragg, Gary Briggs, Peter Buck, Edward Burch, Richard Byrne, Joe Camel, Andy Cirzan, Daniel Corrigan, Wayne Coyne, Heather Crist, David Dethrow, Jay Farrar, Wade Farrar, Rick Gershon, Darin Gray, Josh Grier, Nora Guthrie, Mike Heidorn, Brian Henneman, Matt Hickey, Sam Jones, David Kahne, Chris King, Howie Klein, Peter Koepke, Paul Q. Kolderie, Gary Louris, Scott McCaughey, Joe McEwen, Bob Merlis, Nick Miller, Mike Mills, Thurston Moore, Jim O'Rourke, Jeff Pachman, Jonathan Parker, Frank Riley, Elliot Roberts, Eric Rujanitz, Nick Sakes, René Saller, Steve Scariano, Sean Slade, Laurie Stirratt, Ken Waagner, Janet Weiss, and Neil Young.

Thanks also to my small but dedicated team of researchers and assistants, especially Sandy Travers, who transcribed endless hours of interviews, and Chris Castaneda, who tracked down countless hours of Wilco and Loose Fur concert tape that affirmed and sometimes debunked the fuzzy recollections of those involved. Also devoting time or offering research assistance to this effort were Jason Saldana, Cheryl Weissman, Jeff Sabatini, Donna Murphy, John Jackson at Sony Legacy, Daniel Durchholz, John Bitzer, Deb Bernardini, David Morrison, Marty Perez, Joshua Klein, Matthew Lurie, Andy Downing, and my *Chicago Tribune* colleagues Stacey Wescott and Jennifer Fletcher.

David Dunton was a good friend long before he was my agent, and his judgment and counsel have been invaluable. Regina Joskow Dunton was among the first to plant the idea that I could and should be writing books about our mutual passion, music. Gerry Howard was every bit the editor he was cracked up to be and more, and I thank him for shepherding this project at Doubleday Broadway. Beth Haymaker offered valuable comments and guidance on the manuscript when I needed them most.

The writers and editors I admire and count as friends are far too numerous to mention, but I would especially like to cite the following for their advice, inspiration, and prose: Jim Higgins, Tom Moon, the late *New York Times* critic and blues scholar Robert Palmer, Ira Robbins, Jack Rabid, and Greil Marcus (thank you, Greil, for *Mystery Train*). That goes double for Jim DeRogatis: I couldn't ask for a worthier counterpart, even as we butt heads on everything—including Wilco.

All my colleagues and editors, past and present, at the *Chicago Tribune*, especially Jim Warren, Scott Powers, and Gary Dretzka, set a high standard for journalism that I am still striving to attain.

Finally, my admiration for my parents, Len and June, deepens with every year. This book is as much a product of their values as mine. The pride my parents-in-law, Dan and Pat Lyons, took in this effort has not gone unnoticed. My wife's uncle Denny Coll believed in this endeavor even before I did. My daughters, Katie and Marissa, made sure I made my deadlines by asking me nearly every day how the book was coming along. My wife, Deb, supported this effort in countless ways, big and small, that were beyond selfless. She not only stood by her man; she propped him up on many occasions. More than anyone else, this book is for her.

ABOUT THE AUTHOR

Since 1990, Greg Kot has been the music critic at the *Chicago Tribune*, where he has established a reputation not just for his comprehensive coverage of popular music—from hip-hop to rock *en español*—but for enterprising reportage on music-related social, political, and business issues. With his *Chicago Sun-Times* counterpart Jim DeRogatis, he co-hosts Sound Opinions, "the world's only rock 'n' roll talk show," on radio, television, and the Web (www.soundopinions.net). Kot is a regular contributor to *Rolling Stone* and other national periodicals, and his work has also appeared in *Encyclopaedia Britannica* and numerous books, including *Harrison: A Rolling Stone Tribute to George Harrison* and *The Trouser Press Guide to '90s Rock*. He lives on Chicago's Northwest Side with his wife, two daughters, and far too many records. Please visit the official *Wilco: Learning How to Die* website at www.wilcobook.com.